Footprints

An Autobiography

DAVID DOBSON DAVENPORT

PAGE PUBLISHING, INC.
New York, NY

First originally published by Page Publishing, Inc. 2019

ISBN 978-1-68456-939-7 (Paperback)
ISBN 978-1-68456-940-3 (Digital)

Printed in the United States of America

To my father
and to Suzie

CONTENTS

ONE

Let the Chips Fly

I was born March 22, 1948, in Wharton, a small east Texas oil town. I am the second of three children, the elder son of Robert Earl Davenport Jr. and Ernestine Dobson Davenport.

My father, a twenty-five-year-old engineer at that time, had gone to the Lone Star State after World War II to find work in the oil business. He and my mother were children of career naval officers. They had grown up in a variety of places around the world. When they met, as young adults, it was through their fathers, both of whom had been assigned to the naval base in Norfolk, Virginia.

My paternal grandfather, Robert E. Davenport Sr., owned twenty-one acres of oceanfront property at 2700 River Road in Virginia Beach. He was building his dream house on a pine-covered knoll overlooking Lynnhaven Bay. One day in the fall of 1944, he invited my mother's family, the Dobsons, to come out to see the place and have a picnic.

My grandfathers were what the Navy called mustangs, officers who had risen through the ranks to earn their commission. By all accounts, Earnest Edward Dobson was easygoing and likable, but Commander Davenport was a demanding officer. His military record bears this out. Practically the only criticism he ever got was for being too hard on his men. "There are only two sons of bitches in this whole outfit," a fellow officer once told him, "and you are both of them!"

Commander Davenport thought a man's life ought to amount to something. Even his home life reflected that attitude. He always had a project going on around the house, and he loved working with tools. With my young father at his side, he would talk about "making the chips fly" or leaving his "footprints in the sands of time." He had a habit of using lofty clichés.

He was born in Pensacola, the last of nine children. From there, the family moved to Montgomery, Alabama, where the father, my great-grandfather, took off one day and never came back. The deprivation and hardship this created simply made it too difficult for my grandfather to stay in school beyond the sixth grade. Given little else in the way of opportunity, he eventually lied about his age and joined the Navy. He trained as a motor machinist's mate and went on to serve in both world wars.

In peacetime, he did a tour as commander of helium production for the Navy's ill-fated dirigible program. Then, at the peak of his career, he was given command of a destroyer, the USS *Jacob Jones*, which was later sunk by a German submarine.

Given the poverty of his childhood, and the fact that much of my grandfather's career coincided with the Great Depression, he was known to be exceedingly frugal. As an example, my father once told me he had no recollection of the family ever eating at a restaurant during his entire childhood. Doing so was apparently something my grandfather considered wasteful.

And so it was that, together with my grandmother, Gladys Houston Davenport, he was able to accumulate a respectable affluence over the years. By 1943, the two had enough of a nest egg to buy the twenty-one acres of bayfront property near Virginia Beach. Intending never again to go to sea, Commander Davenport put together two Spanish words and came up with the name Nadamar.

One weekend, in the cool autumn of 1944, my twenty-year-old mother, Ernestine, went along with her parents to visit Nadamar. Together with her father, Lieutenant Commander Dobson, and her mother, Dovie Sanders Dobson, she spent the day boating and picnicking on the crabs and oysters that are so plentiful in the Virginia tidewater. That day, as it turned out, was the day she met my father.

What with the Great Depression and World War II, Mom and Dad had grown up in challenging times. As a consequence, perhaps, my mother, a pretty and popular young woman, harbored no reservations about the importance of a man being ambitious and patriotic. How striking an example of both my father, a tall, raven-haired young naval officer, must have seemed. Robert Davenport Jr. was a smart young man who had graduated in metallurgical engineering from the Virginia Polytechnic Institute when he was still only twenty. He had made plans for a career, but with a war on, he set them aside and followed his father's footsteps into the military. For a time, my mother would later say, he must have been one of the youngest officers in the entire US Navy.

The day they met, Dad had already served a year in the Atlantic. His ship, the amphibious assault vessel USS *Henrico*, had participated in the invasion of Italy and in the D-Day landing at Normandy. Years later, Dad would tell me of his experience that June 6 on the French coastline. The American First Army Division soldiers had been crammed into the hold of his transport ship the night before the attack. Few, if any, were able to sleep that night. Early in the morning, Dad watched them climbing down the nets into the landing boats and pushing off from the ship. They hadn't counted on hitting a sandbar a hundred yards or so from the Omaha Beach, but they did. What easy targets they must have made as they desperately tried to reach the shore. That section of beach, ironically code-named Easy Red, was so heavily defended that not one of the two thousand soldiers from the Henrico was believed to have made landfall. The lucky ones were those wounded near enough the landing craft to be evacuated back to the ship. Dad would never forget the gruesome carnage that returned in those boats.

After Normandy and the brief furlough home, during which he met my mother, Dad was ordered out to the Pacific. There, in August 1945, the Empire of Japan became the last Axis power to surrender in history's greatest military conflict. Under orders to pick up American prisoners of war, Dad's escort carrier, the USS *Lunga Point*, was among the first Allied warships to dock in postwar Japan. When starving prisoners began arriving, they were deloused and brought aboard for a first meal. Sadly, some of the men gorged themselves and went out to vomit over the side. Then, they went back to the galley and ate even more.

Sixty-one countries took part in World War II. It was so big that, for the rest of their lives, those who lived through it would simply call it the War. Three-fourths of humanity had been involved, and something like sixty million people were killed.

In the years that followed, America would be the predominant power in the world, militarily, culturally, and economically. Outwardly, this would be expressed in benign, even charitable acts toward her former enemies. These included the Marshall Plan, which provided funds for the rebuilding of Europe, and the Japanese-American Treaty, which restored full sovereignty to Japan under their Emperor Hirohito. No other military victor in history had been so generous to the vanquished.

Perhaps, America could be forgiven if a sort of national hubris arose out of the victory. Justifiably, most Americans viewed the war as a triumph of good over evil, of American virtue over the malevolent aims of the dictators. Hitler, Mussolini, and Hirohito—all three had been defeated. The cost of their ambitions to the US alone measured in the hundreds of thousands of lives and hundreds of billions of dollars. For many, victory in this greatest of all conflicts was confirmation that American power was now indomitable and that American motives were beyond reproach. Indeed, by the time President Kennedy made his inaugural address in 1961, few would challenge his assertion that Americans would "pay any price, bear any burden, meet any hardship, support any friend, oppose any foe, in order to assure the survival and the success of liberty." How misconceived his words would seem only a few short years later, when my own generation would be summoned to fight in Vietnam.

Anyway, by war's end, Mom and her parents had moved to Seattle, where her father had been assigned to prepare the new destroyer-tender USS *Yellowstone* for service. Throughout 1945, Dad and Mom had been conducting a romance through the mail. Upon disembarking from his ship at the port of Los Angeles, Dad caught a train for Seattle, where it had been agreed the two would marry. Dad arrived to find the invitations sent, the flowers ordered, and so on. Everything was set, in fact, except, as it turned out, for the bride. In the final days before the ceremony, Mom simply had gotten cold feet. Applying all his powers of persuasion, Dad tried to change her mind, but she would not bend. Everyone had to be notified. The wedding was off!

Dejectedly, Dad arranged for a flight home to Virginia and caught a cab to the airport. But then, while boarding the plane, he heard his name being called, and he turned around to find my mother and her parents racing toward him. She had reconsidered.

The next day, the guests were reinvited, flowers were reordered, and on November 27, 1945, the couple was married at the home of a Seattle friend. As reported clear across the country in the *Norfolk Virginia Pilot*, the twenty-one-year-old bride wore "a lace and net gown over taffeta, fashioned with bouffant skirt with a full train." The paper didn't say so, but the twenty-three-year-old groom was dressed in his slightly sea-stained Navy dress blues. He had pressed them carefully himself and tried to conceal the age of his trousers by lightly sandpapering them in the seat. The bride's parents were in attendance. The groom's were not. But for their love letters, the newlyweds had known each other for all of three weeks.

Nine months and five days later, Dad was still in the Navy, assigned to St. Simon's Island, Georgia, when, on September 2, 1946, my sister Dana Victoria was born at the naval hospital in Norfolk. Her middle name was taken from the site of Mom and Dad's honeymoon in British Columbia. Dana was the first grandchild for both sides of the family.

It is hard to imagine how Americans might not have foreseen the economic boom that lay ahead in the decades after the war. In defeating Germany and Japan, the nation had just demonstrated the awesome potential of American capitalism. Yet this was a population accustomed to hard times. America might be the richest country on earth, but the lessons of the Depression would not be easily lost. When it came to financial security, Americans had learned to take nothing for granted. And so it was with Mom and Dad. They were on the verge of better times, but they didn't know it. Mom's parents, whom we children would come to know as Nanny and Bumpa, were living in San Diego now and about to retire. Dad's were hard at work finishing the house at Nadamar.

Nadamar, by the way, was more than big enough to accommodate houses for every member of the family. Commander Davenport, in fact, had encouraged my parents to settle and raise their children there. But Virginia Beach held little opportunity for a young engineer bent on making his own way in the private sector. When the war began, Dad had been working for Curtiss-Wright, an airplane manufacturer and an important defense contractor. But with the war over, he now saw his greatest opportunity in the booming Texas oil business. Anyway, with family on both coasts, he figured it might be a convenience to live halfway between. So shortly after Dana's birth, Dad resigned from the Navy and left to seek work in Houston.

He found it at the Texas Company (Texaco), which started him in El Campo, a tiny backwater community seventy-five miles southwest of town. The job offered none of the perquisites he had been used to as a college-educated naval officer. Instead, he started at the very bottom, doing things like mowing weeds and cleaning septic tanks.

At first, the family lived over a shabby auto supply store. The place was nearly surrounded by "nodding donkeys," the nickname people gave to the seesawing oil pumps that pervade East Texas. But by March of 1948, when I was born at the hospital in nearby Wharton, they had moved to what was only a slightly nicer garage apartment overlooking a cow pasture. What a relief it must have been, a few weeks afterward, when the company offered Dad a transfer to Texaco's office in Santa Paula, California. Finally, he would be doing the work of a real engineer.

So we moved to California, and things were looking up, though not for long. That July, we received a telegram from Dad's only sibling, my aunt Dorothy. The night before, my grandparents had gone into Virginia Beach to see the Cary Grant movie *Mr. Blandings Builds His Dream House*. Years earlier, the Navy had given Commander Davenport a medical retirement when he was diagnosed with angina. Nonetheless, for months he had been building his own dream house, lifting concrete blocks into place and constructing a fifty-foot pier out into the bay. A man whose passion it was to build things, he had done much of the labor himself. Midway through the movie, he slumped over in his seat, giving Gamma (my grandmother) what must have been a horrible fright. The movie was stopped, and an ambulance came, but it was too late. At fifty-three, and after only four months living at his beloved Nadamar, he was dead of a heart attack.

In those days, the model American family was a patriarchy. If a man didn't rule the roost, he might at least be allowed to think he did. For military families, this might have been particularly so. When it came to giving orders, Commander Davenport was a professional, but in Gamma, he had a wife who was anything but submissive. Having been orphaned at an early age by her mother and neglected nearly always by a seriously alcoholic father, Gamma, too, had grown up fending for herself...and a younger sister to boot. As such, she had never developed much respect for the male-dominated scheme of things. In marriage, her suspicion of men and their motives, plus my grandfather's male ego, had long ago combined to foster a mutual impassivity, which, unfortunately, was to echo in the relationship between my father and his sister, Dorothy, for the rest of their lives.

Like a lot of sons, Dad emulated his father, but Commander Davenport was so often at sea, and both Gamma and my aunt Dorothy were such strong-willed women, that Dad often felt over-powered. Particularly as an adolescent, he came to see himself as the family underdog. In time, he would deal with his frustration by over-achieving and by concealing anything from his mother and sister that might be perceived as weakness or failure.

Thus, when Aunt Dorothy's telegram brought the distress-ful news of my grandfather's death that day, Dad wanted to go to Virginia for the funeral, but he didn't want to admit to his family that he had no money for plane fare. In those days, before credit cards, he could not simply charge a ticket either. Disheartened, he decided to ask my mother's parents for help.

Unlike Commander Davenport, Dobie Dobson (Bumpa to us kids) was a softhearted man, given to acts of generosity. Back in

1938, when his wife's only sister, Blanche, died, Bumpa had gladly taken in her eleven-year-old boy, Glenn, and raised him as if he were his own son. Buster, as Glenn was always called, was only a couple of months younger than my mother, so at Christmastime, Bumpa, and Nanny, too, always made sure that Buster got just as many gifts as Mom did. Bumpa never had a lot of money, but what he did have always seemed to be enough. It was only natural that Mom and Dad would turn to him in this hour of need.

And so it was set. The next morning, my parents packed some clothes, loaded Dana and me into the car, and took off for San Diego. Dad would borrow the needed funds from Bumpa and then fly out as soon as possible. Mom, Dana, and I would remain in San Diego until he returned. As we all left the house in Fillmore that morning, the plan seemed to make perfect sense.

The drive south to San Diego was a six-hour trek through the city of Los Angeles and the dozen or so little seaside towns that dotted the Coast Highway. Along the way, Dad had plenty of time to think about what he was doing. By the time we arrived, he no longer felt right about asking Mom's parents for money, so instead, he picked up Nanny and Bumpa's phone and gave the operator Gamma's number. The voice that answered was Dorothy's.

The two agreed that my grandfather's death was terrible news, but they spent little time sharing their grief. Dad asked to speak to Gamma, but Dorothy told him their mother was too upset to come to the phone. "But," Dad insisted, "I need to talk to her about how I am going to get to the funeral."

"You'll have to work that out for yourself," said my aunt.

With little more to discuss, Dorothy said goodbye and hung up the phone. Feeling he'd been spurned by his own family, Dad was now too embarrassed to turn to Mom's. He retired to a bedroom, and for the first time since hearing the news, he wept. A few days later, Commander Davenport would be laid to rest at Arlington National Cemetery, but his only son, and namesake, would not be there.

That Christmas in 1948, Nanny and Bumpa drove up to Fillmore for a visit. They brought along Buster, who was now a handsome young ex-hospital corpsman who many thought resembled the actor Tyrone Power. Having recently been discharged from the Navy, Buster was headed for San Francisco, but he decided to spend the holidays with us along the way. Even fifty years later, my mother would find what happened next to be too sensitive a subject to discuss, so I don't know all the details, but apparently, on New Year's Eve, Buster made some disparaging remark about his own deceased mother. The Dobsons became very upset, and a terrible argument ensued, pitting the three of them against Buster and my father. It ended with Mom and her parents angrily departing for San Diego and taking Dana and me with them.

Early next morning, Buster got his things together and asked Dad for a ride into Pasadena. It was New Year's Day, and he said he wanted to watch the Rose Parade. So the two of them jumped into Dad's car and drove into the city, where crowds were already gathering. Dad asked if Buster would be able to get to San Francisco okay, and Buster assured him he would. The two of them shook hands and said goodbye. That morning, on a street corner in Pasadena, Buster walked out of our lives forever.

Eventually, my parents bought their first home in nearby Santa Paula. It was a brand-new but very small ranch-style house at 204 Arthur Avenue. They had to borrow the $300 down payment from Nanny and Bumpa, but they paid it back thirty days later. My earliest memories are of living there.

The house in Santa Paula would be our home only until 1952. Then our universe would change forever. Texaco offered Dad a job with their Caltex Pacific affiliate in Indonesia, and after discussing it with Mom, he accepted. We were going to go halfway around the world to live at a place called Rumbai, a remote oil camp deep in the jungle on the island of Sumatra. There was no telling how many years we might have to live there or how difficult our lives might be, but none of that really mattered. This was just the sort of career opportunity Dad had been longing for, and he wasn't going to let it go.

Two

Sumatra

Caltex wanted Dad to show up in Sumatra right away, even though they didn't have a house yet for the rest of us. So he got himself a passport and visa and all the shots he needed for travel to Indonesia, and off he went. Mom, meanwhile, stayed behind with Dana and me, waiting for word that we could be accommodated.

It was a long wait—seven months, in fact. During that time, Mom applied for and got a single passport for the three of us. Then she arranged our visas and shots.

Dad's first contract was for three years, so Mom went on a shopping spree, buying up enough clothes and personal items to see us through. There would be few opportunities to buy such things once we got where we were going.

Then there was the matter of our house. It had to be sold. Mom took care of that, too, and at a handsome profit, as it turned out. After a short period staying with Nanny and Bumpa in San Diego, we received word that Dad was ready for us. Through the company, he had arranged passage for us on an ocean liner.

When the day of our departure arrived, we loaded our luggage into the trunk of Bumpa's new two-tone, green-and-white Cadillac and headed north toward the harbor in San Pedro. It was just a few days before Christmas 1952, and I was only four years old, but my memory of it is remarkably clear. I can still see the five of us standing on the dock, hugging and kissing and crying. Mom was Nanny and

Bumpa's only child, Dana and I their only grandchildren. We were going to a very remote spot on the other side of the world, and it was clear there would be no seeing one another for at least two years. It being 1952, there would be no phone calls or e-mails either, no contact at all, in fact, other than handwritten letters. For Nanny and Bumpa especially, this was not a happy occasion.

As travelers did in those days, Mom had dressed as though it was Easter Sunday and she was going to church. What was more, she had attired Dana and me, two little towheads, in matching navy-blue sailor suits. Together, we headed up the gangplank and found a space for ourselves among the other passengers at the deck railing. Members of the crew were handing out streamers, which, as soon as we spotted Nanny and Bumpa below, we started throwing. It was like a scene straight out of an old movie.

The SS *President Cleveland* was a fine ship. Having been launched only the year before, it was almost brand-new. Dana and I set about exploring every inch of her as soon as we could. This was a whole new world for a couple of little kids. There were ship's stewards everywhere, their brass buttons gleaming against their dress white jackets. Dinner chimes rang throughout the ship every time there was a fresh seating in the dining room. Midmornings, hot bullion was served out on the deck, and in the afternoon, it was time for tea and shortbread. Always, there were activities. People played shuffleboard or swam in the pool. Dana and I could come and go at the ship's movie theater as often as we pleased, no tickets required!

To top it off, it was Christmastime. On the twenty-fourth, there was a talent show for the kids, and everybody won a prize. That night, after we were safely asleep, Mom had our cabin steward bring a surprise up from the hold. She had secreted aboard a live Christmas tree on the day of our departure, and now she set about decorating it with lights and some tinsel she had hidden away in our steamer trunk. In the morning, when we awoke, the only light in our windowless little cabin came from that tree. Seeing it sitting there on the night table, right before our eyes, we thought we were gazing upon pure magic!

Along the way, our ship put in for a day at Honolulu. From there, we sailed to Hong Kong, where we parted company for good with the *Cleveland*. It was about time, too, as far as the other passengers were concerned. Unthinkingly, Santa had given me a very noisy pull toy with which I had tormented nearly everyone on board for days.

In Hong Kong, we boarded a second ship and set sail across the South China Sea to Singapore, where we finally met up with Dad. Having just spent seven months raising two small children and shepherding them across the Pacific without any help, Mom could not have been happier to see him.

In those days, there was no commercial air service to where we were going next; instead, we took off from Singapore aboard the company-owned Caltex Star, a military surplus DC-3, and we flew west across the Strait of Malacca toward Sumatra. We were headed for a rough-hewn landing strip at the remote town of Pakanbaru,[*] near the very center of the island.

Pakanbaru (literally "market town that is new") was hardly more than a kampong. Situated some thirty-nine nautical miles north of the equator, on the southern bank of the Siak River, it had been inhabited since the seventeenth century. Indeed, it was the capital of Riau Province. But it had no more than one or two paved roads, and it was still small enough for a person to get around easily on foot. During World War II, Pakanbaru was the site of the Sumatran Death Railway, an atrocity that is little known to the rest of the world but was nonetheless horrific. Much like the Burmese railway in the dramatized story of *The Bridge on the River Kwai*, it was built by a combination of POW and contracted romusha[†] laborers under conditions of extreme cruelty and deprivation. When the track was completed after two years of work, it stretched 215 kilometers westward

---

[*] The name has been spelled in different ways. Most common recently is *Pekanbaru.*

[†] Romushas were laborers acquired mostly from Java. Initially, they came in response to offers of employment, but they were soon forced to work as slaves. When the supply of volunteers dried up, new recruits were simply kidnapped and taken to Sumatra against their will.

through dense jungle, dangerous swamps, and rugged mountains. Unfortunately, there was little construction equipment available to the Japanese other than the conquered human beings whose lives they considered expendable.

At least 10,000 people are known to have died building that railway, most from disease and malnutrition, but many from the inhumanity of their volunteer Korean guards. A few were even killed by tigers. Some 5,800 were drowned when unwitting British submariners sank the transport vessels that were carrying them to work on the railway. With tragic irony, the final spike was driven on the very day in 1945 when the Japanese surrendered. The railway was never put into service.

Peering out the windows from above, we could see a jungle down below that was so dense I wondered how we might ever find an opening big enough in which to land. Eventually, though, after about two hours in the air, our plane did begin to descend. Below us, there was a clearing with two small runways, both paved with Marsden mats, the perforated metal alloy plates used by the Allies during the war. Our pilot managed to bring the Star down smoothly, and soon we were unbuckling our seat belts and gathering our things. When the door of the plane swung open, the air around us became hot and humid with a suddenness unlike anything I had experienced before.

We were led to a tiny building where a couple of men in uniform examined our passports and tried questioning us in Bahasa, ‡which, of course, we did not understand. They got us to open our bags and then went through them, looking for who knows what. Indonesia was still very new as an independent nation, and people in positions of authority might have been, as yet, a little unclear on just what was expected of them. Nonetheless, we were respectful and complied with every instruction.

---

‡ *Bahasa* is a frequent misnomer for Indonesia's most widely spoken language. The term actually refers to Bahasa Melayu, which literally means "language of Malay."

From the airport, we took a short ride in a jeep down to the Siak River. There, we boarded a launch, setting off for our final destination, the Caltex camp at Rumbai.

Rumbai was only one five-kilometer-long S-curve downstream, but what we saw along the way was a whole new world to us. First, there was the river itself, the water in which was mostly leached from decaying jungle matter. It looked astonishingly like Coca-Cola. The foam rising in our wake added to the illusion in a way that might have made us thirsty were it not for the smell of diesel exhaust in the air.

Then, of course, there was the jungle, punctuated here and there by native shanties built out over the water on stilts. Even this far from the sea, fish was the most important protein in the native diet. These people, in fact, lived almost entirely by subsistence, perched above their food supply in houses made mostly from sticks and roofing thatch. We stared at them as we passed. They were little clothed, and they possessed nothing we could see in the way of modern convenience. Yet as fascinated as we were by them, they gave no sign of interest in us. Obviously, they were used to seeing passersby.

Soon we arrived at the Rumbai landing and we were helped ashore with our luggage. Dad's jeep had been left there waiting, so we climbed aboard and Dad steered us onto a black tar road. We were headed uphill and away from the river toward what was to be our new home.

It would be many years later before I would appreciate the historical significance behind our arrival in this strange and distant place. Sumatra is the third largest of Indonesia's six thousand inhabited islands. Its strategic location off the coast of Southeast Asia places it directly on the equator along the Strait of Malacca, one of the most important shipping lanes in the world. Like much of Indonesia, the island is loaded with natural resources. In addition to petroleum, it is blessed with natural gas, tin, copper, and even gold. It has a climate highly conducive to timber production and to the growth of such crops as sugar, manioc, rubber, and various spices, including nutmeg and cloves.

Spices, in fact, are what originally brought the Dutch to the island. In order to capitalize on the enormous profit potential that existed, Holland had established the world's first ongoing shareholder-owned enterprise, the Dutch East India Company, in 1602. Through a tenuous relationship with local sultanates, the company governed the whole archipelago from that time until the end of 1799. Then the company was liquidated, and on January 1, 1800, the territory was claimed as a colony by Holland and formally given the name Dutch East Indies.

In those days, lamps around the world burned various types of fuel. Many used oil rendered from whale blubber. But whale blubber was difficult to acquire, and the flame it produced was excessively smoky. Then, in 1853, a Polish pharmacist figured out how to distill kerosene from petroleum. Much to the chagrin of the whaling industry, oil wells began springing up everywhere.

Sumatra came into the picture in 1885, when oil was first discovered there by the Dutch. Ironically, Thomas Edison had already demonstrated the first incandescent light bulb in 1879. After only two decades, kerosene lamps were already becoming obsolete. Without another use for the stuff, petroleum was once again a substance without much of a purpose. All that changed, however, in 1908, when Henry Ford introduced his affordable, mass-produced automobiles to the world.

The growth in sales of all types of automobiles was so rapid, particularly in the 1920s, that a worldwide search for more petroleum was inevitable. Not all nations were found to be equally blessed with reserves. Some, such as Germany and Japan, were well on the road of industrialization yet they were found to have little or no oil at all. America, on the other hand, was more fortunate. In 1930, the new East Texas field was discovered near Dallas. It was so massive that it caused a serious drop in prices worldwide.

But the East Texas discovery also coincided with the early days of the Great Depression, a period of enormous challenge to businesses everywhere. By 1936, two well-established major companies,

Standard Oil of California and Texaco,[§] decided to reduce the cost of expansion by establishing a joint subsidiary and calling it Caltex.

One of the first places of interest to managers of the Caltex exploration department was Sumatra. Royal Dutch Shell was already producing oil in heavy quantities from their wells near Palembang, at the southern end of the island, so Caltex sent a team of geologists to explore farther north in 1936. For five years, the geologists tramped around, often deep in the jungle, but they found little to pique their interest. Then, one day in 1941, their efforts paid off and news was sent to headquarters that an important discovery had been made in Riau Province at a field they called Duri. Of additional interest was a geologic formation they discovered at a nearby place called Minas. Clearly, things were looking good, at least for the moment.

But just as Indonesian spices had once brought the Dutch, Indonesian oil was now about to bring the Japanese. Never blessed with much in the way of natural resources, Japan was desperate to secure a dependable source of energy to sustain its growth. For years, the Japanese had sought to build an empire in the Orient, calling it a Co-Prosperity Sphere and promoting it as a boon to all of East Asia. By way of conquest, the Japanese had already acquired Taiwan, Korea, and the southern half of Sakhalin decades earlier. Then, in the 1930s, they invaded Manchuria and went on to occupy most of China. When word spread to the West of unspeakable Japanese cruelty, particularly to the people of China, Americans started clamoring for an embargo. Then, in 1941, when the Japanese invaded French Indochina (Vietnam), President Roosevelt finally ordered one.

America was by far the world's largest oil producer, and Japan had become dependent upon the US for 80 percent of its petroleum needs. If the Japanese did not do something fast, their plan for economic expansion was finished. So the decision was made in Tokyo to invade Japan's most important alternative petroleum source, the Dutch East Indies. The only thing standing in the way was the American Navy. If any plan for conquest of the Indies was to succeed, that one big obstacle would have to be neutralized. And what

---

§   In 2001, Chevron and Texaco merged into a single company.

better way to accomplish that than to pull off a surprise attack on the American Pacific Fleet at Pearl Harbor? This was how the oil fields of Indonesia were at the very heart of America's entry into World War II.

Compared to the many other fronts of the war, little historical attention is given to the battle for Sumatra. In part, that may be because it happened so early on and because it was over with so quickly. It was only ten weeks after Pearl Harbor that Japanese troops began landing on the island. A spirited defense was put up by a badly outnumbered and ill-equipped combination of Dutch, British, Australian, and native forces, but within three months, all organized resistance was crushed. Fleeing Western oilmen did what they could to scuttle their equipment and operations. Some were unable to get away in time and were taken prisoner. Bep Gerrits, a cigar-smoking Dutch doctor, who was later a close friend of my parents, was among them. He was one of the Dutch Caltex employees who were captured and held throughout the war at the prison camp in Pakanbaru.

In short order, with captured prisoners as labor, the Japanese were able to get oil operations running again. They used Caltex rigs to drill at both Minas and Duri, and they found oil, lots of it. The Minas field, in fact, was, and still is, the largest oil deposit ever discovered anywhere in Southeast Asia.

But just as oil, or the lack of it, brought on the war in the Pacific, it also contributed to the eventual Allied victory. By 1944, American submarines had become so adept at sinking enemy tankers that Japan was simply running out of gas.

Not until 1950 did Caltex manage to get the necessary permission to restart operations. One of the company's first priorities was to make a livable expatriate community out of Rumbai. Up until then, the camp had been little more than a convenient Siak River transit point for traffic going to and from Minas, but by the time we arrived, in 1952, the rudiments of a town were coming together.

A crew of Dutch employees had begun shipping oil, but Dad was the first American engineer on-site. At thirty-two, he had been given a career-building opportunity by Caltex that a lot of senior oilmen might have envied.

Fewer than two dozen houses, prefabricated in Scandinavia (of all places), had been assembled and made ready for occupancy. All were single-story and were set above the ground on concrete pillars, plantation-style. Each pillar was capped by a sheet metal collar to keep out the bugs and snakes. Each house had three bedrooms, one bathroom, an ample living/dining room space, a kitchen, and a covered patio. Basic furnishings were provided by Caltex. Around the back, each house was connected to a smaller building that featured a godown (storage space) and, as incongruous as it seems, a servants' quarters. Roofs were ringed by gutters that drained into rain barrels in the back. This would be our drinking water.

As soon as we pulled into the unpaved driveway, we could see we were going to like the house we were given. It sat high above the road and was surrounded by a large expanse of grass. From the patio, one looked directly across the street into virgin rain forest.

Right away, Dad introduced us to the man he had hired to serve as our houseboy. Like virtually all indigenous Indonesians, Mochtar was small, little more than five feet in height. He smiled bashfully and nodded when Dad told us his name. We would learn that few natives on Sumatra ever learned any English, and Mochtar was no exception. Instead, as time went on, he was going to teach us to understand and speak Bahasa.

House servants could be hired so cheaply, as it turned out, that hardly anyone from the West would resist employing them. A month's wages here, in fact, might not exceed what one paid a maid in the States for just a day or two. What's more, as awkward and foreign as our way of life must have seemed to these people, they could be remarkably easy to teach. Mochtar, in fact, would turn out to be a pleasantly dispositioned sort, always anxious to please. In time, he would learn what Mom and Dad expected of him and come to be seen almost as a member of the family.

Of course, Dana and I had some learning to do too. From the outset, Dad would be leaving first thing in the morning to go to work each day, and Mom was no early riser. So it would be up to Mochtar to get our breakfast. All we had to do was take our seats at the table and he would ask us what we wanted. After a few minutes in the kitchen, he would appear with whatever it was we had requested. In no time at all, he mastered the art of making French toast, which I tended to favor, and eggs fixed any way we liked. Sometimes he would treat us to an Indonesian favorite, fried bananas sprinkled with powdered sugar.

After breakfast, Dana and I would dress and head out to play. From now on, we would little concern ourselves with who was going to make our beds or clean our rooms. We knew it wouldn't be us.

Rumbai and Pakanbaru were totally surrounded by jungle. There was not another town in any direction for almost two hundred kilometers. Consequently, Caltex would have to provide us with most of our essentials. To this end, the company had set up a commissary in a Quonset hut on the road up from the river. Here, one could buy a reasonable variety of provisions. No frozen foods were available, of course, and there wouldn't be any fresh milk either. Much to our chagrin, Dana and I were going to be raised on powdered milk, something neither of us would ever learn to like.

Even back in the States, television was just getting started, so we certainly weren't going to have a TV. And there weren't going to be any radio stations either. Eventually, Dad did bring home a shortwave unit, and it was capable sometimes of picking up a solitary signal all the way from Australia. In the morning, he would tune into that one station as best he could, and through crackling static we would listen while we ate our breakfast. The station had a recording of Gordon MacRae singing "Oh, What a Beautiful Morning" from the musical *Oklahoma!*, and they played it every day, rain or shine.

There was an elementary school of sorts. It was fashioned from a group of bungalows that had been built before the war. We had a single school bus, too, to serve the whole community. There was a small company hospital, and a pretty nice one at that. It had both private and semiprivate accommodations, and it was equipped with a modern operating room. Dr. Bep Gerrits was chief medical officer for the whole community, and he had a competent staff of nurses.

We were even provided with a clubhouse. It had an outdoor screen for projecting movies that Caltex brought in from the States, but who could view the movies was a matter carefully controlled by the Indonesian censors, and this was a continuing irritant for the kids. The ratings being given were so completely random that we were sometimes excluded from movies that were clearly intended for children. I remember being turned away, for example, from seeing Jerry Lewis movies, goofy comedies that couldn't possibly offend anyone. This was not our country, however, so we stuck by the rules.

In time, the old clubhouse was taken over by the growing elementary school, and an even better clubhouse was built. It featured something meant to pass for a golf course, though I don't recall anybody ever actually playing on it. There was also a large swimming pool that all of us did use, a lot! Indoors, there were a full-service restaurant and an ice cream parlor. Imagine being deep in one of the world's remotest jungles yet having an ice cream parlor where you could eat all the banana splits you wanted. Amazing. And of course, we were never going to run out of bananas either!

Before the completion of the new clubhouse, we always swam at a water hole out in the jungle. It was a dammed-up stream, and it was where I first learned to swim. Neither Dana nor I would ever risk going down there without our parents, of course. Instead, we would all go in the jeep, often accompanied by another family or two. It was a good place to picnic. While the kids splashed around in the water, the grown-ups would set up card tables and play bridge under the trees.

It still fascinates me the variety of tropical fish that swam in that stream. We might easily have captured a few of them for our living room aquarium, but I don't think we ever did.

Of course, there were all sorts of animals to inspire our curiosity. Sometimes, before dinner, we would sit outside on the patio and marvel at the show being put on by the many kinds of birds. Among the most memorable were the six o'clock birds, or at least that was what Dad took to calling them. Every night, around six o'clock, they would fly around overhead, singing out the same three syllables in repetition, "Six o'clock...six o'clo-o-ock."

The hornbills were the real stars of the aerial show, however. Some three feet in length, they were by far the largest birds around. Their plumage was black and white, but each bird had a colorful red-and-yellow casque about the size, shape, and color of a banana, which grew out of its beak and up over its head. This gave these birds a startling appearance, which we always found entertaining. In the evening, they would soar over the house and swoop into the trees, honking and clacking as they went.

Mornings, the show would continue, only now it was the apes and monkeys who took to the stage. Most notable, perhaps, were the gibbons, which were large and black and made such a racket with their whoop-whooping that one could hardly ever sleep in.

There were macaques, too, thousands of them. One day a man came down the street with one and Dad bought him, thinking he would be a fun pet. We kept him chained up on the patio, but not for long. He made such a terrible mess. Besides, we had also acquired a dog, a female named Jojo, and the monkey so antagonized Jojo that she broke her leg one day jumping up at him. In the end, we took the monkey for a jeep ride down to a spot near the river. We thought it would be an easy thing to let him go. To our surprise, he chased after us, almost desperately, as we pulled away. Like humans, of course, monkeys are social, and I guess we had underestimated how much our family meant to this one.

As time went on, much bigger animals also showed up around the camp. We had a neighbor named Wimpy Klopp, a Dutchman who was always going hunting. One day, Wimpy came home with a baby elephant, and he paraded it around the neighborhood. My guess is he had killed its mother, though I don't remember anyone saying so.

Sometime later, in fact, Dad went out with some men on a deer hunt. When a group of elephants tried to cross the road in front of them, one of the men senselessly shot and wounded a female, and Dad wound up finishing her off with his rifle.

But Dad was no hunter. In fact, he only went out one other time that I can recall, and he never shot anything other than that elephant. Maybe doing so had turned him off to the sport for good. I don't know.

In those days, men were hunting for trophies, particularly tiger skins and elephant tusks, but they hunted for the sheer sport of it too. I don't know that reservations were ever expressed about the morality of it all. For one thing, the wild in those days was truly wild. For example, even though Sumatran elephants are smaller than the ones in India or Africa, they could still do enormous damage to villages and crops. Tigers were known to kill people's dogs around camp from time to time. Occasionally, we would even hear of one killing a native Indonesian. When that happened, the animal was called a man-eater and the natives would live in fear until someone hunted it down and shot it.

Lots of tigers were shot too. One morning, Dana and I heard that Wimpy had killed two of them, so we went running over to his house to see. There was a bunch of people standing around on his patio, and as we drew closer, we saw the animals stretched out side by side on Wimpy's picnic table. We got so close we could see the ticks embedded in their skin.

On occasion, though, it was the animals who got the better part of an encounter. One day, someone who had borrowed Dad's jeep came upon a small herd of elephants in the road. Thinking he could outmaneuver them, he managed to get cornered instead. One of the bulls went into a rampage and crushed the front half of the jeep. Fortunately, the man made it back to camp with his life.

On the other hand, a Dutchman named Leo Gervin was not so fortunate. He and four other men were out hunting tigers when a big cat walked right out onto the path in front of them. Before the men could get off a shot, a second tiger came up from behind and took Gervin's life.

Klopp was the product of a Dutch father and an Indonesian mother. But most of the big-game hunters, like Gervin, were purebred Dutch. Many had been born and raised in Indonesia during the colonial period, and the company found them particularly desirable as employees. They knew the culture, of course, but more importantly, they were fluent in the language.

In time, we, too, became familiar with the culture and the language. Largely, this was thanks to Mochtar. Before long, he had all of us getting by with a few words of Bahasa, though, I confess, I never learned to speak it as well as my mother or my sister did. Still, I knew enough to get by. Sometimes, when Mochtar wasn't busy, Dana and I would visit with him in the breezeway between his quarters and the main house, chattering away in our new vocabulary.

Of all the things that interested us about Mochtar, his food is what really stood out. For one thing, no matter what meal he was eating, it was always mostly rice. That, he would consume with a generous portion of sambal, a hot red pepper paste he made by grinding red chilies together in a hollowed-out stone. For protein, he mostly ate crispy dried fish, which he could purchase on his day off in Pakanbaru. On occasion, when he brought home fresh fish, he would lay it out on the roof and dry it in the sun.

Once in a while, Mochtar would have rice cakes. They were just little cubes of rice sweetened with sugarcane juice and wrapped in banana leaves. They were the only food of his I ever remember tasting.

This was the peasant diet, of course. Over the years, we would have other servants, but all of them ate the same meal over and over, or at least that is how I remember it. What's more, they always ate with their fingers. For special occasions, though, Sumatrans had a wonderful cuisine, which, in no time at all, Mom was learning to prepare. Most commonly, we would have nasi goreng (fried rice) or mei goreng (fried noodles). Mom always served them with sambal and fresh krupuks, which are hard, dry chips normally made either from shrimp and tapioca flour or from peanuts. Krupuks blow up when cooked in hot oil into something light and airy and crispy many times their precooked size. Indonesians eat them as commonly as Westerners eat bread.

The fruits, too, were somewhat different from what we had in the States. Yes, there were papayas—at one point, they even grew in our yard. And we had bananas, too, though they were usually much smaller than the ones Americans normally eat. But we also had rambutans, a plum-size tree-growing fruit with a soft, spiny covering and a large pit. They were okay, but for a real treat, we liked to eat mangosteens. Mangosteens are about the size of a tangerine. They are constituted of a purple husk containing a circle of white kidney-shaped segments that are as tasty as one can possibly imagine.

My favorite food discovery of all, though, were the satays. They were marinated meat, normally pork at our house, grilled on bamboo skewers over hot charcoal and served under a mound of heavy peanut sauce. Whenever Mom and Dad had a dinner party, plenty of satays were served, and I would sneak out among the adults and steal them. I couldn't get enough of those darn things!

For the ultimate Indonesian meal, we would dine on something called a rijsttafel (literally "rice table" in Dutch). Indonesian food comes in many varieties, and it is heavily influenced by the cuisines of other Asian nations. At a rijsttafel, these many exotic and wonderful dishes are presented all at once in what amounts to a feast. The labor that goes into preparing such a meal is, of course, great, so rijsttafel wasn't something we got to experience very often.

One of the first things Mom and Dad did in Indonesia was to plan a trip to Bali. Everyone said it was the most enchanting island in the world, so when Mom and Dad's birthdays came around that September in 1953, going there seemed like just the thing to do.

Once again, we would be flying aboard the Caltex Star, only this time we headed southeast toward Java and the capital city of Jakarta. Before, we had seen only jungle canopy beneath our wings, but now the terrain was more varied and more interesting. For one thing, Indonesia has more active volcanoes than any other country, and we were seeing lots of them. At one point during the flight, Dad got the pilot to descend over the top of a particularly beautiful volcano so that he could get a picture. Looking down from above, we were surprised to see a large caldera filled in by a beautiful turquoise-blue lake. For Dana and me, the sight of it all was just incredible, but Mom never got to see it. She was so scared she couldn't look out the window. After landing in Jakarta, we boarded a Garuda Airlines flight, which took us the rest of the way to our destination. Looking down on Bali from the sky, one might have thought it little different from the rest of Indonesia, but we soon found that not to be the case. Where Sumatra, for example, was large and was shrouded in nearly impenetrable jungle, this island was much smaller and more cultivated, in every sense of the word.

Bali is literally a Hindu island in a sea of Islam. Hinduism had, in fact, predominated throughout the East Indies prior to the late Middle Ages. But when Muslim traders began arriving from Western Asia, Islam gradually took over. Bali somehow got excepted, and for centuries, it was a magnet for those who wished to keep to the old ways. What developed was a concentration of artisans, painters, musicians, and theologians, all located in a place of extraordinary beauty. By blending Hindu influences from India with the animistic traditions of their ancient past, these marvelously creative people evolved a highly religious, artistic culture, making Bali one of the most exotic places on earth.

Everywhere we went, we saw open-air temples carved from stone in the most ornate detail. Each was adorned with small offerings of flowers and food wrapped in leaves of banana or palm and left in sacrifice for the various Hindu deities.

The center of the island is dominated by volcanoes, the tallest of which is Gunung Agung (Mount Fire). On its slopes, we visited the Pura Besakih, the most important of the Balinese temples. Nearby, we saw Lake Batur, the ultimate source of most of the irrigation water that serves Bali's famous terraced rice paddies.

The paddies were the most beautiful topographical features we saw on the island, but beyond being beautiful, they also constitute a remarkable system of irrigation that has always functioned farmer to farmer, without any central control. The rich volcanic soil is ideal for growing rice, yet farming on Bali is almost entirely subsistent and most of the growers live in houses without floors and without access to basic utility services.

Virtually everyone we saw on Bali was dressed in batik. This, we were much accustomed to seeing already from living on Sumatra. What we were not accustomed to, however, was the near ubiquity of toplessness among women. Young ones, walking along the road, exposed themselves in this way as they carried enormous parcels on their heads. Old women, too, betel nut juice trickling from their mouths, went about naked from the waist up!

At night, gamelan musicians set up outside our hotel and played their odd assortment of mostly percussion instruments. There, in the firelight, we stood, spellbound, listening to the jingle-jangle of the music and watching as costumed dancers performed magical dramas of good and evil. Always, it seems, the stories included an elaborately costumed dragon or witch. When they appeared, Dana and I would move closer to our parents.

Most mysterious to me, though, was something they called the monkey dance. It is performed by three dozen or so half-naked men seated on the ground in concentric circles. They appear to be in some sort of trance as they lean forward and back, left and right, chanting and whooping in unison. At the end, some of the dancers get up and walk barefoot over hot coals.

Why it was called the monkey dance, I don't know, but to be sure, the island was overrun with monkeys. Unlike the ones in Sumatra, these were brazen, if not outright aggressive, around humans. When approached, they expected to be fed, and when we had no food to offer, they grabbed at Mom's purse and at everything else they thought they could get away with. We all found their antics enormously entertaining.

Of equal interest to us, of course, was the beach. Nowhere else on a tropical island is the feeling of being in paradise stronger than it is where the sand meets the sea. We frolicked with Dad in the surf and learned to make sandcastles. By the end of our visit, Dana and I each had a nice bag of seashells to carry home. Of course, Mom and Dad weren't empty-handed—they took home as many batiks and works of art as they could carry.

By the end of 1954, our first contract in Indonesia had come to an end. Once again, it was time to board the Caltex Star. Only this time we were taking a long leave back to the States. We flew from Pakanbaru to Singapore, where we enjoyed a brief stay at the beach-front Seaview Hotel.

In a world where nearly every community boasts of being a crossroads, Singapore really is such a place, more so, in fact, than anywhere else I can think of. An island sitting just off the southeastern tip of the Asian mainland, Singapore was, even then, one of the busiest seaports in the world. Sooner or later, nearly every oceangoing vessel in the Eastern Hemisphere puts in there.

Accordingly, the Singaporean culture is an amalgam of many others, with British, Chinese, Indian, and Malay being most predominant. Unlike Indonesia, which was now independent of the Netherlands, Singapore was still an old-style colony of the British Empire, and it felt like it too. Meals in the sea-view dining room were white-tablecloth affairs, and midafternoons, tea and biscuits were brought to our room. At bedtime, lying under a whirling ceiling fan and mosquito nets, Dana and I laughed at the cicaks⸀ running up and down the walls. We loved the place.

From Singapore, we flew nearly halfway around the world to Rome. There, we picked up a little Fiat Dad had prearranged with an Italian rental car company, and we set off on our first European vacation. We made stops in Venice and then in Innsbruck, where we all went to a performance of *Cosi Fan Tutte*. Then we drove all over Switzerland and Bavaria before returning to Italy. Each morning we would find a delicatessen and provision ourselves for a picnic lunch, which we would later consume on the side of the road somewhere. Salami and cheese with a crusty loaf of bread always made up our menu. For Mom and Dad, there was always a bottle of red wine. I have no fonder memories than these.

In Genoa, we turned in the Fiat, boarded the SS *Constitution*, and set sail for the States. By now I was discovering something wonderful about traveling. At home, Dana and I tended to have our separate friends. I'm sure this was due, in part, to her being a girl and me being a boy. But another reason was that we often just didn't get along. On vacation, though, things tended to be better between us. Everywhere we went, we had lots of exploring to do together, and we delighted in it. The *Constitution*, for example, like the *Cleveland*, had lots of nooks and crannies that needed to be checked out, and this was something we could do together. Again, as with the *Cleveland*, I particularly enjoyed the onboard movie theater. We saw Leslie Caron

---

⸀ Cicaks (pronounced "chee-chucks") are beige-colored lizards about six inches long. Their feet are tacky enough to enable them to walk upside down on the ceiling.

in *Lili*, and I was captivated by it. For months afterward, I went about singing "A song of love is a sad song, hi lili, hi lily, hi lay…"

Our first crossing of the Atlantic wasn't to be all fun, however. The ship's swimming pool was filled with salt water, and the first time we went in, I swallowed a mouthful. Of course, I immediately vomited, and everybody was ordered out of the pool! Now the whole thing had to be drained and refilled. None of the passengers was allowed to swim for the next twenty-four hours, and nobody was very happy about that. But they had no idea! No sooner did the pool reopen the next day than I went right back in the water and did it again.

Fortunately, we were soon sailing into New York harbor. From New York we flew to Norfolk, Virginia, where, for the first time, I was about to meet Gamma and see Nadamar. I was only six years old, so I had no idea that Nadamar was, in any way, an extraordinary place to live. But of course, it was.

In order to provide herself with a neighbor, Gamma had, by now, sold four of her twenty-one original acres. She still had seventeen, though, all of which were shaded by towering pine trees that grew right down to the water's edge.

The house our grandfather built was chalk white. It stood on a lofty point that thrust out into the bay from the center of the property. Because the water off the point was too shallow for boating, he had built a fifty-foot pier, and Gamma still had his two rowboats, which Dana and I were free to use.

We took a liking to Gamma right away. She had a pleasing round face and a ready smile. She was only sixty, but her hair was exceedingly white. It had been, we were told, for half her life. Living alone in these woods by the sea, she seemed to us entirely happy and self-reliant, though we were too young to perceive otherwise. What was more, she treated us with the kind of warmth that is expected of grandparents, and that was something we greatly enjoyed.

For the first time in our lives, we also got to meet the only cousins we would ever have. Aunt Dorothy and Uncle Hank (Henry Weller) came down from Norfolk the first day, and they brought their two daughters. Buz (Elizabeth) was just a few months younger than Dana, and Jen (Virginia) was eighteen months younger than I was. If the two of them felt any jealousy over having strangers suddenly move in on their grandmother, they didn't show it. Rather, they seemed as happy about getting to know us as we were about getting to know them.

Over the next two weeks, Buz taught Dana and me how to row a boat and how to gather oysters from out of the muck near the shoreline. She showed us how, by using a string, a chicken neck, and a net, we could catch crabs off the side of the pier.

Crabbing was a delight! The first time we tried it, the four of us little kids hauled in a harvest big enough to feed everybody. We carried our catch up to the house in a bushel basket and watched while Gamma dropped them, still alive, into a large pot of boiling water. Then, the whole family gathered around Gamma's picnic table, and we ate our bellies' full. Imagine feasting on something so delicious caught right off your own front yard. It amazes me still!

But we couldn't stay forever, and soon we were pulling away from Nadamar in Gamma's DeSoto. She drove us back to the Norfolk airport, where we said our goodbyes and boarded the flight that would start us on our way to California.

After changing planes in Washington and Los Angeles, we arrived in San Diego late in the evening. Nanny and Bumpa were at Lindbergh Field to meet us. We were tired, of course, but very excited to be back after such a long absence. With all the hugging and laughing that took place, I don't know if anyone even realized we had just completed our first circumnavigation of the world!

Someone must have said something to the newspaper, because a few days later, a reporter called at Nanny and Bumpa's house, and our story, complete with a picture of Mom, appeared in the *San Diego Evening Tribune*. It was January 24, 1955.

Once again, Dana and I were not used to having relatives, but we had no trouble adjusting. Nanny and Bumpa were living now in a rented bungalow on El Cajon Boulevard while their own new house was being built a couple of miles away. Somehow, we all managed to squeeze in.

Dad could only stay for a week. He had scheduled himself to return to Sumatra ahead of the rest of us, knowing Mom would want more time with her parents. Then, Mom did something that would become a pattern over time. Even with just a few weeks left to our stay in San Diego, she enrolled Dana and me in school.

Being temporarily enrolled in an unfamiliar school is not a pleasant experience for a young kid. Trying to fit in among children with whom I had no past and no future was something I found intimidating. One day, when another boy teased me about wearing short pants, I knocked him to the ground, and I got sent home. When the time finally came for us to return to Indonesia, I was relieved.

Apparently, Mom's fear of flying was no longer sufficient to require a ten-day ocean crossing, and that is saying something. After all, flying across the Pacific in a propeller-driven DC-6 was quite an undertaking. As the crow flies, we had a distance of almost 9,000 miles to cover, but with a top speed of 350 miles per hour and a range of only 3,800 miles, our journey wasn't going to go as the crow flies. Instead, we made a forty-eight-hour stop in Hawaii, where Dana and I both got a blistering sunburn on the beach at Waikiki. Then we boarded a second plane that made refueling-and-refreshment stops at Wake Island and on Guam. Taking off from Guam in the middle of the night, we flew on to Hong Kong, where we had a twenty-four-hour layover and then another plane to catch. By the time we got to Singapore, we had been traveling for four days and had spent some thirty-five hours in the air.

Flying might have been slower (and bumpier) in those days, but it was also more refined. For one thing, the cabin was far roomier than in today's economy class, and normally there were diversions of one kind or another for children. These particular planes were even more comfortable than most. They had beds that dropped down from the ceiling, Pullman-style, enabling at least Dana and me to get plenty of sleep.

We got back in Rumbai to find that a few changes had taken place. For one thing, Dad was now officially chief petroleum engineer. While the responsibilities of that job had been his all along, at least now he had the title. I imagine he had a bigger paycheck to boot.

To go with his new stature, we were assigned a new house, though it was really very little different from the old one. Jojo, our dog, was now gone. She had been a good pet, even gave us a large litter of puppies once, but when a friend in Minas had expressed interest in her, Dad had turned her over.

Gone, too, was Mochtar. Not able to remain unemployed during our two-month absence, he had found another family. Fortunately, someone knew of a man and wife who were available for us. Their names were Hierman and Muchina, and Muchina had a teenage brother, Tokijo, who could work as our gardener. All three had been highly regarded by previous employers, so Mom hired them as soon as they came around to the house.

Hierman was tall for an Indonesian. He had sharper features, too, than what we were used to seeing, almost as though he was from some other tribe. His bearing was erect, almost regal, and he had an integrity about him that became apparent as soon as he spoke. Muchina, too, had a pleasing appearance, though, unlike Hierman, she was of average height and had the smoother facial features more typical of Sumatrans. Man and wife both were neatly dressed and very polite. Meanwhile, Tokijo wasn't nearly as tall as Hierman—at least not yet—but he was quick with a laugh and had a smile that seemed permanently affixed to his face. We liked all three of them immediately.

Nobody was happier about the new servants than Mom. She was used to having a houseboy, but now she had a cook too. This gave her more freedom during the day to go about camp and social-ize with her friends. She could always count on Muchina to have a large platter of sandwiches and a tureen of soup ready for our lunch.

Having Hierman and Muchina also made it easy throwing par-ties, and Dad's position in the company gave Mom a reason for doing so, particularly whenever Caltex bigwigs were in camp. Dana and I had been told that children should be seen and not heard, so we stayed in our rooms. Still, there were always heaping platters of satays out there smothered in peanut sauce. Who could blame us for creeping out among the guests and snatching a few? Which we invariably did!

Even at thirty, Mom was already an excellent cook. Night after night, she turned out the most wonderful dishes for our candlelight dinners: lamb curry, chicken paprika, veal parmesan…the list went on. But now, with Muchina's help, Indonesian specialties were pouring out of our kitchen as well. It was marvelous!

Hierman would serve at table, and he took the job very seriously. He always dressed impeccably in a starched white shirt, and he had a black turban that he wore neatly wrapped around his head. Mom began keeping a little bell by her dinner plate, and whenever she rang it, he would emerge from the kitchen. Serve from the left, take away to the right—he knew just what to do.

Dana and I always had healthy appetites. We never balked at eating even the most exotic dishes. In fact, we relished them. We dined with great care, however, as our table manners were the subject of constant scrutiny by our mother.

After dessert, Mom and Dad usually finished their wine out on the patio, where they sat talking in the dark. On occasion, they would come into the living room instead. When they did, Dana and I would climb onto the couch, pin Dad between us, and expect him to read to us or tell us a story. Most fondly, perhaps, I remember listening to Tennyson's "Charge of the Light Brigade" and Kipling's "Rikki-Tikki-Tavi" in this way. But many other stories stick out in my memory as well. The most outlandish, of course, were the ones Dad made up as he went along. Dana and I would listen in utter amazement, never sure whether we were hearing the truth or not.

On one of these nights, in early December 1955, our front door suddenly flew open and a menacing-looking black man carrying a large burlap bag sprang into our living room. In school, Dana and I had already encountered the legendary Dutch character and Saint Nicholas companion Zwarte Piet (Black Peter), so we recognized him immediately. But when this Dutchman in blackface grabbed me and forced me into his sack, I didn't know what to make of it. Suddenly, I was being carried off down the street, and I was scared. Of course, he quickly took me back into the house and let me go. He also passed out homemade gingerbread men before he left, so I guess I had to forgive him. Nonetheless, I think everyone else found the experience a lot funnier than I did!

Into this happy mix, a few weeks later, my brother Mark was born at the Rumbai hospital on the twenty-ninth of January 1956. Because he was the fifth member of the family, Mom chose Quentin as his middle name. Dana and I were delighted to have this little brother, as sweet an infant as you could ever want.

I was no longer the baby now, and that was fine with me. I was about to turn eight, and I had been given a new bicycle for Christmas. I was half a head taller than anyone else my age, and I was free to roam around and play wherever I pleased, as long as I showed up on time for meals. As unlikely as it seems, I was even allowed to play in the jungle, which I frequently did either with Dana or with some of the other boys.

At the old house, I had palled around with fellows named Allen White and Stevie Yetter. But then Allen's family moved to Duri, and the Yetters left Sumatra altogether. So now I had new friends coming into the picture. Denny Bales moved in across the street. He had a million toys, or so it seemed, and he always made me laugh. We played together in a big drainage ditch, which was down at the end of our street. It was a great place to make roads for our miniature cars.

My parents didn't pay much notice, but I had started carrying a hatchet around. Just for the fun of it, I was going into the jungle and cutting down trees. One day, Denny was using the hatchet to carve little roads into the side of the ditch when it slipped from his hand and struck me in the arm. I wasn't hurt. He didn't even break the skin. But I went into a rage anyway, grabbing the hatchet and chasing him down the street. Thank goodness he could run faster than I could, or who knows what terrible thing I might have done.

When Denny wasn't around, Mary Lou Caywood usually was. She lived around the corner, and she was such a tomboy, more daring, I'd say, than any of the guys. At least she was more daring than I was. I know that for sure. Once, she coaxed me up onto a roof, and then she jumped off. I felt no desire to follow her, but I was embarrassed not to. "Come on, come on!" she pleaded. "You can do it!" So I finally did, hurling myself out into the air.

Another time, the two of us were riding our bikes down near the hospital when Mary Lou discovered a way to climb up into the attic over the nurses' apartments. Like a fool, I followed her. Neither of us knew wallboard ceilings aren't meant to hold any weight. As soon as we stepped off the joists, both of us punched right through into the apartments below.

Fortunately, my arms caught on the joists, keeping me from falling all the way to the floor, but most of my body was dangling from somebody's bathroom ceiling. Mary Lou, meanwhile, had gone all the way through, though luckily she fell into an easy chair and was unhurt.

We got out of there in a hurry, of course, and I never told a soul about it. I still wonder what those nurses must have thought when they got home that night.

In December 1956, it was time for another long leave. This time, after flying to Singapore, we boarded a plane to India. We spent Christmas in Old Delhi at the wonderful Maidens Hotel, a charming remnant of the British colonial period. Santa managed to keep track of us, however. When we awoke, Dana and I found maharaja shoes by our beds, and they were filled with candy. We were also given Kodak Brownie cameras, which we happily put to use right away. Over the days that followed, when we weren't exploring the hotel together, we were off with our parents, taking pictures at the Red Fort and at the Taj Mahal.

From Delhi, we flew to Pakistan for a brief visit in Karachi. Then we boarded another plane for Lebanon. By this time, though, Mom was taking ill, so ill, in fact, that she had to be hospitalized when we reached Beirut. What started as a cold had turned into pneumonia, and that was enough to throw us off our itinerary for a couple of weeks.

Once again, our first European stop was Rome, where we rented another Fiat. This time, we stopped in Pisa, spent a couple of days at Lake Como, and then headed over the Alps in time to spend Mark's first birthday at the wonderful Hotel Walliserhof in Zermatt. While we were there, the hotel provided us with babysitters for Mark so that Dad could take the rest of us out for ski lessons.

My arm was in a cast, owing to an accident I had falling off the high dive at the Rumbai pool. Even so, I managed to do well enough skiing to know I wanted to try it again someday.

Next, we went to Paris, where Dana had heard there were lots of lovers. While she kept a watchful eye out for them, we all managed to make it to the usual tourist attractions. Then we turned in our Fiat and flew to London.

In London, too, we saw most of the big attractions. Dana and I missed out on one of the biggest, however, Westminster Abbey. That day, our parents were unable to get us away from the television in our hotel room. Televisions, you see, were already commonplace in the US, but we had never had anything more than a glimpse of one before.

Finally, we left Europe, flying to Norfolk, via New York and Washington, DC. Since our last visit, Gamma had given Aunt Dorothy and Uncle Hank enough ground on which to build a house at Nadamar, and they were now living there. So this time, our cousins were closer at hand, and the four of us kids had another wonderful time rowing Gamma's boats around in the bay and catching crabs off the pier.

Then, of course, we flew to San Diego, just as we had done two years before. Once again, Dad was there only a week or so before returning to Sumatra. The rest of us stayed on with Nanny and Bumpa, who were in their new house now on 8553 Lucille Drive. We were there about a month, just long enough for Mom to put Dana and me in school.

By early 1957, when we returned to Indonesia, Dad was well established as a company *tuan besar*, or big boss. His job was to program and direct all drilling and production activities, and that encompassed most of the company's mission on Sumatra. Meanwhile, our family had been moved into yet another new house half a kilometer farther up from the Siak River.

Our new yard was one of the largest in camp, so Dad decided it was a good place to apply some of the knowledge he had gained helping his own father grow food many years earlier. As a first step, he had Hierman and Tokijo build a picket fence enclosure next to the servants' quarters. He filled it up with ducks, a couple of dozen or so. Next, he dug out a strip of ground outside my bedroom window, and he built a small but fairly sophisticated hydroponic garden. Of course, none of the rest of us had any idea what a hydroponic garden was, so we were pretty impressed. In no time at all, we were eating lots of duck and a lot of endive salads, too, among other things.

Another perk that went with Dad's increasing importance was his new Willys Jeep Wagon. Unlike most of the other vehicles in town, which were conventional army-surplus open-air jeeps, the wagon was fully enclosed.

One evening, Dad told me he was going to drive up to Duri and Dumai, spend the night, and then take care of some business before returning the next day. Would I like to tag a long?

"Sure," I said. "I'd love to!"

Dumai had forever been a small coastal town on the Strait of Malacca, but its proximity to the Duri field was about to make it an important loading dock for oil tankers. Dad had talked about it a lot, but none of the rest of us had ever been there. After dinner, Dad filled his thermos with coffee, and he said, "Let's hit the road!"

As the crow flies, Dumai and Rumbai are only about 150 kilometers apart. But the road between the two was a wavy and winding 200 kilometers at least. It was only eighteen feet wide, and except for the two small settlements at Minas and Duri, it passed through nothing but virgin jungle. Like all company roads, it was topped with a mixture of tar and sand, which, in the tropical heat and humidity, could be easily impressed with a footprint or tire track.

It was well after dark when we pulled away from the house. There would be no streetlamps along the way, no painted stripes on the road, no road-condition signs, and probably no other vehicles anywhere in sight. Under such conditions, our drive, if accomplished safely, should have taken nearly three hours.

We passed through Minas at around nine thirty. Then, about thirty minutes later, we came to a wide place where the road crossed over a stream. Dad pulled the jeep over onto the shoulder and braked.

"Son, I need to go to the bathroom," he said, "and I think this is as good a place as any. Do you want to go too?"

"I guess so," I said, not wanting to stay alone in the car.

Of course, I didn't really want to get out of the car either. I had been playing in the jungle near our house for years, hiking on trails, creating hideouts, even swinging on vines. But this was different. We were out in the middle of nowhere, and owing to the absence of the moon that night, it was dark, very dark.

We climbed out and went about our business, peeing side by side near the bank of the stream. In a couple of minutes, we were back in the jeep, and I felt doubly relieved.

As Dad edged the car back onto the highway, we thought we were on our way. But only a few hundred meters passed before our headlamps suddenly illuminated a large yellow snake slithering across the road.

You would think, living in a place like Indonesia for so long, I'd have been inured to these critters by now. They were, after all, everywhere, and we encountered them all the time. But that simply wasn't the case. Just the opposite was true, in fact. With so many deadly serpents about, all children were taught to be afraid, and I was no exception.

Once, when all four of us had gone out for a drive, we ran over an enormous python. It was as thick as a man's thigh and stretched clear across the road, a distance of eighteen feet! To make sure it was dead, Dad backed up and ran over it again. When we turned to look, we barely managed to see it disappear into the jungle. I doubt many animals could survive such a punishment. Later, we looked up pythons in the *Encyclopedia Britannica*. Up to that time, the longest ever recorded was sixteen feet.

There is no telling what kind of snake Dad and I were encountering on the road to Dumai that night. It could well have been a spitting cobra, many of which are yellow, and all of which are very dangerous. But it didn't slow down for our sake, and I didn't want it to, anyway.

Nonetheless, there was something ominous about a long yellow snake on a moonless night. And sure enough, we were about to discover what it was. Rounding a corner and starting down a long gentle slope, we suddenly found ourselves spinning out of control. There was a trench someone had dug along the roadside, and a recent rain had slopped mud from it out onto the highway. The wagon skidded maybe twenty meters or so and then came to rest, both right side wheels deep in the mire.

Our four-wheel-drive Willys Jeep was, of course, designed for such emergencies. But somehow, this particular challenge proved to be more than it could handle. Over and over Dad tried to break us free by shifting back and forth between forward and reverse, but it was no use. We were only sinking deeper into the mud.

Soon, Dad gave up and turned off the motor. It was past ten o'clock now. We were stuck deep in the jungle, at least forty kilometers from the nearest settlement. We had no flashlight, no food, no blankets, no pillows, just a thermos of coffee, which I was too young to drink. We both knew there was little chance of anyone coming around to find us, at least until morning.

"Dad, what are we going to do?" I asked.

"Well, I guess we're just going to have to spend the night in the car," he said. "I don't know what else we can do."

Fortunately, both of us had just gone to the bathroom, so the only thing left was to try to make ourselves comfortable. I climbed into the back seat, and Dad stretched out in the front. To keep the air fresh inside, he cranked two of the windows down several inches. I protested, of course, thinking we would surely die, but there really wasn't much choice.

Neither of us slept very much that night. Just as the sun was coming up, we were startled awake by the sound of an approaching vehicle. It was Harlan White, the father of my friend Allen, who had moved to Duri ages ago. Thankfully, Mr. White's truck was equipped with a winch, and in no time at all, he had us out of the ditch.

Dad thanked him heartily, and then the two of them chatted briefly. Mr. White had a habit of using colorful language, and it occurred to me that Dad had responded in kind. Well, sort of, at least. In describing how we got stuck the night before, he uttered the word *damn*, and that was the closest thing to an expletive I'd ever heard him say.

In October that same year, 1957, news arrived in the jungle that something earth-shattering had transpired on the world stage. The Soviet Union had launched a man-made satellite into orbit. Called Sputnik, it weighed 184 pounds and was eight times heavier than a satellite America had been working on. Everyone in camp was astounded. Wasn't this the era of American dominance? If anyone was to accomplish this feat, shouldn't it have been us?

Long accustomed to evenings spent out on the patio, our family now started searching the sky every night for Sputnik. But none of us ever made out the tiny speck of light we were hoping to see. The satellite was, after all, some five hundred miles away, and it was only twenty-two inches in diameter. The experience, though, awakened in me an interest in current events that would grow as time went on. I was only nine years old, but I began paying attention to the *Weekly Reader* when it was passed out at school.

Always before, I brought home good report cards, but I confess, my grades, by now, were beginning to fade. I fancied myself one of the smarter kids in class, but my lessons were requiring more effort and more concentration as time went on, and these were two qualities I seemed to lack. Instead, I was a nearly constant daydreamer, and I think Dana might have been too. Her grades were no better than mine.

For our parents, each report card, when it came, was a source of increasing consternation. "I don't understand this," Mom would say. "I always had good grades in school, and my parents never had to make me do my homework!"

At first, Dad handled the problem by imposing formal study times, which we were to spend in our rooms. Temporarily, at least, the plan seemed to help, but when our report cards came out again, they were worse than ever. A couple of times, Dad became so exasperated he took off his belt and spanked us both.

Spanking is something, I suppose, that most parents succumb to sooner or later. It isn't pleasant for parent or child, and it certainly wasn't pleasant for Dad (or Mom either, for that matter, who usually could be heard getting upset out in the hallway). But for Dana and me, it was terrifying. Once, after a particularly bad spanking, I checked my bottom in the mirror and was surprised to see red welts where Dad had broken the skin. When I told Dana about it, she said she had them too. Neither of us ever told our parents, though. Best just to leave it alone.

After a while, Dad put away his belt and never spanked us again. He just didn't have the stomach for it anymore, and anyway, it wasn't working. As frightened as Dana and I were of the spankings, neither of us ever cared enough to do much better in school. I can't speak for Dana, of course, but in my case, the reason was pretty simple. Lost in my own thoughts, I was having trouble listening to my teachers and often had no clue to what was going on.

In another respect, however, my intellectual development wasn't being neglected. Thanks, in part, to all of Dad's reading to us, I was becoming more and more interested in books. On one of our occasional trips to Singapore, Mom purchased a couple of volumes for me by the English author of children's mystery series Enid Blyton. I read them quickly and then began looking for more Enid Blyton books in the small library we had at the company school. Soon, I had read all her Secret Seven novels and was devouring the Famous Five series. At year's end, when our Christmas package came from Nanny and Bumpa, six Hardy Boy mysteries were included for me, and in a matter of weeks, I had read all of them.

The following year, 1958, I checked R. D. Blackmore's *Lorna Doone* out of the library and read it. It was a big book for a ten-year-old, but I loved every page. Like me, John Ridd was taller than everyone else, and the beautiful Lorna, with her flowing black hair, presented an image of feminine perfection that stays with me to this day.

Even though the fully independent Republic of Indonesia was only eight years old, there was already talk of rebellion on Sumatra. Regional commanders of the national army, not happy with the heavy hand of President Sukarno, were demanding greater autonomy for the island. When their demands were refused, they took control of the island by force and set up a revolutionary government of the

Republic of Indonesia. They called it the PRRI. Sukarno sent in loyalist troops to put down the rebellion, and though we never actually saw, or even heard, any fighting in Rumbai, we did, for a time, have soldiers bivouacked around town.

At about the same time, Dad and Mom had gone in as partners with some friends in buying a boat they had moored down on the Siak River. When the fourth of July came around, Dad got a brainstorm.

He ran down to the river in the wagon and snatched up all the emergency flares and smoke bombs that were on the boat. Then he brought them back to the house, and as the sun dipped below the horizon, he began setting them off for us in the front yard.

We were lucky we didn't all get killed. Thinking they were under attack, the federal army showed up in a matter of minutes. It was really only a couple of jeeps, one of them bearing a ranking officer, but their guns were drawn, and they were ready for trouble!

That year was notable for two other events that happened in our lives. First, my mother lost what would have been her fourth child when the baby she was expecting was born too early to save. Dad was up at Duri or Dumai or someplace the night it happened, but he hurried home when he got the news. The next morning, he explained everything to Dana and me and asked us not to bring it up to Mom when she came home. He said it was not something she would want to talk about. In all the years afterward, I never once even mentioned it, not even to express my sympathy, and as far as I know, Dana never did either.

The other event was something that happened to Mark, our little two-year-old brother. While kicking a ball in the front yard one day, he fell awkwardly and broke his leg. Because he was so young, the break was what Dr. Gerrits called a green stick, where the bone isn't hard enough yet to snap very cleanly. For that reason, it was put in traction, and poor little Mark was kept on his back in the hospital, his leg sticking up at a ninety-degree angle, for seven long weeks.

In March 1959, our third contract in Indonesia was nearing an end. With only a week to go before our third home leave, we were struck by yet another misfortune. Coming home from school on the bus one day, I was surprised when we were stopped by a couple of men who were standing in the middle of the street. One of them boarded the bus and announced there was a house on fire around the bend. All of us, he said, would have to get out and walk the rest of the way home.

"Whose house is it?" someone asked as we filed off the bus.

"Davenports'," he responded, and that was all, just "Davenports'!"

The mere suggestion of our house burning down was so alien I thought the man must be mistaken. But I alighted from the bus and took off running to see for myself. I ran hard the entire distance, and when I came around the last corner, I saw in an instant that he wasn't.

Out on the street in front of the house, vehicles, including the camp fire truck, were strewn about, and there were people all around. A couple of fire hoses lay stretched across the lawn, and blackened clutter was everywhere. I saw no one from my family.

I saw no flames, either. The fire had already been extinguished. What remained of the house was little more than a burned-out shell. Across the rooftop, a thin mixture of smoke and steam was rising, and the air all around me was heavy with the musty, unpleasant odor that burned coals make when they are doused.

The loss of the building itself, of course, was no real tragedy for our family. After all, we didn't own it. But nearly everything we did own was either seriously damaged or gone forever. It was almost as though we had suddenly decided to start life over.

No one said for sure what started the fire, but it appeared to have ignited in the bedroom Mark and I shared. Just about every closet in Rumbai was equipped with a caged light bulb set down near the floor. These lights were kept on to prevent mildew on clothing, a problem in the tropics. Perhaps Mark or I left an article of clothing on top of the light in our closet. Thankfully, though, neither of us was ever accused of being responsible for what happened.

With only a few days to go before our home leave, Mom and Dad accepted an offer for us to stay temporarily at a neighbor's house. We salvaged what we could of our charred belongings, and Dad secured a place to store them. Friends came around with donations of clothing and personal items, and in no time at all, we had enough to fill our aluminum suitcases, which had survived the fire just fine.

We departed Sumatra as passengers aboard a handsome yacht cruising down the Siak River. Once before, we had spent an entire day boating upstream to visit the one-hundred-year-old sultan of Siak Palace. The most prominent feature along the river, the palace had once housed the rulers of Central Sumatra. On that trip, we kept seeing crocodiles in the water, and I worried about them when it got dark. As small as our boat was, I kept wondering what would happen if I fell overboard. It gave me the willies.

This time, though, the boat was a lot bigger, and we reached the mouth of the river before the sun went down. All day, we saw nothing but jungle.**

Dana and I both spent time that day talking to the pilot. I was fascinated by the constant steering necessitated by so many turns in the river. Speaking mostly in Bahasa, he explained how he watched for landmarks along the way, a sandbar here, a giant tree trunk there. This was how he judged his progress. After six years in Indonesia, we had little trouble understanding him.

Late in the afternoon, our boat passed out of the river and turned southward into a much broader channel. As evening came on, pleasant aromas began coming from the galley. Soon, it would be time for dinner.

By nightfall, we were docked at Karimun, our only stop before crossing the Malacca Strait to Singapore. Dana, Mark, and I were sent off to sleep in the largest cabin, which was in the stern.

At sunup, we awoke to hear a great commotion outside. There were laborers loading cargo on the dock. To see what was going on, we opened a window and leaned out. Then, suddenly, Dana pointed down at the water and said, "Look!"

Just below the water's surface, in the shade of our boat, dozens of the most exotic fishes in all different shapes and colors were swim-

---

** Sadly, that would not be true today. Much of the rain forest along the Siak, and throughout Sumatra, for that matter, has been burned away by fires that were set to clear the land for farming.

ming about. I had never seen such a sight. It was like gazing into the most beautiful saltwater aquarium, only it was real.

That morning, a calm sea, and bright sunshine prevailed as we crossed the strait and sailed into Singapore harbor. Along the way, Dana and I ate breakfast on deck with Dad. He was having caviar on toast, and for the first time ever, we had it too. Unbeknownst to either of us, it would be many years before we would ever see Indonesia again.

That afternoon, we checked in to Singapore's famous Raffles Hotel. The Raffles was, and is, a marvelous old relic of the British colonial period. One half-expects to see Rudyard Kipling or Phileas Fogg striding through the lobby. Kipling, in fact, as well as a lot of other famous people, actually had been a guest there. Legend has it that the last wild tiger on Singapore island was shot under the billiard table at the Raffles in 1902! We stayed just long enough to replace some clothes we had lost in the fire and to catch up on our curry at a nearby restaurant.

From there, we boarded a series of planes in places like Saigon and Bangkok, which ultimately delivered us to Cairo. There, Dad had booked us into another historic hotel. This time it was the Shepheard's Hotel, which had just been renovated. The luxury we found there surpassed anything I had experienced before. The beds, in particular, were magnificent!

Our first morning in Egypt, Dad took us out to Giza to see the pyramids and the Sphinx. Dana and I climbed a good distance up one of the pyramids. Then we managed to have our pictures taken sitting on a camel.

The next day, we all went to the main souk. Mom wanted to shop for Egyptian perfumes and jewelry. Soon, we were deep in a labyrinth of passageways and crowded stalls selling brassware, camel saddles, sheepskins, Arab clothing, and all manner of foodstuffs. We found a small shop selling unbranded perfumes in tiny vials containing the purest essence of real flowers. The proprietor passed around samples for us all to smell, and Mom picked out the one she liked.

From there, we flew to Vienna, where, after a couple of days, we rented a car and drove to Stuttgart, the site of the Mercedes-Benz factory. Months before, Dad had preordered a pea soup–green 190. It might have been their least-expensive model, but we were all aware of what a special car it was, and we were very excited. Dad stopped at the first hardware store and bought a pail and chamois to wash it with, something he would do almost every day for the rest of the trip.

We spent the next week or so driving all over West Germany. In Frankfurt, we saw a store that sold china. Mom picked out a set with a lovely rose pattern, and all of us thought she had made the perfect choice.

Our last stop in Germany was an overnight stay in Hamburg, a city that had been mercilessly bombed out by the Allies during the war. Fifty thousand people, mostly civilians, had lost their lives there, most during a horrifying firestorm that was bomb-induced in the summer of 1943.

Now it was 1959, a full sixteen years later, and Hamburg was back on its feet. Yet driving through town, we saw that many buildings still lay in ruins.

After Hamburg, we crossed into Denmark. We visited Odense and then came to rest for a few days in Copenhagen.

What a marvelous place that was, especially to Dana and me. We had recently seen the movie *Hans Christian Andersen*, starring Danny Kaye singing "Wonderful, Wonderful Copenhagen." The song was in my mind and on my lips the whole time we were there. We stayed in a nice old hotel on the grand circle of the wharf at Nyhavn. From there, we could walk to just about all the important attractions, and we did. We visited the statue of the Little Mermaid, and of course, Dad took us all to the Tivoli amusement park. When we left Copenhagen, all of us felt we had been somewhere special.

We took a ferry to Sweden, and then we spent several days touring Norway as far up as Geiranger Fjord. Driving along steep mountainside roads, over glaciers, and through tunnels by the score, we looked down upon the great fjords and saw beauty almost too great to comprehend.

For three nights, we stayed in a fine hotel in Geiranger, right on the fjord. Each morning we experienced one of Scandinavia's greatest pleasures, the smorgasbord breakfast. Then, Dad exposed us to a variety of activities. The first day, we tried waterskiing. No, neither of us could get up. We were just little kids, and you can imagine how cold the water was in a Norwegian fjord. Then Dad took us hiking in the woods and showed us what was purported to be a Viking burial mound. The next day, he and I went out onto the fjord to fish for salmon, and while I don't recall that we caught anything, it was great sharing the experience alone with him.

After Geiranger, we made our way down to Bergen. There, we drove our little green Mercedes onto another ferry and sailed across the North Sea to Newcastle upon Tyne, England. From Newcastle, we drove up to Scotland and checked in for three nights at a charming old country inn near the village of Bridge of Allan. The hotel had a large garden in back, where most of the fruits and vegetables were grown. I particularly remember having homemade jam in the dining room at breakfast.

After a quick jaunt farther north to see Loch Ness (but not the monster), we turned south and headed back toward England. We stopped for lunch at the home of a very gracious couple named Watson, who had befriended Mom and Dad two weeks earlier in Scandinavia. When Dad told Mr. Watson how much we appreciated the "local color" we were getting, Mr. Watson responded, "Local color, hell! I'm the laird!"

Driving away that afternoon, Dad laughed and said, "You know what? I'll bet he is the laird!"

Next, we stopped at Stratford, where Mom and Dad saw a performance of *Othello* and we visited the cottage of Anne Hathaway. Then, after a quick day trip into London, followed by a visit to Stonehenge, Dad checked us into a resort hotel at a beach in the south of England. We spent three nights there.

After more than a month's traveling, which had taken us halfway around the world, we drove to Southampton and boarded the German cruise ship *Hanseatic*. Finally, we were on our way to the States.

A week later, we were standing on a dock in New York, watching freight being unloaded. Sure enough, after about an hour, we saw our little green Mercedes rising into the sky from out of the hold. The crane swung around and set it gently on the dock.

Back in our car, we headed south through New Jersey. We spent the night at a roadside motel in Delaware and arrived at Nadamar the next day.

Nadamar, it seemed, was a place where very little ever seemed to change. Sure enough, we found most things just as we had left them. Now, though, there was a corral on the property and a horse that Gamma had given Buz for her birthday. Buz had named the horse Star.

Dana and I were delighted. In addition to everything else there was to do at Nadamar, now we could go horseback riding. And Buz, always the teacher, was only too happy to show us everything she knew about doing so.

Star, as it turned out, wasn't the only recent example of Gamma's generosity. Aunt Dorothy was now driving a new car and making no secret about who had paid for it. Neither Dana nor I could have cared less, of course. We were too young to consider the implications, and besides, we were having too much fun.

Still, Mom and Dad noticed. Inexplicably, Gamma had never sent any of us so much as a card for our birthdays. And a card was just about the only thing we ever got from her at Christmas. Yet here she was, lavishing these wonderful gifts on Dorothy and Buz.

As the day of our departure from Nadamar approached, Mom must have told Dad she didn't want to drive clear across the United States with Dana and me in the back seat. She had, evidently, had enough of our chatter and our arguing while driving around Europe for more than a month. So they put the two of us on an airplane, and they, along with Mark, set off for California in the Mercedes.

When we arrived in San Diego, Dana was twelve years old, and I was eleven. We had been traveling for two months and had just completed our third trip completely around the world. Nanny and Bumpa, meanwhile, had well established themselves in their new home on Lucille Drive. Inside, their freshly painted and wallpapered house was filled with Chinese rugs and furniture they had acquired during their years stationed in the Orient. Outside, Bumpa had already created a yard so manicured and resplendent, with its dwarf citrus trees and its blackberry vines, that one almost felt it was magical. Along the back wall was a small koi pond he had built, with a little waterfall and lily pads. On his small back porch, he had placed two director's chairs, from which he could sit with Nanny and look out with satisfaction over the fruits of his labor.

Nanny and Bumpa always seemed as excited by these visits as we were. In a few days, when Mom and Dad arrived, there was even more excitement, because they were bringing Mark, whom they hadn't seen since he was a baby. Now he was running all over the place and having the time of his life.

At breakfast, Bumpa liked to eat grits, so the rest of us did, too, while we were at his house. One morning, soon after Mark arrived, Bumpa surprised us all by taking his dentures out at the breakfast table. He was doing it, of course, just to get a reaction out of Mark, who was only three years old. And boy, did he ever get a reaction. Mark's jaw dropped wide open. He was stunned!

As was customary, Dad left for Sumatra first. Then, sometime afterward, Mom unloaded something of a bombshell on Dana and me. She had decided to leave us behind. Dana would stay in San Diego with Nanny and Bumpa, and I would be sent to a military academy in Long Beach.

Neither of us objected to this news. On all our trips to the US, Dana had been excited about the trappings of life in America. Hula-Hoops, pizza parlors, television, neon lights, roller skates—none of these things existed in Rumbai. And besides, Nanny and Bumpa always gave her more attention than she was used to at home, and she loved it.

Meanwhile, I would get to play soldier. Mom had enrolled me once before as a temporary day student at a military academy in San Diego, and I hadn't found that too distasteful. In fact, it was the one school I kind of looked upon as an adventure.

And so it was set. In November, as the time drew near for Mom to leave, she drove me up to Long Beach. Dad had sold the Mercedes before going back, so we rode up in Bumpa's Cadillac. There was no interstate highway yet between San Diego and Long Beach, so it took a while to get there.

Mom had a list of necessaries, including uniforms and the name of the store where we would find them. There, I was outfitted with khakis, dress blues, a brown leather bomber jacket, neckties, caps, a pair of black oxford shoes, and so on. We also bought a school blanket. It was navy blue and was emblazoned with the letters SCMA on a large school emblem.

At a second store, we bought toiletries and a marking pen for identifying my laundry. Then we found a bookstore, where Mom bought me the final item on our list, a Bible. Bound in black leather and sold in its own little box, it seemed special to me, perhaps because it was something I knew so little about.

Having completed our shopping, we headed up Cherry Avenue in the direction of the campus. Fittingly, the Southern California Military Academy was located near the top of Signal Hill, the site of what, until the 1930s, had been the biggest oil strike ever in the United States. In fact, the entire 2.2-square-mile town of Signal Hill, an enclave within the city limits of Long Beach, had once been a forest of oil derricks. Now, though, the derricks were gone. Over the years they had been replaced by nodding-donkeys, oil pumps that labored incongruously among a growing number of private homes and commercial buildings.

We pulled into the lot in front of the administration building and parked the car. The campus was a collection of a dozen or so rectangular buildings. All were one- or two-story stucco. All were pre–World War II. There were two large parade grounds, both paved with asphalt. Altogether, the campus embodied about fifteen acres, the whole thing enclosed by a chain-link fence topped with barbed wire. Except for a small patch of grass and some flowers at the entrance, there was no greenery anywhere.

We parked, got out, and then followed the signs to the campus headquarters. There, a cheerful woman greeted us from behind a reception desk. She ushered us into the office of the commandant, a Captain Tate. Sharp-featured and about fifty, he had a flat belly and was wearing a crisp uniform. We exchanged pleasantries, and then

Tate told us a little about what to expect. Mom asked a question or two and then got out her checkbook.

A uniformed upperclassman was summoned, and he led Mom and me, my things in hand, out to C-1, the barracks to which I was being assigned. We reached the building, climbed a small stoop, and went inside. We were in a large room, maybe thirty-six feet long and sixteen feet wide. The two longer walls were lined with white metal-framed twin beds. At the foot of each one was a locker. All but one of the beds were made up. It was already two months into the school year, so as usual, I was going to be the new kid.

Hearing us, a pleasant woman of about seventy appeared and introduced herself as the housemother. She said her name was Mrs. Saxton, and just meeting her helped put me at ease. Having a sweet old grandma type to turn to, in an environment as foreign as this, was bound to make things a little easier.

Mrs. Saxton showed us to my bed, and Mom helped me unpack. Using the marking pen, we put my name inside my uniforms and stowed them in the footlocker. Then, Mom showed me one last time how to tie a necktie.

With that done, we left the barracks and walked back up to the front of the campus. When we reached the parking lot, she hugged me and offered reassurance. I would be fine, she said. She would write me, and she expected to hear from me too. Then, I watched as she climbed into Bumpa's Cadillac and drove away.

That evening, I ate my first dinner in the mess hall. A hundred or more cadets were there, a dozen or so at each table, sitting on long benches. Large bowls of food were brought in and passed from boy to boy.

After dinner, I returned to the barracks, where Mrs. Saxton was waiting to explain some of what was expected of me. She said there would be frequent inspections, the consequences of which would be serious if I failed. This would apply for such infractions as not having my bed made according to strict regulations or not keeping my shoes and brass perfectly shined. Then, she demonstrated how to make the bed using hospital corners.

With sundown approaching, she dismissed me to join the other boys. They were headed for what was called the canteen, which was really just a snack shack. There, we lined up to receive what was a nightly ration of candy or chips. When my turn came, I chose a bag of Fritos and headed back to the barracks. Climbing the steps, I stopped and turned to admire the sunset. The other boys were laughing and sharing their treats with one another. I wondered if I would ever fit in.

By nine thirty, Mrs. Saxton had all of us in our pajamas and climbing into bed. Making it clear there was to be no talking whatsoever, she flipped off the lights, and the room went dark.

For a time, I lay there in my bunk thinking about Mom and Dad and Indonesia. Only a few months earlier, our home in Rumbai had been completely destroyed by fire, and I thought about that too. I thought about the friends I had left behind. I thought about Dana and what it must be like staying in San Diego with Nanny and Bumpa. How different our circumstances would be now.

As sleep overcame me, a gentle breeze drifted through the window above my bunk. With it arrived the soft strains of something sweetly somber and melodic. As if to reassure me, somewhere in the distance, a lone bugler was playing Taps.

THREE

Toy Soldier

At six o'clock the next morning, the bugler was at it again. Reveille was piercing the air, and in an instant, boys in pajamas were everywhere, running around as though trying to keep up with the music. This was my first day of classes, and no less importantly, it would be my first day in uniform. I couldn't wait.

The bathroom was already crowded when I got there. I managed to get my turn at the urinals and then found a spot at a sink to brush my teeth. Then, I was back making my bunk, hurriedly folding and tucking in the hospital corners, just as I had been shown the night before. I stretched the covers as tautly as I could. "So you can bounce a quarter off them," Mrs. Saxton had said. She had warned me about how tough inspections were going to be, and though she didn't explain the consequences, I was taking heed.

Next, I removed my pajamas, folded them, and stowed them in the footlocker. I put on my underwear and socks and started dressing in my crisp, new khakis. I tucked in my shirt and threaded my belt around my waist, carefully centering the bright brass buckle. I squeezed my feet into the black oxfords and tied them. Then I picked up a necktie and my collar pins and headed back to the bathroom for another turn in front of the mirror.

After a couple of tries, I got my necktie acceptably knotted. Then I folded the ends neatly into my shirt just below the second button and started applying the pins to my collars. They were shiny brass school insignia, one for each side. Crossed rifles went on the right, and the letters SCMA went on the left. I centered them and pushed them through the fabric, fastening each on the backside.

There was only one item left: my cap. It was a simple garrison cap, the kind that fits on the head like an opened envelope. Standing squarely in front of the mirror, I set it in place and shifted it about until the angle seemed right.

Now, I was ready, and oh, what a sight I was! Only, there was no time to stand there admiring myself. Other cadets were already scrambling out the door and onto the parade ground. The bugler was sounding assembly! *Tah-tah-tah-tah-tah-tah-tah…*

Formation had begun, and cadets were running around, trying to find their proper places. My company, C Company, was forming up directly in front of the barracks, so I had no trouble falling in. A cadet sergeant was there giving orders. He pointed to where he wanted me, and I quickly took my spot.

As soon as everyone was in place, the sergeant straightened us out, rank and file, by ordering us to extend our right arms, first to the cadet in front, then to the cadet on the right.

"TEN HUT!" he ordered, and everyone came to an immediate attention. Copying what I saw, I thrust out my chest as far as it would go, pinning back my shoulders.

He walked among us for a minute, pausing here and there to check a detail or two. Then he stepped out in front and turned to face us. Looking down at a clipboard he had in his hand, he began to call the roll.

"BASSLER?"

"Here!" someone answered.

"BERRY?"

"Here!"

"CARROLL?"

And so on.

The whole battalion was comprised of six companies, A, B, C, D, E, and F. Each company consisted of about fifty cadets. Standing there stiffly in the morning air with our backs to the barracks, we gazed across the parade ground toward the mess hall. Facing us, from a few yards away, was an upper-class boy, a high-ranking officer who was apparently the battalion commander. He was flanked by two lesser support officers, and all three of them were in front of a microphone stand.

As soon as all the companies had completed the roll, the battalion commander leaned into the microphone and called for reports.

"Company a!" he said.

The Company A sergeant snapped a salute and shouted, "Company a, all present and accounted for, sir!"

"Company b!"

The Company B sergeant likewise saluted. "company b, all present and accounted for, sir."

"Company c!"

And so on.

Next, out of the corner of my eyes, I could see Captain Tate, the school commandant, approaching. He made his way to the microphone, where he stopped and gazed out over the assemblage. After a moment, he said something to the battalion commander, who then turned and ordered the entire battalion to execute a left face.

"Battalion," he said, "present huarms!" and every cadet on the field snapped a salute in the direction of the campus flagpole. Then the bugler played reveille again while two cadets raised the Stars and Stripes.

Once that was complete, the battalion was commanded to order arms (stop saluting), right face, and parade rest. Captain Tate was about to speak.

Reading from a clipboard he was carrying, the captain bade us good morning and went over the day's announcements. When he was finished, he nodded in the direction of the battalion commander, and we were all ordered dismissed to report to the mess hall.

Month after month, this routine would be repeated every school day. As winter came on and the mornings grew chillier, we began wearing bomber jackets, but that was the only thing that ever really changed.

Except for our being in uniform, I found the classroom experience at SCMA to be little different from other schools I had attended.

As a sixth grader, I was assigned to Mrs. Alexander's class. She was a warm and witty woman, long experienced at teaching school. Unlike those who would discipline us outside the classroom, she displayed a fondness for the boys that was always reciprocated. I guess we just liked her too much to misbehave.

When classes were over each day, every cadet was ordered out to the parade ground for an hour of what was called drill. Broken up into platoons of a dozen or so boys each, we were taught how to march. "Left FACE!" "Right FACE!" "Forward HUARCH!" "To the left, HUARCH!" "Right oblique, HUARCH!" "Platoon, HALT!"

Sometimes we were ordered to stand at attention and remain motionless on a hot afternoon, just waiting to be inspected. If anything was wrong with someone's posture, or if another's tie wasn't straight, or if someone's shoes didn't shine, all of us would stand there erect while the drill sergeant upbraided the poor fellow. No amount of careful preparation would be enough to spare us this fate. Always, it seemed, there was someone requiring reprimand, even if for the thinnest of reasons. And when the infraction was considered serious enough (for example, talking in the ranks), push-ups were meted out as punishment. In time, all of us gained the ability to drop down onto the pavement and do a hundred or more push-ups without difficulty. Needless to say, I never liked drill!

Afterward, we were allowed free time until dinner. I say "free time" because we were free to dress in civvies and move about the campus at will. But every day, every cadet spent this period shining his shoes and his belt buckle. By the amount of time spent and the ardor with which we approached this task, you'd have thought something enormously important was at stake. Each of us developed his own formula for achieving the perfect shine. The formula always included a particular combination of polish and the right amount of spit applied either by cloth or brush. I spent so many hours at this task that my right index finger became stained black as a result. Still, I never thought my shoes, in particular, were shiny enough, probably because there was always someone there to tell me so.

After dinner in the mess hall, we reported for two hours of study hall, which was conducted in the same classrooms where we took our daytime instruction. Finally, at the end of the day, we were sent to the canteen and then off to bed.

Always we were admonished to be on our best behavior. This meant saluting sharply whenever we encountered Captain Tate or any of the other officers who roamed the campus. It also required meticulous concern with our personal appearance and the condition of our bunks and personal effects. As promised, sudden, surprise inspections were frequent over time, and there was punishment for those who failed to pass. The worst punishment, though, was probably the one used by Mrs. Saxton. As sweet as she seemed, she wouldn't tolerate talking after Taps. If she caught you, she would make you stand in front of your footlocker with both arms extended straight out in front. I didn't consider that so onerous at first, but then it happened to me, and I discovered how much it hurt after the first couple of minutes.

Weekends, a lot of the boys went home to their families. This left no more than fifty or so on campus. Dressed in civvies, we would spend Saturday morning either lounging in the TV room or playing on the parade ground. There was sports equipment available to us, but nothing was ever organized in the way of ball games and such.

After lunch, there would be an outing and a bus would be brought up from the motor pool. Once, we went clear up to Griffith Park in Los Angeles. Other times we were taken horseback riding or to a roller rink. Usually, though, we just went to a matinee at the Towne Theater, which was about five miles to the north on Atlantic Avenue. Once there, we were given a movie ticket and a dollar to spend at the concession stand. I almost always bought either a Charms sucker or a box of Good & Plenty candy.

On Sundays, everybody, regardless of faith, got into uniform and was taken to a local Protestant church. This experience was rather new to me, having hardly ever been to a church service before, and I confess, I was somewhat influenced by it. Before long, I joined the Bible Club and was singing in the school choir.

I think I did pretty well at SCMA, though sometimes I did get homesick. Only once during the entire year did I get to speak to my mother on the phone. I was summoned from my bed late one night to do so. In those days, a phone call from as far away as Indonesia to the United States was expensive, and it took some doing to accomplish. It required the help of multiple operators, and the poor sound quality made it hard to understand what was being said. Nonetheless, I started crying the moment I heard my mother's tiny voice from the other end of the line, and I fought back tears throughout our brief conversation. When I returned to my bunk, I felt lonelier than ever.

Over time, though, homesickness turned out to be less of a challenge for me than did plain old physical illness. For some reason, I kept coming down with a flu that I just couldn't shake. I spent whole weeks laid up in the campus infirmary. When I went to San Diego to spend Christmas at Nanny and Bumpa's, I got sick there too. They had planned a wonderful holiday for Dana and me, and I was so happy to be back with family again, but I got sick anyway and wound up spending much of the time in Nanny's four-poster bed.

Despite all this, my grades at SCMA were among the best I ever got. No doubt, this owed to the two hours of forced study we underwent each night. I was no dummy, but I lacked self-discipline, and being in such a structured environment was benefiting me. In fact, during the winter, my grades and comportment had earned me my first stripe. I was now a private first class. Then, when spring came, I was promoted again. Now I was a corporal, with two stripes on my sleeve. Hey, I could get into this.

The year 1959 was the year Alaska and Hawaii were admitted to the union as the forty-ninth and fiftieth states respectively. But the big news in 1960 was the campaign for the US presidency. President Eisenhower had been in office ever since I could remember, and his second term was coming to an end.

My family loved Eisenhower. We had been, after all, a military family, and there was no greater war hero than Ike. Furthermore, he looked an awful lot like Bumpa, which didn't hurt my impression of him any. His eight years in office had been a period of extraordinary prosperity for the country. My parents didn't want to see that end, so they hoped Ike's vice president, Richard Nixon, would get elected.

Leading the race among Democrats was a handsome young senator, the Catholic blue blood from Massachusetts named John

Kennedy. I knew little about either candidate, of course, but it seemed obvious to me that Nixon would be our next president.

Late in April, everyone was abuzz about the coming execution of Caryl Chessman. Chessman had been convicted on charges of rape and robbery a dozen years earlier. Normally, one probably wouldn't get the death penalty for these crimes, but California had employed what was called the Little Lindbergh Law. Inspired by the kidnap-murder of Charles Lindbergh's baby in 1932, the law provided that any bodily harm committed by a kidnapper qualified the crime as a capital offense. Chessman hadn't really kidnapped his victims, but he did drag them from their cars to rape them. So the state of California prosecuted him for kidnapping, and he was sentenced to death.

Acting as his own attorney, Chessman managed to achieve numerous stays of execution, keeping himself alive throughout the 1950s. Over the decade, he authored four successful books detailing his experience in the criminal justice system and garnering public sympathy for himself. But now his time was running out, and he was destined to die in the San Quentin gas chamber on May 2. I was too young to understand the issues involved, of course, but I listened intently while his death was reported over the radio that night. I didn't know it yet, but days earlier, a death had already happened that was much more important to my family, and my time in military school was all but over.

The morning after Chessman was executed, Mrs. Saxton stopped me heading out to roll call. "David," she said, "don't go to class this morning. Right after breakfast, I want you to come straight back here. Do you understand?"

"Why? What's going on?" I asked.

"I'll explain when you get back, but don't forget! You are supposed to come straight here after breakfast," she repeated.

I did as I was told, and when I returned, Mrs. Saxton was waiting for me. "David," she said, "they want you to pack up your things and take them to headquarters right away. You are going home this morning."

"What's wrong? Why am I going home?"

"I don't know," she lied, "but I don't think you're coming back. They want you to take all your belongings with you."

I was perplexed. Why was I going home? Nobody else was going home. But then, I thought, any opportunity to get out of school is a pretty good deal. So I pulled my suitcase out from under my bunk, and I started packing.

As soon as I had everything transferred from my footlocker, I stripped my bed and folded up my blanket to carry along. Satisfied that I had everything that was mine, Mrs. Saxton led me to the door. I stepped out into the sunlight and started off across campus toward headquarters. When I got there, a driver was waiting with instructions to take me to the Greyhound station in downtown Long Beach. Except for Mrs. Saxton, I had said goodbye to no one.

San Diego is only about eighty miles down the Coast Highway from Long Beach, but the route is dotted with seaside towns like Laguna, San Clemente, and Oceanside. Each had traffic to negotiate and a depot where the bus would stop to let people on and off. I had made this trip three times before, at Thanksgiving, Christmas, and Easter, so I knew it would take a while. I bought a ten-cent candy bar and a couple of comic books at the Long Beach terminal and settled in for the ride.

In Laguna, we pulled up in front of a coffee shop for thirty minutes, long enough to go inside and get a sandwich. I was eating mine when a scruffy-looking man with shoulder-length hair came in and sat at the counter. He drank a cup of coffee, paid the cashier, and then departed. I stared at him the whole time. I'd never even imagined long hair on a man before, much less seen it. How odd. Then, I was back on the bus. Next stop: San Clemente.

In midafternoon, we passed through Del Mar and La Jolla. Before long, San Diego Bay was coming into view, and I saw the familiar sight of tuna boats moored along the water's edge. We reached the Embarcadero, turned left on Broadway, and pulled into the terminal.

I stepped off the bus, hoping someone would be there to pick me up, and I wasn't disappointed. Immediately, Dana's face appeared, looking at me through the glass doors from inside the station house.

"Hi, Dana!" I said as I entered.

At thirteen, Dana was so young, and the news she carried was so big she had trouble restraining her smile. Searching my face as she spoke, she simply blurted it out.

"Bumpa died."

FOUR

Oh, Mexico

To the west and southwest of the Embarcadero, beyond the assortment of tour boats and Navy ships that ply the San Diego harbor, is the Coronado Peninsula. There, one can see the flat expanse of the North Island Naval Air Station, where military aircraft take off and land. A little farther in the distance is Point Loma, a massive promontory rising 422 feet from the water's surface. At its highest point stands the Old Point Loma Lighthouse. They call it "old" because it sits up so high it often wasn't seen in a fog, so it was replaced by a newer one decades ago.

A thousand feet or so from the Old Lighthouse is the military cemetery at Fort Rosecrans. On the seaward side of that cemetery, where the grass slopes down toward the ocean, among the rows of white headstones, one stone bears the following inscription:

Ernest Edward Dobson
Missouri LCDR
US Navy Ret
World War I and II
June 20, 1896
April 24,1960

Not everything on that headstone is correct, however. Bumpa wasn't born in 1896—he was born in 1897. Like my grandfather

Davenport, and many others of their era, Bumpa had fibbed about his age to get into the service.

While there were numerous parallels in the lives of my grandfathers, the two were actually quite different from one another. Having grown up in humiliating poverty, Commander Davenport was a man on a mission to see how much he could accomplish in life. Bumpa was ambitious, too, of course, but he wasn't out to prove anything. Commander Davenport dominated people, whereas Bumpa was more a man of warmth and compromise.

Back in the 1890s, Bumpa's father, Ira W. Dobson, had owned a successful haberdashery in Salisbury, Missouri. Bumpa might have grown up there, too, had it not been for a single incident that occurred when he was two years old. One day, someone saw Ira riding down the street with a "working girl" seated beside him in his carriage. Who knows, maybe he was just giving the woman a lift, but that would have made little difference to his wife, Laura. She was a Linville, daughter of the prominent Missouri preacher John Riley Linville, and she was not about to accept such public disgrace. Laura sued for divorce, and then, perhaps to escape humiliation, she pulled up stakes and took my young grandfather to live in Reno, Nevada. The two of them were only in Reno long enough for Laura to meet and marry a brickmason named Frank Snyder, and then the family moved to Lake County, California. Someone said there was a prune ranch for sale there, and Laura had enough money from her divorce settlement to buy it.

In time, though, raising prunes wouldn't prove to be everything she had hoped. So one day, when Laura's brother Clarence offered his handsome three-story house in Berkeley in trade for the ranch, Laura accepted.

The Linvilles were an aspiring bunch. As time passed, Laura's three sisters and one remaining brother all moved to the Golden State. Each of the four girls had at least attended college, and one of them even completed medical school. Another one married a physician, which put the whole family "knee-deep" in doctors, as Bumpa would later say.

Of course, none of this put Frank Snyder in a very good spot. Some in the family were saying that Laura, in choosing a man who laid bricks for a living, had married beneath herself. Years later, in fact, Laura would claim the only man she ever loved was Ira W. Dobson. What was more, she wished she hadn't acted so precipitously in divorcing him.

So Frank Snyder never did get his full measure of devotion from Laura. But then, he never got it from Bumpa either. That was because the man was so often mean to my young grandfather that Bumpa came to hate him for it. Maybe that was why Bumpa took off and joined the Navy the way he did.

Starting in 1913, he trained to be a machinist's mate, the job he was to perform throughout the First World War. Then, in 1920, while stationed in Charleston, South Carolina, Bumpa fell in love with an auburn-haired sixteen-year-old wisp of a girl named Dovie Sanders. Dovie was from Coal City, Alabama, but she and her mother, Elizabeth, were now living in Charleston, where they leased a big house and rented out the bedrooms to Navy folk. One of those Navy folk was Bumpa, and on April 2, the two were married.

In 1924, after Bumpa was transferred to San Pedro, California, Dovie gave birth to their first and only child, my mother, on September 16. With Bumpa off on a long voyage to Australia at that time, Nanny decided to honor him by naming their baby Ernestine Elizabeth.

There were far worse career choices a man could make than being in the Navy, particularly during the Depression. For one thing, Bumpa always had a steady and dependable income, something millions of other people lacked. For another, being in the Navy enabled Bumpa to show his family places around the world that most people only dreamed about. In 1931, when he was ordered to China, Bumpa took along his family. Each morning for two years, my mother was transported by rickshaw from the family's hotel apartment on the Bund, through the streets of Shanghai, to a convent school.

In 1933, they moved to Manila, where they would live for another two years. After that, from 1935 to 1937, they were stationed in Washington, DC. They were living in DC when Nanny's sister

Blanche died and Buster joined the family. In 1937, they moved to San Diego, and then in 1940, they shipped out to Honolulu, where Bumpa was stationed at Pearl Harbor. No, they weren't there for the Japanese attack. By that time, in December of 1941, they had already moved again, this time to Pensacola. Pensacola was where Bumpa spent most of World War II, and it was from there that my mother went off to college at the University of Alabama.

Eventually, Bumpa retired to San Diego. He and Nanny bought and lived in several houses before they finally settled into the pink-and-gray stucco house on Lucille Drive that I remember. It was not a large home, but it was brand-new, and it had a very nice view over-looking one of the side canyons above Mission Valley.

Bumpa had two important passions. First, he loved the out-doors. In retirement, he would spend many days either hunting pheasant or going fishing. He had his own ten-foot aluminum boat with an outboard motor, and sometimes he would take Nanny along. They bought a movie camera, and she would film him streaking back and forth on the water or holding up a string of fish he had caught. In every frame, he wore a necktie, a wide one, which was the style in those days.

Bumpa's other great passion was his garden. In it, he grew poin-settia, oranges, lemons, blackberries, and roses, and all were kept lush and healthy. He didn't have much room for a lawn, but what he did have was dichondra, and it was always carefully manicured.

In one corner of his backyard, Bumpa built a beautiful little waterfall. It fed into a kidney-shaped pond with water lilies and a few koi, which were a source of great fascination to Dana, Mark, and me. It was on a Sunday morning, when Dana was helping him clean his pond, that Bumpa suddenly fell over dead of a heart attack.

Bumpa had, in fact, suffered several heart attacks before the one that took his life. Like nearly half of all American adults at that time, he and Nanny were cigarette smokers. His doctor had warned him about it, but Bumpa said he enjoyed smoking too much to quit.

So it was that Mom and Mark were with Nanny and Dana when they came to get me at the bus depot that day. After six months away at school, I suddenly found myself back in the arms of my family. I should have been overjoyed, I know, but I don't remember it that way. Bumpa's death was such a shock. I had never experienced the loss of a family member before, and I was dazed. I did understand one thing immediately, however. Mrs. Saxton had been right: my days at the Southern California Military Academy were over.

The next morning, the five of us rode down to the University Heights section of town where the Colonial Mortuary was on El Cajon Boulevard. We were going to view Bumpa's remains, something I was squeamish about doing. "But don't worry," Dana said on the way over. "He looks really nice. He looks like he just got dressed up to go out for dinner, and he's resting." When we entered the room, it was just as Dana had said. Bumpa was laid out on a table. He was wearing his best suit and one of his wide ties.

A couple of days later, we returned for the funeral. Walking in, I recognized almost no one among the mourners. Bumpa's casket was open, and in it I saw something else I didn't recognize. In his hand, someone had placed a trowel, and around his waist, there was a small white apron. I asked my mother what that was all about, and she whispered to me that Bumpa was a Mason, something she would have to explain later.

When the service concluded, we stepped outside and watched while Bumpa's casket was carried out and placed in a waiting hearse. We were then directed to a black limousine directly behind the hearse. We rode in a procession of a dozen or so cars, headlamps glowing, down Washington Street, onto Harbor Drive, and out toward the cemetery at Fort Rosecrans.

At graveside, folding chairs had been set up for our family, and we took them. A Navy chaplain waited for everyone to congregate before expressing a few words of sympathy and encouragement to the family. Then he asked us all to bow our heads, and he gave the benediction. Next, Bumpa was given a seven-gun salute, as three rifle volleys cracked loudly in the morning air. Two sailors removed the American flag that had been draped over Bumpa's coffin at the mortuary. Working together, they folded it into the triangular shape of military custom, and one of them presented it to Nanny with a salute.

Nanny, of course, was completely grief-stricken. The life she and Bumpa had made together for forty years had ended so suddenly she didn't know what to do with herself. Unwilling to leave her alone in this condition, my mother made the decision not to return to Sumatra. Dad, as it happened, wasn't going to be stationed there much longer, anyway. He had just been promoted and was due for transfer back to corporate headquarters in New York City. What, though, were the rest of us to do in the meantime?

The simple answer would have been to wait in San Diego, long enough, at least, until Nanny could decide about her future. Following that, we could take off for New York, where Mom could start looking for a house. For reasons I cannot explain, though, Mom chose not to do those things; instead, she wanted to find a nice vacation spot in Mexico and keep all of us down there, including Nanny, until Dad's return.

I don't know that she was all that certain about where in Mexico we should go. Maybe she just closed her eyes and pointed at a map. But by whatever means, she soon had us all checking in to a large hotel in downtown Guadalajara. For Dana and me, this meant being back living the life of world travelers, and we liked it. For a while, at least, there would be no schoolwork and no chores for us to do. And for Mom, who was used to having her needs met by other people, the arrangement made sense.

We spent each morning exploring the shops around the hotel, and in the afternoon, we napped, as was our family custom. In the evenings, we went down to the hotel bar, where Mom would consume her requisite pair of martinis. She and Nanny both, I'm afraid, were rather fond of their liquor, but Dana and I didn't mind. We thought it was fun being among the adults, sipping away at our Shirley Temples.

After only a week of this, however, Mom realized we were going to need something a little less urban. Someone told her about a place called Ajijic (Ah-hee-heek), a rustic little town on Lake Chapala, some fifty miles to the southeast. Summertime temperatures there were supposed to be moderate, and rental units were apparently easy to find.

The next day, we got into a taxi and headed out to see for ourselves. Sure enough, we found Ajijic to be inviting, though rustic, to be sure. Except for the highway, not a single street in the town was paved. But we had no trouble locating a spacious adobe house to rent and a woman to do the cleaning and cooking for us. The house was surrounded by a high wall enclosing a big backyard, and it was shaded almost entirely by a very large mango tree. Everywhere, there were mangoes, either hanging from the tree or rotting on the ground.

Inside, the house was sparsely furnished, and there were separate water heaters located in the kitchen and the bath. Both were operated on demand by placing a bread-loaf-shaped block of combustible material into the burner, lighting it, and then waiting for the water to get hot.

The housekeeper, meanwhile, turned out to be an excellent cook. Right away, she started presenting us with the most wonderful Mexican dishes. Our favorite: chile rellenos. She would roast Anaheim chilies on an open flame, then sweat them in a paper bag before peeling off the burnt skin. Then she stuffed them with cheese, coated them with flour, and dredged them in egg batter before frying them in a skillet. Wow, they were good.

So that part of Mom's new arrangement looked to be pretty promising. What had to be worked out next was what to do with Dana and me. Mom had always told us we made her nervous. In fact, in Rumbai, we alone among our friends had been allowed to run all over town without ever reporting our whereabouts. As long as we showed up in time for dinner, Mom never seemed to care what we were doing. She just wanted us out from underfoot, and that, by the way, went down just fine with Dana and me. What she called nervousness came across as irritability to us, and we didn't like being around it.

That was exactly what Dana and I had in mind when, on our first day in town, we put on our swimsuits and headed eagerly out the door. The nearest beach was only three blocks away, but we were astounded by what we saw when we got there. There were people swimming, all right, all apparently locals. But there were water snakes swimming around among them! No one seemed to be the least bit concerned, but we were. After some hesitation, we did go in, but only briefly. Then we left and never went back.

The lake having lost its appeal, Mom found another way of keeping Dana and me occupied. With such a big fenced-in yard, and all those mangos lying on the ground for animal food, she decided we ought to have horses. There was, after all, a stable just down the road, so she arranged a weekly rental for each of us.

We couldn't believe our good fortune. True enough, Mom had always been generous to us at Christmas, seeing we got more presents than any of our friends. But other than that, we had learned through experience that her needs came first. There was just no way having two horses in the yard would accomplish that. So we were pretty surprised.

Each day, we took off riding up and down our street and out into the countryside. We would stop at the stable to buy oats and hay, and when we weren't riding, the horses meandered in the yard, gobbling up the fallen mangos. After every ride, we curried them, just as Buzz had taught us at Nadamar, but we never did get around to cleaning up after them. We didn't have to. In less than a month, we were on the move again.

Mom was getting antsy. For some reason, Ajijic was just not the answer she had hoped for. So we repacked our things and headed back to Guadalajara. In Guadalajara we boarded a plane for Mexico City. We arrived and checked in to a large luxury hotel on the Paseo de la Reforma, a grand boulevard that runs northeast to southwest, bisecting the city. Almost immediately, Dana found out there was a Hollywood production company staying at the hotel. They were making *The Last Sunset*, starring Rock Hudson and Kirk Douglas. From that moment on, whenever we weren't out seeing the sights, the two of us were down in the lobby, trying to catch a glimpse of anyone famous. The only actor we ever met, though, was Regis Toomey. He had only a character role in the film, and neither of us recognized him, but we got his autograph anyway. It wasn't until much later that I discovered Toomey had been in scores of movies over the years.

Meanwhile, just as in Guadalajara, Mom was asking around for ideas about where to go next. Someone told her about Cuernavaca, a charming resort town with cobblestone streets and a daily temperature that always seemed to peak at seventy-two degrees Fahrenheit. That sounded pretty good to her, so we were off again, this time riding by taxi the fifty miles or so to our destination.

We quickly discovered that Cuernavaca was a lot nicer than Ajijic. Ajijic was a dusty backwater, but Cuernavaca had charm.

We found and rented a comfortable little bungalow in a good location. It was one of a half-dozen or so in an enclave that featured a well-manicured lawn and a swimming pool. The best thing about it, though, was its easy walking distance from the Zocalo, a leafy old town square with colorful tourist shops and a large movie theater. At its center, the Zocalo featured a forty-foot-tall parasol-shaped pavilion covering an elevated bandstand. Street vendors peddled their souvenirs there, and men with electric blenders made tropical fruit drinks for the tourists. Down the road was Las Mañanitas, a famous restaurant where the dining was done al fresco among peacocks and other exotic fowl in a lush tropical garden.

I was still an avid reader of books. Many times, my mother had bragged to Dana and me about reading *The Good Earth* by Pearl S. Buck when she was only twelve. Being twelve myself now, and anxious to prove I was just as smart as Mom was, I found the book in a bookshop and read it. You might have thought that a pretty good way for a boy to spend part of his summer vacation, but Mom managed to come up with another idea. She announced one day that she had found a school for us, and even if temporarily, Dana and I were going to have to go. Apparently, we were getting on her nerves again.

So off we went, but the school Mom found proved to be a miserable experience for me. Even though I had only finished the sixth grade, I had already attended five different schools. This was the sixth, and by far the worst. Classes were in English as well as Spanish, which could have been of value, but there was little structure and not much of anything really being taught. To top it off, lunch was a slice of baloney between two slices of stale bread and a bowl of exceedingly thin soup. Most of the kids were Mexican. As usual, everyone around me would be well-acquainted with one another, and I would be the stranger. I was so unhappy that, after a few days, I simply walked off the premises.

After going a mile or so, I came to a pay phone somewhere near the Zocalo, and using my lunch money, I called my mother.

"Where are you?" she asked, surprised to hear my voice.

"I left the school, Mom. I hope you don't get mad, but I just can't go there anymore."

"Can you get back here okay?"

"Yes."

"Okay. Well, then, come on back, and we'll talk about it."

I thought I would catch hell, but I didn't. That night she told Dana and me we didn't have to go back.

Ever since I was six or seven, I had been attracted to women. There had been a young married woman in Rumbai that really caught my eye. She had long brown hair that danced in the wind when she rode around in her jeep. Only once did she ever speak to me, but when she did, she touched me on the arm and called me honey. That was it, as far as I was concerned. I was in love. But others, too, had aroused my interest, like the dark-haired girl skating in an ice show Dad once took us to in Jakarta. Now, at twelve, my feelings were intensifying.

There was a convenience store down the street from the bungalows. When I went there, I would glance at the newspapers and magazines. By now, John Kennedy was close to getting the presidential nomination from the Democrats, and his picture was on the cover of the newspaper nearly every day. My parents preferred Richard Nixon, of course, since they were Republicans, but Kennedy had a good-looking wife, and whenever I saw her picture, I would stop and admire her.

There were movie magazines too. One had Elizabeth Taylor on the cover. Her movie *Suddenly Last Summer* had recently come out, and in it she wore a scandalous white swimsuit. She was only twenty-eight, but already she was married to her fourth husband. Gosh, she was beautiful. I bought the magazine and read all about her. Could it be that a woman like her and a kid like me—no, I guess not. But I sure thought about it.

One day, a young American couple moved in to a neighboring bungalow. They were on their honeymoon. She was a pretty young blonde with a nice figure, and she started right away sunning herself by the pool every morning. I, of course, began spying on her, my imagination running wild. One day, she and her husband took off to do some sightseeing. They left their swimsuits hanging out to dry on their front porch. I waited until I thought no one was looking, and then, with my pulse racing, I crept over to get a closer look. I glanced around to make sure it was safe, and then I took her bikini top into my hands and pressed it into my face. For a long moment, I just stood there drawing my breath through the fabric and thinking what a wonderful thing it must be to make love to such a woman.

With the end of summer approaching, it became apparent we would be leaving Mexico soon. A letter came from Dad indicating he was winding things up in Indonesia. He had vacation time coming, and he wanted us all to spend it together near his mother in Virginia. Still, Mom had one more place she wanted to visit before we headed back to the States, and that was the picturesque cathedral town of Taxco.

The journey to Taxco was something we accomplished by riding over a meandering mountain road on a broken-down old public bus that was straight out of the movies. But the town proved to be well worth the trouble. There were silver mines there and stores selling locally fabricated jewelry at attractive prices. Mom bought herself an amethyst ring that day. She also bought a heavy pair of brass doorknobs inlaid with a mosaic of azurite and malachite. No doubt, the knobs were intended to go on some dream house she had suddenly imagined owning someday.

A few days later, we were back at the Mexico City airport, putting Nanny on a plane back to San Diego. She was coping better now and wanted to go home and sell her house. With Bumpa gone, along with much of his retirement income, she would be unable to live that well anymore. Besides, San Diego was too far away from the East Coast, where our family was going to be. An hour or so later, the rest of us boarded a plane and took off in the direction of Virginia.

FIVE

The Second Pitch

Gamma met us at the airport in Norfolk. She and Mom spent the next couple of days looking for a house to rent. They found a furnished place in Virginia Beach on the corner of Myrtle Avenue and Forty-Third Street, just two blocks from the ocean.

Right away, we moved in, and Mom got us enrolled in school. Within a couple of weeks, Dad arrived, pulling up in front of the cottage in a shiny new Mercedes he had picked up at the factory in Stuttgart. It was a model 220S, bigger and more expensive than the 190 we had already owned. In a gesture to changing times, the 220 featured tail fins, though they were modest compared to the ones on American cars. Dad had paid $5,600, which was a lot for a car in those days.

In a way, I guess, he was rewarding himself for all he had accomplished. Having arrived in Sumatra in 1952 as a mere twenty-nine-year-old, he had quickly become the company's chief petroleum engineer. In that capacity, he had programmed and directed all drilling and production activities for nearly eight years, developing two major oil fields and three minor ones in the process. Largely under his planning and management, production levels at Caltex Indonesia had increased from 25,000 barrels per day to 1,500,000. Now he was being rewarded with a nice increase in salary and an office at the corporate headquarters in New York City.

I don't know about Dana, but for me, there was something awkward about having Dad around at first. I had been very excited about his return, that's for sure, but with eighteen months having passed since I had seen him last, I was feeling unsure of myself. All I needed, I guess, was a little reacquainting. Little did I know, but an opportunity for just that was about to blow into town!

Her name was Donna. She was a monster category-4 hurricane, one of the most damaging ever to come ashore in America. Donna had started off the west coast of Africa, then made her way across the Atlantic, and was now moving slowly up the East Coast of America. Before ever reaching us, she had killed hundreds of people and caused hundreds of millions of dollars in damage. Knowing this, Dad thought it best for us to ride her out at Nadamar, where we would be some fifteen feet above sea level inside Gamma's solidly constructed cinderblock house. We packed some things into the car and headed that way on the eleventh of September, a Sunday.

The storm was expected to strike our area during the night, so Dad got right to work shuttering windows and making sure there was nothing left outside that could be ripped loose by the wind. One important task he assigned to me was to go down to the boat dock and tie up Gamma's two rowboats as securely as I could.

When I awoke the next morning, the storm was raging. I wanted to go outside and experience it directly, even if just for a minute, but the grown-ups knew better and wouldn't let me open the door. I couldn't imagine a person being hurt, or even killed, by something as innocuous as wind and rain. Then Dad explained it's the flooding and the flying debris that kills people, not the wind itself.

We spent that whole day huddled inside Gamma's house. We had no electricity, so there was no TV or radio to keep us informed. Instead, we just listened to the ruckus outside and wondered about the damage we might find once the storm had passed. A couple of times, Dad asked me, "Are you sure you tied those boats down securely?" I guess he was worried now and wishing he had checked my work. But then, I was worried too. How could I ever live it down if the boats were swept away?

By nightfall, things were quieting down, but it wasn't until the second morning that we could go out and have a look. When we did, we discovered, thankfully, that Gamma's house was undamaged, but everywhere else I looked, there were branches on the ground and trees that had been uprooted. None of that concerned me most, however. What really concerned me was that boat dock and those two rowboats. I took off in that direction immediately.

When I got there, the boats were nowhere in sight! *Oh no,* I thought. But then I realized, *Oh my gosh, where's the dock?* Thank goodness, I had apparently tied the boats down so well that the storm had swept them and the dock away together!

Dad and I had a quick breakfast, then we got busy surveying the rest of the damage. The worst of it, as it turned out, was over at Aunt Dorothy's house, where a tree had blown over and crashed through the roof. Uncle Hank was already at work making a temporary patch to keep the weather out of what was the bedroom shared by Buzz and Jen.

With seventeen acres of wooded property to account for, we found other trees that were down too. One rather large one had fallen across the drive, making it impossible for our cars to get in or out. It was too big to budge by hand, so Dad found a two-man saw among Gamma's tools, and we set to work cutting out the piece that blocked the way. After that, we continued our inspection tour, piling up fallen branches and pushing away uprooted trees as we went.

Deep in the woods, we discovered something that brought me enormous relief. Somehow, the storm had managed to force the boat dock through a hundred feet or so of trees and underbrush, leaving it in a most unlikely spot. But still securely lashed to their mooring cleats were Gamma's rowboats!

Days later, Dana and I were back in school. The junior high where we were enrolled was just a short bus drive from our rented cottage. I was starting seventh grade, and this would bring to seven the number of schools I had attended. I was finding it hard enough being twelve, an awkward age to begin with, much less having to go through being a stranger again. I had been through this so many times before. I knew how unimportant I was going to feel. These kids even spoke with a different accent from mine. I was so far out of the loop that I felt stupid.

Perhaps, having spent most of my life either in the depths of the Indonesian jungle or locked away in an all-male military academy, I was just underexposed. I don't know. But whatever it was, I was intimidated. From the first day, I sat in class, watching the clock and longing for the final bell to ring. Having little interest in what was going on around me, I resorted to my old habit of daydreaming.

To her credit, Mrs. Turner, our teacher, was all business. Rarely, in fact, did I ever see her smile. But she was tall and slender and beautiful, and I felt drawn to her. She wore expensive-looking clothes, and her light-brown hair and her makeup were always carefully done. She was married to a young naval officer, and I guess she must have been about thirty years old.

My greatest fear was being called on in class. Then, of course, one day I was. We had been given the homework assignment of making a list of plants we knew to be native to the Virginia Tidewater area. I had, in fact, given the matter some thought, but being a newcomer, I didn't know where to turn for help. The only examples I could think of were holly, pine, and dogwood, three species I knew to be present out at Nadamar.

"David, why don't we start with you?" she announced, awakening me from my reverie. "Bring your list up to the front of the class and tell us what you found."

Having practically nothing to report, I was mortified. Immediately I thought, *How can I stretch this somehow?* I wound up fabricating a goofy story about how I had fallen into a holly bush as I was searching for plants the night before. This was meant to distract by entertaining, but nobody bought it. Instead, they sat there, stone-faced, staring at me like I was some sort of miserable cretin.

Then they started laughing, but it had nothing to do with my story. No, they weren't laughing with me. They were laughing at me. I didn't realize it, but in my nervousness, I had pulled my shirttail out and I was rubbing my exposed belly with my hand. When I finished, I was sent back to my seat utterly humiliated.

There were two subjects we covered that fall, however, that I did find engaging. One was the upcoming presidential election. No one my age could remember any president other than Eisenhower. As a seventy-year-old who had led America through years of war and peace, he was very much a grandfather figure to the whole nation. Now, though, a new era was coming, and I think everyone could feel it. Nixon and Kennedy were both a lot younger than Ike. One of them was going to be president, and the contest between them was just too close to predict.

The other matter I cared about was the 1960 World Series. Not having grown up in America, I really found professional sports almost too arcane to comprehend. Nonetheless, a friend of mine in Rumbai had a shoebox full of baseball cards, from which I learned some of the really big names, like Mickey Mantle and Yogi Berra. Mantle and Berra were, after all, the two biggest stars of the New York Yankees, the team that dominated baseball all through the 1950s. In fact, in my twelve years of life, New York had won the American League pennant ten times and the World Series seven.

Playing against the Yankees that October were the Pittsburgh Pirates. If I remember right, I wanted the Yankees to win, at least at first. But as the series got going, something interesting was taking place. The Yankees were winning all right, and in lopsided blowouts. The Pirates were winning too, but their victories were by much smaller margins. By October 13, when the series reached game 7, Pittsburgh had been outscored overall by a whopping 46 to 17. Yet they were still alive, and the games were tied up at three apiece.

Some of the kids were begging Mrs. Turner to bring in a television so we could watch the final, and she agreed, but only if we waited until after lunch. That meant seeing only two or three innings at the end, but hey, that was better than doing schoolwork.

Meanwhile, some 450 miles away, the great city of Pittsburgh had fallen silent. Every person in Allegheny County, it seemed, was either in front of a TV or listening to a radio. The luckiest ones were out in Oakland, watching the game in person at Forbes Field. Schools all over the city had ended early, and kids were streaming home to catch the end of the game. On the Northside, Pittsburgh's oldest multiethnic, multiracial, working-class neighborhood, Father Mastrangelo told the nuns at Regina Coeli Catholic School to send the kids home.

One of those youngsters was a beautiful, dark-haired eighth grader named Suzan Albanesi. Suzie, as everybody called her, was the eldest granddaughter in a family of first- and second-generation Italian Americans living all together in a three-story row house at 1901 Charles Street. She walked straight home that day. When she got there, she could hear the TV from her grandparents' living room on the second floor. She put down her books and sweater and went up to join the family.

So far, the game had been a pitched battle. The Pirates led for the first five innings. Then the Yankees started scoring. By the eighth inning, the game was seven to four, Yankees, and things weren't looking so good for Pittsburgh.

But the Pirates didn't shrink. In the bottom of the eighth, they scored a walloping five runs, taking back the lead at nine to seven. When New York came in to bat, they needed two more runs just to survive, but they got them when both Mantle and Berra scored RBIs.

Now it was the bottom of the ninth, and the score was nine to nine. It was the Pirates' turn at bat. The first man to step up to the plate was the twenty-four-year-old second baseman from Ohio, Bill Mazeroski. Mazeroski was already one of the best infielders in baseball, but he had a career batting average of .261, which, while respectable, meant he was no slugger. After taking a few practice swings, he stepped into the box and awaited the first pitch.

"Ball one!" shouted the umpire as it whizzed past the plate and into the catcher's glove.

People everywhere let out their breath. Nobody needed reminding that just one Pittsburgh run would win the whole thing, but the Albanesis were crossing their fingers and whispering it anyway.

Out at Forbes Field, the crowd fell silent again. On the mound, Yankee's pitcher Ralph Terry went into his windup. Then he let loose with a fastball, and it was headed straight over the plate.

Nothing lasts forever, of course, and so it was with Forbes Field. In 1970, the venerable old ballpark, which had served the Pirates for sixty-three years, was torn down. It was replaced by Three Rivers Stadium, built on the Northside, near where the Allegheny and the Monongahela rivers meet to form the Ohio. Then, in 2000, Three Rivers, home to both the Pittsburgh Steelers and the Pirates, itself came down and was replaced by the separate facilities of Heinz Field and PNC Park. Today, on the river walk outside PNC Park, there stands a section of the old left-field wall, which was moved from Forbes Field. It still bears an original sign painted on it that says, "406 FT."

Out in Oakland, the University of Pittsburgh now occupies the spot where Forbes Field itself used to be. But parts of the old wall remain, and there are bricks in the sidewalk representing where the left-field section once stood. There, on the ground, is a plaque:

> This marks the spot where Bill Mazeroski's home run ball cleared the left center field wall of Forbes Field on October 13, 1960, thereby winning the World Series Championship for the Pittsburgh Pirates. The historic hit came in the ninth inning of the seventh game to beat the New York Yankees by a score of 10-9.

That October day in 1960 was my first real exposure to professional sports in America. But to the people of Pittsburgh, it is nothing less than the most storied day in their history. At the instant of Bill Mazeroski's home run, a euphoria swept over them. All across the city, people poured into the streets to laugh and shout their happiness to the world. On Charles Street, the Albanesi family was among them.

SIX

A Connecticut Yankee

Days later, we were on the move again. Dad's vacation time was running out, and he needed to report for work in New York City. My parents thought Greenwich, Connecticut, would be a good place to live. Only a short train ride from Manhattan, it is a well-known bedroom community for people who work in the city. So we loaded our things into the new Mercedes, said our goodbyes to the folks at Nadamar, and headed north toward New England.

We found a rental house on a gray afternoon in mid-October. It was a pleasant one-and-a-half-story Cape Cod on a leafy cul-de-sac named Licata Terrace. The house number was 25. There were two bedrooms on the main floor for Dana and my parents, and there was a second story with an attic on one side and a finished bedroom on the other for Mark and me. In back, the lawn sloped down to a tree-lined road, and beyond that, by a hundred feet or so, flowed the Mianus River.

The presidential election was now less than three weeks away. Our family, like just about everyone else in America, had already watched three debates on television between Senator Kennedy and Vice President Nixon. They had, in fact, been the first televised presidential debates ever. Now, on October 21, 1960, from our living room in Connecticut, we watched the fourth and final debate. In those days, of course, the broadcast was done in black-and-white.

By the time Election Day arrived on November 9, the race was widely considered too close to predict, and boy, was it ever. We all stayed up as late as we could that night, watching the returns, but we still didn't know who had won when we went to bed. By morning, though, all doubt had been removed, and John F. Kennedy was our new president-elect.

At his inaugural, Kennedy would say, "Let the word go forth from this time and place…the torch has been passed to a new generation of Americans." Given the disparity between Kennedy's age and Eisenhower's, that was certainly the truth. In a way, though, the torch was being passed not only to his generation but also to mine. Yes, my contemporaries and I were only children, but we were the products of the post–World War II baby boom, a massive bulge in the population, which, from its beginning, had altered nearly everything about American life.

For me, the real changes taking place were the ones affecting me personally. Connecticut, like the military academy in California, and like the schools in Cuernavaca and Virginia, was a whole new environment, filled with unfamiliar faces and uneasy social encounters. If anything, my awkwardness was going to get even worse.

The weather, too, was something new and different. Except for our week in Zermatt in 1957, neither Dana nor I had ever been in snow. Now we were having to bundle up every morning to walk down to the school bus, which stopped at an old stone bridge a quarter mile or so down the road.

The prospect of standing there in the cold every morning with a group of kids who were strangers to me was something I dreaded from the start. Yet Dana seemed unfazed, joining in conversation with the other girls as though she had known them forever. Meanwhile, I would walk back and forth across the bridge, speaking to no one and wishing the bus would hurry up and arrive.

Unsurprisingly, the other boys soon began to make fun of me. I don't know why, but they started calling me Badger. "Hey, Badger," someone would holler out, "how many stones on that bridge?" Then they'd all laugh.

Things weren't going much better the rest of my day either. The Central Middle School in Greenwich was a nice-enough place, all right. I had good teachers, too, and the other students all seemed happy enough. But I just didn't have a friend.

And I was daydreaming again. Right away, my grades were terrible. For the first time in my life, I had a locker, and I went to different classrooms for different subjects taught by different teachers. Other kids were taking notes, but I didn't even have a notebook. Was I going to need one? I simply didn't know. I was in serious need of guidance, but once again, I just thought I was stupid.

At home, my sister and I were having to do the evening dishes now. Normally, Dana would wash and I would dry. Having always had servants in the past, I found this chore to be very unpleasant. There were dishwashing machines on the market, but we didn't have one. Once our job was done, we would try to join Mom and Dad in the living room to watch TV. Invariably, one of them would ask, "Don't you have homework to do?"

"No," I usually answered. "I already did it at school." Or I'd say, "We didn't have any."

Of course, I was lying. I hadn't done my homework at school, and yes, I'm sure I had plenty. I just didn't know what it was.

Once, when my math teacher started to call on me in class, he stopped himself and said, "No, don't tell me…your dog ate your homework again." Everybody laughed. Then, one time, I brought home a report card and my science teacher had written on it that I was "lethargic."

"Do you know what that means?" Dad asked me.

"No, I don't."

"It means you're lazy," he said.

After that, Dad called me Lardy a few times. Having looked back at pictures of myself from that era, I later realized, in fact, that I had been overweight. But I didn't know it at that time. I guess Dad was trying to shame me out of being lethargic.

Thankfully, though, the days of Dad spanking us with his belt were gone forever. Dad said once that we had grown too big for such treatment, and I was glad to hear it.

Looking back on it now, I realize how seriously I lacked self-esteem. Always being the strange new kid in school, coupled with having parents who couldn't figure out how to inspire me, destroyed any ambition I might otherwise have had. Once, my father even said to me, "Well, you are either stupid or lazy. Which is it?"

Neither of my parents ever went to a parent-teacher conference that I can remember. "I don't understand," my mother kept repeating. "I had good grades when I was in school, and nobody ever had to tell me to do my homework!"

To be fair, there were bright spots at school for me, though. In music class one day, my teacher announced in front of everyone that I had a beautiful singing voice, something I had never been told before.

Another time, our English teacher asked us each to write an abstract poem. She liked mine so much she had it printed in the school newspaper. It was called "The Hour of Defeat." Many years later, I can still recite a few lines from it.

When all of us were told to come up with something to do for the school talent show, I simply ignored it. I thought no one would force me to get up onstage if I simply had nothing to offer. But I was wrong. When the time came, I was shoved out onto the stage anyway.

Having nothing prepared, I improvised myself into an inebriated cowboy who was depressed about having lost a gunfight. The whole thing was pretty silly, but for some reason it worked, and for once, I had everyone laughing *with* me. At the end of the school year, I was asked to perform it again, which I did, at an assembly of the entire student body and their parents.

I remember seeing a really beautiful black woman in the audience that day. Her clothes, her makeup, her hair, everything about her was so striking that I couldn't stop looking at her. She was what polite people called a colored woman. Of course, she must have been some other kid's mother, so shame on me, I guess.

Having grown up in Indonesia, I was used to everybody being either white or brown. To me, "colored" people were a curiosity. I don't think, in fact, I had ever even spoken to a black person before. I do remember hearing Nanny and Bumpa talking about them, though. Nanny grew up poor in Alabama, where just about everyone used the term *nigger*. She didn't know any better, and neither did Bumpa, I guess. Bumpa even told me once that he had watched a "nigger" get lynched when he was a kid. Maybe he was just making it up. I don't know. But my only experience of black people was limited to the skycaps I had seen at the airport in New York and to a woman in Virginia who took in Gamma's ironing.

There was an eatery in downtown Greenwich in those days. It was on Putnam Avenue, and it was called the White Diner. Our family went there for casual dinners a couple of times. It was really nothing more than the name suggests, just a place to get a hamburger or maybe a hot turkey sandwich. But on its door, there was a sign that read, "Whites Only." That seemed a little odd to me, but I confess, it never stopped us from going in.

Once inside, of course, we kids knew to sit up straight and demonstrate our very best table manners. Good manners, of course, are important, but to our mother, a woman raised during the Depression by Navy parents, they were a lot more important than anything as abstract as social justice.

In the spring of 1961, Mom and Dad decided it was time we had a home of our own. At first, they considered making an offer on the Licata Terrace house, but soon they changed their minds and started looking for something nicer. They found a new development of expensive homes in nearby Stamford. It was a beautiful place, set among a series of ponds connected by a quiet country brook. There, at 77 Rocky Rapids Road, they bought a building lot and started construction on a house they would actually own, for a change. When it was done, it had a full unfinished basement and about five thousand square feet of finished floor space divided equally between the first and second floors. The exterior was shake shingle all around, and inside there were four bedrooms, a formal entry, and a separate dining room. The yard, which was maybe three-fourths of an acre, had a large lawn in front but was mostly virgin forest in the back. It was everything Mom could have hoped for, or so she thought.

We moved in just in time for Dana and me to start the new school year at yet another school. Dana was in ninth grade. I was in eighth. A construction delay at our intended middle school meant our classes would be held at Rippowam High School, a large rectangular two-story building on High Ridge Road, some five miles away.

Mom took us down in the car to get enrolled. There, an administrator gave us placement exams, and when we were done, she told Mom and me that I would be assigned to the highest of four different eighth-grade class levels.

"I'm not sure that's such a good idea," my mother responded. "His grades haven't been very good." And so it was decided I would go into 8-2-L. The *L* stood for Latin, something Mom had taken when she was in school.

For me, the most noticeable (and most wonderful) difference about this new school was the girls. Rippowam, after all, was more than just a middle school. It was also a high school. There were a lot more girls around than might have otherwise been the case, and many of them were years older than I was. They wore makeup. They wore stockings. Some wore heels. Most of them either teased their hair or combed it up in a beehive, which was popular back then. They dressed, in other words, to get attention, something I was increasingly happy to provide.

Of all the girls, my favorites were the Italian Americans, and at Rippowam, there were a lot of them. With their dark hair and their olive skin, I found some of them irresistible. Of course, there wasn't much I could do about it. I was still afraid of my own shadow.

There was a boy my age, named Mark Hughes, who lived up the street from us. Right off, he and I became friends and began hanging out together. One day, I noticed him in the hallway at school. He was talking to the one girl I considered hottest of them all. Her name was Linda Sericchio. She had a beautiful Mediterranean complexion and black hair that was all teased up on top of her head. Like an idiot, I said something to Mark about her on the school bus that afternoon.

The next day, he told me he had spoken to her about it, and I was mortified. "What? Why did you do that?" I demanded. I couldn't believe it!

"Don't worry," he pleaded. "It's no big deal."

But then, for the next few days, he teased me about her. He said she was curious about me and wanted him to point me out. I was so embarrassed. Now I would have to sneak around the hallways between classes.

Then, one day, they caught me. At the end of my last class, I headed for my locker and found the two of them waiting there. Hoping they hadn't seen me yet, I ducked into a classroom and just stood there in a corner, my heart racing. Within seconds, though, I heard Mark's voice.

"Go ahead," he was saying. "Go ahead, take a look! He's in there."

I was a frightened animal caught in a trap. If there was any way I could have walked through those walls, I surely would have. To satisfy her curiosity, Linda Sericchio, by my reckoning the prettiest girl in school, stepped halfway into the room and then leaned over to find out who I was. For two seconds, or less, she looked at me, and I looked at her. Then she turned and walked out of the room.

At this stage of my life, I'm afraid this was the nature of my relationship with girls. I loved them to death, lusted for them, in fact, but I had no courage whatsoever to do anything about it.

Another new friend who lived on my street was a kid named Dennis Seymour. In some ways, he was just as awkward as I was, which was okay by me. Dennis and I walked into town after school one day, and mostly out of impulse, we shoplifted a couple of packs of chewing gum at a supermarket. Theft was something brand-new to me, but frankly, I was instantly exhilarated by conquering my fear in this way.

The next day, we went back and did it again, only this time we hit two supermarkets, swiping several packs of gum at each. *Man,* I thought, *I can get into this!*

For the next week or so, we went into town every afternoon and repeated the crime, each time taking more gum than the time before, and a lot more, I might add, than we would ever be able to chew ourselves.

In school, I was passing out gum to any and all takers and, most importantly, to girls! For the first time, I felt like I was getting noticed, and I liked it. I thought I was finally somebody!

Well, I was somebody, all right. Especially the day Dennis and I got caught. We were walking out of a grocery store with whole boxes of chewing gum concealed in our jackets when we heard a manager's voice calling us back. Too scared to run, we dutifully followed him back inside and into his office to wait while he called our mothers on the phone.

Boy, was I ashamed. As far as I knew, no one in the history of my family had ever stolen anything. My parents, of course, had no idea of the part my failure with girls had to do with this sorry episode. But thankfully, they let it pass without much of a lecture and no punishment that I can recall. I guess they figured my embarrassment alone would teach me a lesson. But then, they couldn't foresee, and neither could I, that there were going to be bigger larcenies in my future. Much bigger.

We only lived on Rocky Rapids Road for two years. While there, I was responsible for washing both our cars every week and mowing the lawn. We still had the Mercedes, but we also had a baby-blue Volkswagen Beetle Dad had bought to get himself to and from the Stamford train station every day. Between washing both cars every week, mowing the lawn, and helping Dana with the dishes at night, I felt overworked. But with the new house, at least we now had an automatic dishwasher, which greatly simplified that chore. We also had a power lawn mower Dad bought at Caldor's discount store in Greenwich for forty-three dollars. In the summer of 1962, Dad let me use that mower to make money cutting grass around the neighborhood, which I did for five dollars a yard.

That money came in handy whenever I wanted to go into town to see a matinee. Usually, I would do so either with Dana or one of my friends, but sometimes I just went by myself. I remember seeing *Rome Adventure* that way, sitting all alone in the theater. It was a love story filmed in Italy, with Suzan Pleshette and Troy Donahue. I was probably the only kid in the audience that day who had actually been to Italy, and I recognized all the landmarks in the background.

Mostly, though, I just sat there drooling over Suzanne Pleshette and wishing I were her boyfriend.

When I wasn't at the movies or doing my chores that summer, I was usually out in the woods with Mark Hughes, working on a tree house we were building from pilfered lumber scraps. It was a pretty good one, too, standing about ten feet above the ground. Of course, neither one of us had a level, so the whole thing was hopelessly crooked.

We built it far enough into the woods so as not to be visible from the street. But then, one day, some bulldozers arrived and they started clearing the way for a new street through the forest. Before long, our secret hideaway was in somebody else's front yard.

With so many ponds around, all the kids were into ice-skating, and Dana and I were no exception. We skated all three of the winters we were in Connecticut, but the most memorable experience for both of us, I think, was in December 1962, when we spied our friends one morning on the pond across the street. We had been waiting patiently, just as they had, for the ice to be thick enough to skate on, and we took this to be our signal that it was.

"Hold on a minute," Dad said as he caught us going out the door. "I'm coming with you." He wanted to make sure the ice really was ready.

The three of us headed over to the pond, with Dana and me both wishing Dad had something, anything, else to do. When we reached the ice, he cautiously walked out to the middle, found a spot, and stopped. Then he turned around and jumped straight up in the air, coming down with a thud. Our friends had been having such a lovely time skating, but now they stood and watched as a great crack began to spread out from under Dad's feet in both directions. And that was it. All skating was now canceled for the rest of day. Thanks, Dad. I guess.

Even though two years had passed since Bumpa's death, Nanny was still having a difficult time. Not wanting to be alone in San Diego, she had sold her house in the fall of 1960 and followed us to Connecticut. She moved in with us in Greenwich initially, but that just didn't work out. She and Mom were both, shall we say, enthusiastic drinkers, but Nanny would get a little too enthusiastic. Before long, Mom was having to put her to bed every night.

When we moved to Stamford, Nanny moved with us. But her move was into an apartment in town. It was nice, though. It had only one bedroom, but there was a big picture window in the living room offering a nice view over the town.

From the fall of 1961 until the spring of 1962, that apartment was where Nanny lived. Sometimes we would visit her there, and she always seemed happy when we did. When Christmas came, she bought me a sweatshirt and monogrammed it for me with "Brave Dave," a nickname I had chosen for myself.

In truth, though, Nanny could not have been very happy. Late that winter, she presented us with a surprise announcement. Somehow, she had managed to locate a long-forgotten relative who was living down in Miami. Taking little time for reflection, Nanny had decided she wanted to live down there.

Almost immediately, she hired a moving company, and by the end of the month, she was on her way to the Sunshine State. With just enough money left from the sale of her San Diego house, she bought a place and moved in.

Of course, things aren't always what they seem, and soon that distant relative proved to be no company at all. At sixty years of age, Nanny was now alone, living far away from family and in an unfamiliar place. Because Bumpa had chosen to maximize his retirement income for his life only, she would be getting by from now on with very little savings and income. After all those years traveling the world as a naval officer's wife, she was back where she had started, poor and living deep in the South.

For the rest of us, though, things couldn't have been much better. We were living in a large luxury home in a magnificent New England setting. In fact, you might think our mother, after so many years occupying company houses in the middle of a hot and humid jungle, would be delighted. And I suppose she was pleased for the most part, though not always. Heretofore, Mom's life had been mostly one of privilege. She had started out as the only child in a family where the father was frequently away at sea. His long absences conferred upon her a degree of importance in the family that went well beyond what most children experience. True, the Great Depression prevailed from the time she was five until she was seventeen, but by being Navy, and by being abroad much of the time, her family had escaped most of its effects.

Then, as if by some bizarre coincidence, her fortune had been much the same for seven years living in Indonesia. Once again, pleasing Ernestine had been a key priority for nearly everyone around her. Her servants, her kids, her husband, even her friends, most of whose husbands worked for my dad, all had treated her with deference.

Mom was used to spending her time planning cocktail parties and traveling the world, but now we were in Stamford, and a different reality had settled in. Now she had clothes to iron and bathrooms to clean. The servants, the adoring friends who laughed at all her jokes, all were just a memory.

Sometimes, at dinner, Mom would complain about how hard her life had become. She even broke down crying about it a couple of times. How ironic it was. She had achieved the dream of owning such a beautiful and expensive home, yet it wasn't the joy she had expected. The fact that two of her three children were now teenagers and becoming more difficult to control didn't help either.

What was more, Mom was having to manage her situation with progressively less help from Dad, as he was now traveling abroad more often on company business. Sometimes he would be in Bahrain, the site of Caltex's original and most productive operations. Often, though, he was out in the middle of the Sahara Desert, at the company's newest and most promising oil fields. This was Libya, where oil hadn't even been discovered until 1959. That country was so promising as a supplier of oil, and it was so close to the European marketplace, that it was expected to play an important role in the company's future.

One Saturday, in the early spring of 1963, Rippowam held a special guidance session for all ninth graders. The purpose was to familiarize students with and help us choose among the various educational paths we would be offered as entering high school students. I knew beforehand I would be asked to indicate a preference for either the college prep curriculum or vocational school. When I told my father about this, he dropped a bombshell on me.

"David," he said, after drawing a breath, "if I were you, I would choose vocational school."

"Why?" I asked.

"Well, your grades aren't very good, and vocational school would at least give you a skill you can make a living with someday."

"A skill?" I asked. "Like what?"

"Well," he said, "like being a plumber, for example."

One lesson I have learned in life is that no job, providing it constitutes moral and productive employment, is any less noble than any other. However, as the son of a college-educated executive, I had always envisioned myself going in the same direction. Granted, I was no academic, but I wasn't ready to give up on myself.

Maybe Dad was making an honest appraisal of my future, or maybe he was just trying to scare me into trying harder at school. I guess I'll never know. To be fair, though, he had tried repeatedly during my junior high school years to encourage in me the same kind of ambition he had always felt.

I remember Dad taking me to an antique shop once. We found an old tube radio there from the 1930s. It was a tabletop model, cased in wood, and it was just what Dad was looking for. Of course, it didn't work, but that was the whole idea. Dad was thinking that getting it working again might nurture in me an interest in electronics.

After we got home, he showed me how to remove all the tubes. Then we took them to an electronics store for testing. This was all new to me, of course, but Dad showed me how to work the tube tester, and soon we had identified and bought replacements for the tubes that were bad. When we got the radio put back together, it worked fine. We set it up in my room, and I listened to it a few times, but I'm sorry to say, it never instilled an interest in electronics in me.

Another time, Dad bought me a chemistry set for Christmas. It had little vials in it filled with substances that I guess I was supposed to mix together. I don't know, because I never read the instructions; instead, I just left the whole thing sitting in a pile on my desk, under a bedroom window.

That same window, by the way, was where I often spent hours staring through binoculars at one of the houses a hundred yards or so across the pond. A very pretty, chestnut-haired girl named Barbara Gommi lived over there, and what I took to be her bedroom window was clearly visible from mine.

For all the time I spent watching, though, I never even caught a glimpse of her. One Saturday morning, in frustration, I asked my brother, who was only seven at that time, to go over and knock on her door. Many years later, when I was in my sixties, Mark would remind me of what happened next. He was supposed to tell her he had lost his cat in her yard. Would she mind helping him look for it? He followed my instructions to the letter, and she did come out to have a look. But she never came around to a spot where I could see her from my window.

This was still the state of my love life as a fifteen-year-old, and I'm afraid, it was the state of my father's efforts at implanting me with intellectual curiosity. Maybe that was why he was urging me to sign up for trade school, which I dutifully did. But as disappointed as I was about this unexpected turn, something soon happened that made me wonder if Dad's motive wasn't of the ulterior variety. Could it be he was trying out a little reverse psychology on me?

Less than a week after I made my selection known at school, Dad came home one night with an announcement to make. Our time in Connecticut, he said, was nearly over. Amoseas had chosen him to take charge of developing the company's newest oil field at a place called Beda, some two hundred miles deep in the Sahara Desert. He was going to be responsible for everything from drilling wells to setting up a pipeline and treatment facilities and providing living quarters for the men who were going to do the work. Clearly, this was to be a very major undertaking for Dad and a life-changing event for all of us.

After three years of a near-normal existence living in Connecticut, suddenly we were all world travelers again. All of us were excited, but no one more than I. My future at trade school had just been canceled!

There were preparations to be made, of course. For one thing, we all needed immunizations again, and we needed new passports too. It was May of 1963, and I was barely fifteen. My height and weight were measured and recorded in my new passport. I was six foot one, and I weighed 170 pounds.

Because we always knew how possible it was for Dad to be transferred, Mom had been circumspect about the condition of the house. Consequently, no repairs or paint were needed, and my parents were able to sell it quickly. Just about everything, in fact, seemed to come off without a hitch. There was just one issue left, however. Dad needed to get a work visa from the Libyan government, and this was something that might take time.

"No problem," said Dad. "I don't think it'll take very long, and anyway, the company will put us up in a hotel while we wait."

Well, it really didn't prove to be much of a problem. In the end, though, Dad's prediction about how long it would take was a little off the mark. It was early June when we checked in to two rooms at the Roger Smith Hotel, a three-star establishment on Lexington Avenue in New York. We wouldn't be checking out until the first week of August. Mom and Dad were in one room, while Dana, Mark, and I shared a suite.

The hotel was at a great location. Just half a block away, on the other side of the street, was the Waldorf Astoria, and we were easy walking distance from Grand Central Station, Times Square, and Rockefeller Center.

All three of us kids were out of school for the summer. Thankfully, Dana and I were old enough to be turned loose on the city. Each day, Dad gave us five dollars apiece, enough money to buy lunch and maybe amuse ourselves just a little. Together, we would set off to have as much fun as we knew how. Mostly, this meant exploring, and before long, we were very familiar with midtown Manhattan.

Dad, meanwhile, was still going to work every day. Of course, he was doing so at much greater convenience, since his office was now right down the street. Good thing, too, because he had a big job ahead lining up the staff and equipment he would need to get things rolling in Libya.

As always, Mom would sleep in in the mornings, so Dana and I were usually on our own for breakfast. We got in the habit of going over to Horn & Hardart, an automat, where one purchased food, item by item, using quarters to open little windows. When we didn't go there again for lunch, we would usually take that meal up in Mom's room at the Roger Smith. She would order sandwiches over the phone and have them delivered from a delicatessen down on the street.

We always took naps in the afternoon, but afterward, Dana and I would usually head right back out the door again. Sometimes we would walk over to Times Square and take in a movie. We saw *PT 109* and *Mutiny on the Bounty* with Marlon Brando. We saw *How the West Was Won* in Cinerama, and perhaps best of all, we saw *Lawrence of Arabia,* something that foreshadowed the life we ourselves were about to experience in the Sahara.

At night, the five of us would go out for some of the most memorable dinners we ever had together. Around the corner from our hotel, on Forty-Seventh Street, there was a great little French restaurant called Marnel's. It probably got more of our business than any other.

Another place we frequented was the Stockholm, a midtown Scandinavian smorgasbord that featured chilled lobster. Then, way down in the Bowery, there was a Spanish place that Dad took us to one night. He had heard it was pretty good, but none of us had any idea what Spanish food was all about. Shortly after we were seated, a waiter walked through the dining room, delivering a large and colorful pan heaped with yellow rice and seafood. In an instant, we knew what to order, and paella has been a family favorite ever since.

As we usually did during our travels, we declined restaurant desserts in favor, sometimes, of a sweet we might purchase on our walk back to the hotel. When that didn't happen, we could each take an apple from a bushel basketful kept in the lobby at the Roger Smith. Before long, though, Dana and I began abusing that privilege by sending our little brother down to get more apples long after we were all supposed to be in bed. Not wanting to get ourselves in trouble, I guess we thought Mark was young enough to be forgiven. When he came back to the room one night spilling apples out of his overfilled pajama top, all three of us laughed hysterically. After that, we cooled it for a while.

June stretched into July, and still there was no work visa forthcoming, so Mom and Dad decided to send for Nanny. Not knowing for sure how long we would be out of the country, Mom must have been feeling guilty about taking off without seeing her first. So Dad bought her a ticket, and Nanny caught a Pullman train, riding up the coast from Miami. For those few days, it was happy times for her again. She was able to set her loneliness aside and enjoy being in the company of family. Then, when her visit was over, we all went down to Pennsylvania Station to see her off. It was late in the evening, and I remember waving back to her through the window as she sat on the bed in her little sleeper compartment.

Then the first week of August arrived, and so did Dad's passport. His work visa had been approved by the Libyan embassy, and it was stamped inside. With nothing left to hold us back, Dad made the earliest possible flight arrangements, and we all started packing again.

SEVEN

The Shores of Tripoli

Arriving at the new TWA Flight Center at Idlewild Airport (later John F. Kennedy International) was like taking a step into the future. Before the building ever opened, less than a year earlier, it had already been called a historic landmark. The *New York Times* described it as the Grand Central of the jet age. Its streamlined, organic shape recalled a giant manta ray floating in the ocean.

There were no direct flights to Tripoli, so this night we would go only as far as Rome. For all of us except Dad, this crossing of the Atlantic, from west to east, would be a first. Meanwhile, Dana and I had never even flown on a jet before. This one was a Boeing 707, and I was pretty excited about it.

Our late day departure meant our arrival in Rome would be the following morning, which would be standard even today for commercial flights from the US to Europe. There would be a movie shown on board, something else that was entirely new to us. It was *Bye Bye Birdie*, a film about teenagers and rock and roll, perfect for entertaining Dana and me. Clearly, air travel had changed since our Indonesia days.

After landing at Leonardo da Vinci Airport, we took a taxi to the Roman seaside suburb of Fiumicino. We rested there until the following morning at a comfortable pensione just a few blocks up from the beach. We were too sleep-deprived for a swim or to go into Rome.

Next morning, we boarded an Alitalia Caravelle for the short flight across the Mediterranean into Tripoli. Seeing the lovely stewardesses on board, and hearing their melodic Italian through the airplane speakers, reminded me of how much I fancied some of the Italian American girls back in Stamford.

This would not be our first experience of North Africa. We had, remember, vacationed in Cairo four years earlier. This time, though, it was August outside, and the searing heat is what I remember most about our arrival at Tripoli's Idris International Airport in bin Ghashir. I didn't know it yet, but the highest atmospheric temperature ever recorded on the planet earth, 136 degrees Fahrenheit, was at Al 'Aziziyah, just twenty miles from where we landed.

In the Middle East, Dad's company was known not as Caltex but as Amoseas, and it was an Amoseas employee who met our plane. He waited as we went through customs and immigration and then helped us with our bags. We followed him out of the terminal to a black Mercedes, surprisingly similar to our own, which, by the way, was itself in shipment to Tripoli.

Pulling out of the airport, we turned north onto a hot, dusty road. The trip into town was going to be about thirty-five kilometers long, mostly through agricultural land that had been claimed from the dessert through irrigation. It was surprising to see such lush dirt farms here growing produce in such abundance. Most impressive were the many rows of fruit trees that lined the way. Our driver explained that these were blood oranges, planted during the Italian occupation prior to World War II. When ripe, they might have a coppery blush on the outside, but inside the flesh was dark and red.

Soon, flat-roofed, sand-colored stucco houses started appearing. They were modest at first, quite apparently the homes of native Libyans, but as we drove deeper into the community, we saw larger, more well-appointed Mediterranean-style villas with high walls around them and iron gates in front. Almost all were duplexes. Some had bright splashes of bougainvillea cascading over them in shades of red or purple. This was Giorgimpopoli, a seaside neighborhood to the west of Tripoli, home mostly to Americans and other expatriates brought here by the oil boom.

Our villa, as it turned out, was still under construction and not quite ready for us, so our driver delivered us to the nearby home of another Amoseas family that was away on leave. We would be staying there temporarily.

Except for one highway through the center of town, all the streets in Giorgimpopoli were unpaved, including our own. Each was a sandy white passageway between mostly white walls surrounding mostly white villas. In the midday sun, one could hardly open his eyes for the glare.

And was it ever hot! Right away, we learned there would be no air-conditioning—practically none, in fact, in the entire town. Instead, portable fans, oscillating in every room, were how people coped. I wondered how this could be adequate in temperatures exceeding 110 degrees every day.

One consolation did offer itself, however. This villa, like the one we were about to rent, was just a short walk from a private cove on the Mediterranean. There, at water's edge, was the improbably named Tripoli Golf Club. It had a decent restaurant and a cocktail lounge with large windows overlooking the sea. Outside, there were tennis courts and a private beach. In short, just about everything you might want from a private club was there, except for a golf course. It was the perfect place for expatriate teenagers to make friends and hang out at the beach.

In a few weeks, Dana, Mark, and I would be back in school. Collectively, the American oil companies had established a combined elementary / junior high school nearby. Mark was ready to enter the second grade, so he would be going there. Dana, meanwhile, was a high school junior. I was a sophomore. For us, school was twenty kilometers away, east of Tripoli, at Wheelus, an American Air Force base.

Our first day of school, Dana and I walked up to the corner where we were told the bus would stop. We waited a while, but it never arrived. Finally, a couple of cars appeared and pulled up to where we were standing. The driver of the first car, apparently an American, told us the bus wasn't going to come. He and the other driver were there to take us to the base. Seeing that some kids were already in the cars, I reached for a door handle.

Oh my gosh! I thought. Looking up at me from the back seat was the most incredible face. Her hair was nearly black, her eyes dark and lovely. She had to be a teenager, I knew, but how was that possible? I had never had a close encounter with such a beautiful woman in my life.

How convenient it would have been had this lovely creature smiled and slid over to make room for me. A boy with any poise at all would have introduced himself on the spot and wound up marrying her someday. You never know. But none of that was going to happen here. Instead, her eyes said it all. *Un uh, buddy! This is my window seat. You can go around to the other side!*

Dana and I had enrolled at Wheelus a week before, so we already knew the route through downtown Tripoli and beyond. It ran parallel to the coast, past the old walled city and its labyrinthine downtown souk, where tourists shopped for the usual camel saddles, ornamental brass, and sheepskin rugs. There, atop the ancient Red Castle, stood the mast of the USS *Philadelphia*, a 160-year-old trophy of the Barbary pirates. Then, the route turned right onto the date-palm-lined Sharia al Fatah, the harbor boulevard, which ran past what was Tripoli's finest hotel in those days, the Uaddan.

It was another ten kilometers beyond the city before the American air base came into view. This morning, though, all that was of little interest to me. Instead, I kept thinking of the girl sitting two feet away.

Classes at Wheelus were conducted in a rectangular one-story building of a dozen or so classrooms. They faced inward onto a large rectangular courtyard where crabgrass and a few date palms struggled to survive. To connect the classrooms, sidewalks crisscrossed the common area in the same pattern as the stripes on the British Union Jack.

I was signed up for French, biology, English, Geometry, and European history. I also had an hour of physical education on my schedule, which was to be conducted across the street in a large public park.

Perhaps half of the students were oil kids, the other half Air Force. Air Force families lived mostly on the base, so Dana and I were acquainted with none of them at first. Nor for that matter, did we know most of the oil kids yet. Two we did know were Bill Keane, a senior who lived near us, and his sister, Diane. Diane was a little overweight, perhaps, but she was a modest sort with a cheerful demeanor. Bill, on the other hand, was a self-proclaimed lothario, God's gift to women, to hear him tell it. With his comb always at the ready, he never passed a mirror without stopping. Even though he was just seventeen, he claimed to have had many sexual conquests under his belt (including Sandra Dee, who was a big Hollywood star at that time). Despite all this, Bill was a good-natured character who laughed a lot. Dana and I liked them both.

A half-dozen or so of the boys at Wheelus, I soon discovered, were getting to and from school on bright-red Gileras, Italian motorcycles I had never heard of before. I immediately wanted one, of course, but there was no point saying so to my parents. I was, after all, only fifteen.

Bill didn't have a motorcycle either, but what he did have was the frequent use of his parents' Volkswagen. It was a baby-blue Beetle that he called the Messerschmitt, and Dana and I were quick to become two of his favorite passengers.

Right away, Wheelus seemed to have a party atmosphere. When we arrived every morning, there would be rock and roll music playing in the courtyard. Between classes, everyone passed through this common area. Girls in their crisp white blouses and knee-length skirts looked so sharp to me, particularly the extroverted ones. It seemed like they flirted with every boy but me.

Short-sleeve shirts with button-down collars were de rigueur for the boys. So were white Levi's. I wore them both.

One thing I accomplished right away was to learn the name of the girl in the car. She was Mary Wray, and not surprisingly, every boy at Wheelus had his eye on her.

How well I remembered that day in Stamford and the humiliation I felt at being exposed to Linda Sericchio. You'd think I would know by now to keep my feelings to myself, but I didn't. Like a fool,

I blabbed the whole thing to Bill Keane one day just a week or so after school had started. I was horrified by what happened the next day at lunch.

We had a choice of places to go: there was an indoor cafeteria just around the corner, or we could eat outdoors at a base-operated hamburger joint down the street. It was called the Oasis, and just about everyone was there that day.

I had just arrived when Bill walked up to me with Mary Wray in tow and introduced us. Then, without any further comment, he turned and walked away. Clearly, he had said something to her about me, but I didn't know what, and I was scared to death.

There she stood, looking up through those beautiful eyes, waiting for me to speak. But I could only stammer. My face started twitching, and my mouth went dry. I wanted to run, but how could I?

Finally, she said something, though I don't remember what. Then she smiled and went back to her friends.

I had lots of awkward experiences that autumn at Wheelus. One morning, I was on the athletic field with a group of other boys, waiting for our physical education class to begin. Not far from where I stood, a large beetle was slowly crossing the sidewalk. I went over to it and was going to step on it. One of the other boys saw what I was about to do and stopped me.

"Hey, Dave," he said, "why don't you live and let live?"

How that boy knew my name, I don't know. And how odd was it for a guy in gym class to be asking another guy not to kill a bug? Nonetheless, his words were an early lesson to me about having the courage to speak up when something isn't right.

In all of Libya, there was only one TV station. It was operated by the Armed Forces Broadcasting Service at Wheelus Air Base. The picture was black-and-white, and at our house at least, it was poor in quality.

One November night, after dinner, I was alone in the living room, stretched out on the couch and watching *The Dick Van Dyke Show*. I don't remember what Dana or Mark were doing, but Mom and Dad were in another room, talking. Suddenly, the program was interrupted by a short news bulletin. Someone, the announcer said, had shot President Kennedy in Dallas. The announcer said he would give more information as it became available. Then, *The Dick Van Dyke Show* came back on.

Overhearing this, Dad came into the room. "What's going on?" he asked.

"I don't know. They just said someone shot President Kennedy."

An assassination attempt on the president? That didn't sound right. Nothing like that had happened since horse-and-buggy days. Could this be for real?

After two or three minutes, the announcer came back on and said the president had died. Then *Dick Van Dyke* returned, and I just lay there thinking I was going to watch the rest of the show. Then, Dad reappeared and said, "Let's turn that off, son. I think we owe the man that much."

I turned it off, but it didn't seem right. The president was dead. So what? What could I do about it? Turning off the TV wasn't going to help. I didn't say so, but I was surprised. When it came to Kennedy, hardly anything ever said in our household, particularly by my mother, had ever risen above the level of contempt. Back in Santa Paula in 1948, Mom had volunteered in the congressional campaign of Richard Nixon. Then in 1952, Eisenhower, a man who physically resembled her father, became president, with Nixon as his running mate. Nixon, as far as Mom was concerned, would have been one of our greatest presidents. Kennedy, on the other hand, was anything but.

Mom always ran either hot or cold on people, but usually it was cold. This was particularly true when someone waited on her at a store or in a restaurant. She always seemed to speak to such people condescendingly, and I was always getting embarrassed by it.

Once again, in Tripoli, as in Rumbai, she had hired a servant to do our housework. This time, the servant was Abbud, our Libyan houseboy. Thanks to Abbud, Mom could sleep in late every morning, if she wanted, and spend most of her time doing as she pleased. That might just mean reading a book or taking a nap. But she was a great cook, and she always made us a good dinner. Then, she would drink martinis, and by the time we sat down to eat, she could become unpleasant.

I made only a couple of good friends that school year. My sister thought them nerds. One was Bob Bevis, an only child who was a year older than I was and almost as tall. Sometimes after school, I would go over to his house and watch him eat hot dogs. I don't remember ever having one myself, though I'm sure it was offered. My sister might have actually been right about Bob. He was a bit of a misfit. He had grown up in Europe, somehow managing to have little interaction with other kids. He didn't dress or behave like the other boys at school. Where they wore Levi's and spoke in teen vernacular, Bob wore slacks and was stilted in his speech.

His parents owned a 190 SL Mercedes, and Bob always talked about having one of his own someday. "It's going to be gunmetal gray and have a tan leather interior," he would say.

He also liked to talk about his college plans. Though still a junior, he had already made up his mind. "I'm going to the Sorbonne," he said. "They want me because of my languages."

They want me for my languages? Why did such an absurd remark seem so plausible to me back then? I knew one thing, though. No college was going to want me, either for languages or anything else. I didn't have the grades.

A closer friendship I soon developed was with a boy named Scott Latham. Scott was an owl-faced kid from Texas who wore horn-rimmed glasses and had pimples even worse than mine. He was really smart, though, and he had a great sense of humor. I always enjoyed time spent with him. Scott and I were both interested in acting, and we both belonged to the drama club. When the club produced a review of one-act plays at the base theater one night, he and I performed in the comedy sketch *If Men Played Cards as Women Do.* The place was packed, and we managed to get some really big laughs.

I guess you could say Scott was an intellectual. He was always reading books, and he had an impressive vocabulary. As far as he was concerned, there was a perfect word for everything, and he tried to use it. His favorite was *indefatigable*, which he managed to fit at least once into every conversation.

Scott used to go to the base library with his mother every week. A couple of times, I went with them, and that was how he got me interested in the science fiction writer Ray Bradbury. I read some of Bradbury's books that year. One of my favorite Bradbury stories was *A Sound of Thunder*, about a group of men who time-travel back to the Jurassic period. One of the men accidentally steps off the path, killing a butterfly. When they get back to the present day, the time-travelers discover that things have changed. Signs are spelled differently, a different man is president of the United States, and so on.

I thought about the beetle I almost killed on the sports field that day. Who knows what difference a person makes?

One afternoon, Scott and I accepted a ride from an Italian man we hardly knew. He had a small record player sitting in his front passenger seat. It was plugged into the cigarette lighter of his car, and he was using it to play the same 45 rpm record over and over. It was by a new English rock group called the Beatles. On one side of the record was the song "She Loves You," on the other side "I Want to Hold Your Hand." We liked them instantly.

As it turned out, we weren't the only ones. In the weeks and months ahead, there was a worldwide explosion of interest in the Beatles, something the media started calling Beatlemania. Every teenager had to have their records, and even the Tripoli kids were a part of it. "Please, Please Me" and "Love Me Do" were played over our public-address system at school, and formerly crew-cut boys were starting to let their hair grow. That wasn't going to work at my house, though. After all, what would my mother's friends think if they saw her son walking around looking like a girl?

In truth, there wasn't much about raising teenagers that appealed to Mom. Dana and I both got on her nerves, and she said so often. In large part, of course, this was normal. What parent doesn't find teenagers a challenge? But Mom lacked some of the most essential parenting tools. For one thing, she was seldom one for feeling empathy, and this almost always put her needs at odds with ours. It also made it very difficult for her to change her mind about anything. In fact, she was so fixed in her thinking that she often could not even tolerate objective discourse. At dinner, for example, we might be allowed to discuss the when, the where, or the what of a matter, but not the why. Many times, Mom would terminate a conversation not because she disagreed necessarily but because she found abstractions irritating. To her, everything was either right or wrong, and any suggestion of nuance violated her sensibilities. Poor Dad, meanwhile, a contemplative and intelligent man, would go along with these demands just to keep the peace.

Dana was always butting heads with Mom. Boys were Dana's main preoccupation now, and Mom was dismissive about every one she brought around. Of far more interest to Mom were the boys she herself had dated many years before.

"I always played the field," she would say. Or "You know, I was engaged three times before I met your father." Evidently, she had been quite a success with boys when she was young, and I guess by implication, Dana was not.

Only, Dana was! Already there was a nice-looking boy at school who was asking her out. He was a tall and handsome dark-haired German boy, an identical twin named Gunther Pranitch. Numerous times I saw him with Dana at school. He even came to the house a couple of times to take her out. But I doubt Mom even cared enough to learn his name. This sort of thing offended Dana and made her want to rebel. There were times when she would skip school with a friend. I didn't know what they were up to, but when Dana invited me to join them one day, I accepted.

The British Army had an enlisted men's club some distance away, and we set off walking to it that morning. It was a fairly long walk, as I remember, but the girls were hoping to meet young soldiers. Only, no young soldiers appeared, so we spent our day watching the clock and waiting to go home. Needless to say, I never did that again.

Dana had a couple of relationships with local boys that year. One was a young Libyan, and the other an ethnic Italian who had grown up in Libya. Dana would have loved to talk about these relationships at the dinner table, but Mom would never hear of it. As far as she was concerned, Tripoli was just a temporary job assignment.

There was no way she was going to risk having her American daughter stay behind in North Africa, possibly even married to a local.

So Dana conducted her relationships the only way she could, in secret. Instead of coming to the house, her boyfriends might have to meet her somewhere else, and as far as our parents were to know, Dana was just going over to visit friends like Bill and Diane.

Only, Mom and Dad couldn't be fooled forever, and when they finally figured things out, they decided to take action. Putting it all together—poor grades, local boyfriends, and of course, Mom's perennial problem with her nerves—they determined that Dana should be sent away to boarding school.

With a little effort, they found La Chatelaine, a school for girls in Saint-Blaise, Switzerland. Here, there would be no boys, which was just perfect, as far as they were concerned. They applied, and soon Dana's acceptance arrived in the mail.

This was all well and good, but how were they going to make Dana leave home but not me? What kind of message did that send? Besides, I got on Mom's nerves too, didn't I? So while they were at it, they arranged for me to go to the American International School in Vienna, Austria.

The American International School (AIS) would be my eleventh school in eleven years, but it was located in one of my favorite European cities, and I was delighted. Dana was happy, too, and so was Dad. Although he was not as disillusioned with parenting as Mom was, he had nonetheless been worried about Dana too. Plus, he had a lot on his shoulders out in the oil fields. Both Beda and Nafoora were deep in the Sahara. Each needed his full attention, managing the manpower and equipment necessary to drill for, pump, and transport oil by pipeline to the Mediterranean. Purchasing and coordinating all this was entirely Dad's responsibility.

One day, before I headed off to Vienna, Dad invited me to go out to Nafoora on one of his regular visits. At first, I was hesitant about going. I couldn't imagine what there would be for me to do out there, but I wound up going anyway.

Dad also invited Mr. Bagley, one of the science teachers from Wheelus High School. Bagley, a black American, had contacted

Dad and indicated an interest on his own. Together, the three of us boarded a company-chartered DC-3, and off we went.

There was no real road to Nafoora. There was none to Beda either, for that matter. When company personnel made either trip over land, they did so using a compass. Nafoora was in a part of the desert known as the Sea of Sand, where dunes can rise a hundred feet or more into the sky. Four-wheel drive was required for getting there, and the company owned Land Rovers for that purpose. Beda, on the other hand, was on a hammada, or stone plateau. Dad himself had once made that trip, driving some two hundred kilometers with another man into the middle of the Sahara. They did so in a brand-new Volkswagen microbus they had purchased for use at the camp. Along the way, they found and visited the Bedouin oasis of Maradah, a tiny settlement surrounding a big wet hole in the ground.

There are few places on Earth as perilous to travelers as the Sahara. Both Beda and Nafoora are close in latitude to where the *Lady Be Good* went down in World War II, an event that perfectly illustrates the sort of thing that can happen. In that tragic episode, an American bomber crew became disoriented when returning to Libya from a raid over Italy. Unable to see the African coastline in the dark, and with their navigation equipment malfunctioning, they overflew their air base and continued for two more hours out over the desert. Running out of fuel, they bailed out, and even then they thought they were doing so over water. Eventually, all nine airmen died, but not without great suffering. One of them recorded the whole ordeal in his diary, which wasn't found until seventeen years later.

No such fate awaited us, of course, as our plane successfully located and landed on the airstrip at Nafoora. We were met by a half-dozen or so Arabs who were waiting there to unload supplies. One of them approached Mr. Bagley and tried to strike up a conversation, something that made all of us laugh. Thinking a black man could only be Libyan, the man was rattling off at him in Arabic.

"I'm sorry," said Mr. Bagley, to the man's surprise. "I don't speak your language."

My stay at Nafoora was only two days, but I found it interesting. It is normal in the oil business to find oneself in some pretty remote places, and this place was easily as remote as any other. Several trailers were on-site. Some were sleeping quarters for the workers, one a very basic kitchen and dining facility. Another was a small lab for testing the oil and examining the core samples that came out of the various wells. The whole thing was operated by no more than two or three Western oilmen and a few dozen Libyans. All were rotated in and out by Dad.

Before we left, Dad took me for a short ride over some sand dunes in a Land Rover. How magnificent they were, like giant ocean swells. Afterward, he showed me a spot where ancient ostrich shell fragments were lying on the ground. He explained how, ten thousand years ago, during the Ice Age, the Sahara was a land with plenty of rainfall and lush vegetation.

"People used to live out here," he said, and he showed me several arrowheads he had discovered near the water hole that day he had visited Maradah. It was almost too much to believe, but the evidence was right in front of me.

Not long after our trip to the desert, Dad came up with another idea for us to do together. He had learned that classes were conducted out on the air base for scuba certification. He thought the two of us should have a go at it, and I liked the idea immediately. Within a few weeks, we were both certified and had the equipment necessary to do all the diving we wanted. With the Mediterranean practically in our front yard, we were well practiced at snorkeling, something I truly loved. But now, with the ability to go to much greater depths, we looked forward to having more exploring to do. For the first time in my life, though, I soon discovered I was incapable of descending more than about eight feet. The pressure on my eardrums was just too painful, and I was at a loss for what to do about it. After only a couple of outings, I was back to snorkeling for good.

Like me, my friend Scott was planning to do eleventh and twelfth grades at a boarding school in Europe. Only, his parents had chosen a school in Lugano, Switzerland. The two of us spent that summer in 1964 hanging out together, sharing the excitement we were feeling. As big as the Beatles and other British rock groups had suddenly become, American folk music was still very much in its heyday. We were both fans of groups like the Kingston Trio and Peter, Paul, and Mary, but now a new name was popping up. Sitting on the floor in Scott's bedroom, we listened to Bob Dylan for the first time that summer. I thought I didn't care for his sound at first, but my opinion would change over time.

One day, Scott and I were at the beach club when we ran into a freckle-faced, redheaded kid we hadn't seen before. Under a large concrete pavilion where kids would go to get in the shade, he was playing guitar and singing for a group of our friends. Being "folkies," Scott and I jumped right in and started singing along.

Afterward, we introduced ourselves. His name was Andy Dorman. He was the son of an American diplomat, and he lived near the US Embassy in downtown Tripoli. The reason we didn't know him, he explained, was that he didn't go to Wheelus. Instead, he attended a boarding school back in Massachusetts called Winchendon. He was a prep school kid, the very thing Scott and I were about to become.

Andy was loaded with charm, and he was loaded with talent. He knew how to play a lot of songs, and he sang each one out like a born entertainer. What really surprised us though was when he complimented our singing and invited us to join him as a folk group!

"But we don't play guitar," we warned.

"That's okay. I'll play the guitar, and all three of us will sing. Let's do it!"

So it began right there under the pavilion. We were having our first rehearsal. After that, we met and practiced every day. Sometimes we did so at the club while other kids looked on in amusement. Then, we would go for a swim at the beach. Once, when Andy's parents were away, we stayed at his house in the city and practiced all night long.

Andy's dad was the deputy chief of mission at the embassy. This meant he functioned as ambassador whenever the real ambassador was away. Consequently, Andy lived in a fine urban home with a well-kept garden, all of it surrounded by a high security wall.

After a couple of weeks, we decided we were ready, so we approached the golf club about entertaining one night in the dining room. We didn't expect to be paid, of course, and so the manager agreed. Only, the dining room turned out to be nearly empty that night, so we didn't gain much from the experience.

Next, we approached the nightclub manager at the Uaddan Hotel in downtown Tripoli. The Uaddan was the only luxury hotel in town. It had a large roof terrace with a first-class, open-air restaurant/nightclub overlooking the harbor. Every weekend, weather permitting, a dance band would perform there for well-heeled customers from all over the world. Would the manager consider letting us fill in for that band during one of their breaks? "Sure," she said.

That Friday, we showed up with one guitar and three sets of parents who had made dinner reservations. I guess the venue must have gotten their attention, because they hadn't shown much interest before. We had a nice dinner, and then, when the band was about to break, the manager came over to the table and asked us for the name of our group. She wanted to give us a proper introduction.

We really hadn't chosen a name, but for the purpose of this evening, we had agreed to be called Wynken, Blyken, and Nod, after the children's poem and folk song. We told the manager, but she couldn't remember it when she reached the microphone. Instead, she said, "Ladies and gentlemen...the Stateside Singers!"

We only had one microphone. It would have been better to have three, or even none at all, for that matter, because our voices were picked up unevenly. But at least we got to experience what it felt like to sing in front of an audience. And we learned an important lesson about performing. Always do it for an empty room first, and always rehearse at least once with the microphone!

And then, summer was over. Andy left to go back to school, and Scott took off for Lugano. In a day or so, it would be my turn to leave.

There was a small outdoor movie house in Giorgimpopoli. It was hardly more than a courtyard with a projector, really. It had a makeshift screen and about three dozen folding chairs. Mostly, it attracted American teenagers. My last night in town was a Friday. With my friends now gone, I decided to take in a movie alone. I got there and took a seat by myself in the back row. Sitting there in the twilight, waiting for the show to start, I was admiring a group of girls several rows in front of me. Each one was painted up and pretty. Among them was the beautiful Mary Wray, laughing and having a good time. Sitting next to her was, of all people, my sister, Dana.

EIGHT

Vienna

Then, it was Saturday morning, and I was on my way to Austria. There were no direct flights, so I connected in Rome. I was glad, though. Changing planes and hanging out at a major European airport made me feel like such a jet-setter. Besides, the girl watching was excellent.

When I landed in Vienna, it was late in the evening and a steady rain was falling. The airport looked deserted, and I wondered if I might have been forgotten. Then I spied a middle-aged couple with a teenage boy coming toward me and smiling.

"Are you David Davenport?" the man asked.

"Yes!"

He introduced himself as Dr. Parsons, director of AIS. The woman and boy were his wife and son.

I was holding a portable record player my parents had given me as a parting gift, but I needed to retrieve my suitcase, so we set off for the baggage claim. Once that was taken care of, we headed out to the parking lot, where a shiny, new Volkswagen minibus was waiting. It was robin's-egg blue and had the letters *AIS* artfully painted on its side.

The Vienna Airport is in Schwechat, a suburb southeast of the city, and AIS is on the opposite side of town. So our drive of forty-five minutes or so took us right through the heart of Vienna. In the dark and the rain, I could only imagine what it looked like.

Dr. Parsons was at the wheel. He asked about me and my family. He wanted to know how we came to be living in Africa. He talked about the school and the plans that were being made. He seemed as excited as I was about being there. It was, he said, his first year too.

There were plenty of other schools I could have applied to. Amazingly, my father had left the choice up to me. I picked Vienna because I had good memories of our visit there in 1959. Also, AIS was co-ed, which made a difference to me. Many other schools, including Dana's, were not.

Like Berlin, Vienna had been carved up into zones by the Allies at the end of World War II. The city had always been an important diplomatic post, but because it was the easternmost capital on the free-European mainland, it now held more geopolitical significance than ever before. Every intelligence agency was active here. It was the headquarters of the recently established International Atomic Energy Agency. With so many countries represented, a truly international school had become a necessity. AIS was established in 1959 by the American and Canadian Embassies, and kids from all over the world were enrolled.

All this and more was explained by Dr. Parsons as we made our way over glistening wet streets. For the first five years, he told me, classes had been conducted in a single urban building that had been adapted for the purpose. But now, a new school complex had been built on the edge of the famed Vienna Woods, in a neighborhood called Salmannsdorf. Everything about the place was modern, he said, except for an old three-story brick and half-timbered mansion they called the Villa. This great house had been restored and divided into a residence for the director and his family on one side and a boys' dormitory on the other. This was where my room was going to be.

It was past ten o'clock, and the rain had diminished by the time we pulled into a driveway. "Here we are," announced Dr. Parsons, braking to a stop.

I climbed out of the minibus and got my first look at my new home. Even in the dark, I could make out what a grand house it was, its lower reaches covered in ivy and its upper windows set among towering trees. The Villa appeared to be the estate of some bygone wealthy family, which, of course, was exactly what it was. Instead of just one front door, though, it had two.

It being late, Mrs. Parsons said good night. She and her son went inside through the door on the left. Dr. Parsons and I unloaded my belongings from the back of the minibus and entered the door on the right.

Inside, we walked down one short hallway and then another before coming to a door. Dr. Parsons knocked. A man I took to be in his late twenties answered. He had crew-cut hair and an athletic build. "Well, hello!" he said, revealing a toothy grin. "Is this David Davenport?"

Before I could speak, Dr. Parsons answered that it was, and he introduced me to Mr. Anderson. The Andersons, he said, were a married couple, and their apartment was just beyond the door. Together, they were the dorm counselors in charge of all the Villa boys. It was too late to show me around, so Dr. Parsons said good night and headed back down the hall.

"Come on, Dave," said Mr. Anderson. "I'll take you up to your room."

He picked up my bag and we headed back down the hall toward the stairs. There were three floors in the Villa, the main floor, where the front entrance was, a lower floor, and an upper one. My room was on the upper floor, and it was the first room we came to at the top of the stairs. The door was standing open, revealing a large, well-lit room containing two sets of bunk beds. They were framed in white tubular steel that reminded me of the beds I had slept in years earlier at the military academy. Against one wall, there was a bathroom sink with a mirror behind it. Standing before it, holding a toothbrush and wearing pajamas, was a boy of about my age.

"Robert, here's your first roommate," Mr. Anderson said, introducing us.

Few experiences in my life have stirred as much excitement in me as waking up the next morning in Austria. The rain of the night before had vanished now. The white walls of my new room were bathed in glorious sunlight. Compared to the dust of Libya, everything here seemed so bright and clean and fresh. I went at once to the window, and there I gazed upon a scene as different from Giorgimpopoli as I could imagine. Stretching across a valley and onto distant hills was what the Austrians call the Wienerwald, the Vienna Woods of Johann Strauss's celebrated waltz. In the foreground were fine old European homes, each one similar to the Villa in both style and size. No more than thirty meters away on my right was the brand-new AIS school building, three buildings, really, asymmetrically conjoined and sprawled out on the hillside. Below me was a shiny, new parking lot and a patch of freshly sodded lawn. Everything, it seemed, was saying, "Hey, David, you are going to like this!"

As soon as we were dressed, I followed my new roommate out the door and down the stairs. The cafeteria, he said, was in the school building next door, and he would show me the way. We went through the main downstairs hallway into a large dayroom, out a back door, down a fire escape, through a concrete passageway, across a courtyard, and into the new building.

The cafeteria was large and bright. It had brand-new tables and benches, enough to seat hundreds of kids. So far, I had seen only Robert, of course, but I knew others would be arriving. Relatively few would be boarding students. I knew that already. Most would be going home every night and living with their parents. This cafeteria might be bustling at lunchtime on a normal weekday, but the rest of the time it would be the preserve of the few who, like Robert and me, lived in the Villa.

We stepped up to the counter and Robert said, "Guten Morgen," to the two cooks who were there. Dressed as the chefs they were, both greeted us cheerfully, though neither spoke any English. We were given our meal trays and took a seat at one of the tables. "How is it you speak German?" I asked, suddenly feeling inadequate because I didn't.

"My mother is German," he said. "We used to live in Germany when I was a kid."

As we ate, I asked Robert where his parents were living now, and he began to tell me his story. Like mine, his family was in Africa. His father worked for an international relief organization in

Burundi, a landlocked Central African country that was smaller and more impoverished than almost any other. *So we have something in common,* I thought. But as he spoke, I began to realize how different Robert's experience in Africa was from mine. Where I had been going to school on an American air base and hanging out with other expatriates at a Mediterranean beach club, Robert lived in the very heart of Africa, where few white people ever ventured.

"To tell you the truth," he confided, "I'm not sure I can stay here."

"Why?" I asked incredulously.

"I'm homesick," he said. "I miss my mother."

Wow, I thought. What a strange thing for a teenage boy to admit. I couldn't imagine myself confessing such a thing, even if it was true. Of course, in my case, it wouldn't be true. I was feeling liberated, and I had every expectation of enjoying the experience.

"You'll get used to it," I said, trying to provide encouragement. Of course, I had no way of knowing he would.

Robert and I spent our first morning together out exploring the new surroundings. Across the street from the school in one direction was a small vineyard, and beyond that were even more vineyards, none more than half an acre or so. Salmannsdorf, as I later learned, is a village known for its heurigen, taverns that produce wine from grapes grown in their own backyards.

We walked down the hill toward the village and turned onto Hameaustrasse, the main thoroughfare. The pavement was all cobblestones, and the shops, while closed on a Sunday, were small and quaint. Every sign we passed was in German, and Robert translated each one for me as we walked along.

Afterward, we took another direction, walking aimlessly out of the village and along a forested stretch of road. Just before we turned back, a red fox appeared in the road up ahead. He paused, getting a good look at us, and then he took off into the underbrush.

Late in the afternoon, an hour or so before dinner, Robert and I were back in our room when we heard voices and footsteps coming up the stairs. Another roommate had arrived, and with him he brought his mother.

He was tall boy, almost as tall, in fact, as my six feet and three inches. He was round of face and had a heavy shadow of whiskers. His hair was thick and black. I wouldn't say he was overweight, but he had the soft appearance of someone more interested in books than sports.

"I'm Elias Menkes," he said as he reached out his hand. "And this is my mother."

I suppose I would have been embarrassed had my mother arrived with me, but Elias didn't seem to care. She was there to unpack his clothes and put them away, something that seemed natural enough to him. And when it was time for her to go, she gave no appearance of wanting to do so. I wondered if she might have stayed the night had someone not appeared and reminded us to change into our dinner clothes.

That, by the way, was one little bit of incongruity. Even though dinner would be in the same cafeteria where the entire school ate lunch every day, even though it was served on trays and we sat on benches, jacket and tie would be required every night.

I got my first look at some of the other boys as we filed into the cafeteria that evening. There were eleven of us in all. Only two were seniors, Steve Remp and Alex Mehdevi. Neither was new to the school. Steve was a tall and impressive Texan who, like me, was the son of an oilman. His father worked in Saudi Arabia.

From the start, it was apparent that Steve was the natural leader of the group. He seemed older and wiser somehow than the other boys. Alex, meanwhile, was a dark-complexioned multinational boy from Mallorca. He was badly pigeon-toed, a fault that caused him to walk awkwardly, and his posture was so poor you might think him shorter than he really was. Nonetheless, I would come to know him as a born iconoclast with a powerful intellect.

There were two other juniors in addition to my roommates and me. Mike Nassie, an Israeli, was a kid with a good heart. He was also very smart, though he would prove to be a tiresome practical jokester at times. Mike's much older brother, Ron, who was studying at the University of Vienna, was going to be living at the Villa and assisting the Andersons as a dorm counselor. Mike and Ron's father was the Israeli legate in Prague.

The other junior was Jim Ward, the son of a Marine colonel who was stationed at the American Embassy in Moscow. Jim was a tall, gung ho, all-American type with a butch haircut who nonetheless had a decent command of German by virtue of having spent several years already at AIS.

So far, only one sophomore had arrived. He was Barry Newton, the awkward and eccentric son of a State Department official who worked mostly behind the iron curtain.

Then there were two freshmen. Nick Reynolds, the youngest of the Villa boys, would turn out to be one of the smartest. The son of the head of consular affairs for the US Embassy in Prague, Nick had a cynical sense of humor and a gift for repartee that stood him well with the older boys. Michael Shaw was the other freshman. He was very good-natured and likable, but he was more immature by far than any of the other boys. Mike's father was some sort of an international businessman from New York.

Not until the next afternoon would my third and final roommate arrive. George Levine was an entertaining New Yorker who, like Elias and Mike Nassie, was Jewish. He spoke with a heavy accent that placed him right in the center of the Bronx, but he'd spent enough time in Austria by now to have acquired nearly flawless German. George was no older than I was, but already he claimed to be a seasoned Casanova, a man of the streets who somehow ought to be looked up to by the rest of the boys. Perhaps it was a measure of my naivete, but I would come to believe in and admire his stories of sexual conquest.

Several weeks would transpire before the final two Villa boys would appear. One of them was Jan Homan, a good-looking, blondheaded Dutch boy who arrived one night unable to speak a word of English. Late on another night, one Peter Ruziska would show up. He didn't speak any English either. Peter was a Czech who had literally been smuggled out from behind the iron curtain. He was still fearful of being caught when he arrived. You could see it in his eyes.

Anyway, after dinner that first night, I set up my new little phonograph and played the only record I had brought to Vienna. It was the soundtrack album from the Beatles' brand-new movie, *A Hard Day's Night*. While the music played, Elias, Robert, and I shared more about ourselves with one another. Elias said he grew up in Margaretville, a small town in the Catskills. He was the only child of parents who had emigrated from Germany and become naturalized Americans. When his father died at an early age, Elias's mother decided to move back to Munich, taking Elias along. But Elias was all New York. In fact, he had long ago made the decision to go to college at Columbia University, and that was largely why he was at AIS now. Getting into the Ivy League, he reasoned, would be easier if he took all the qualifying courses offered at an American high school.

I soon discovered that Ivy League aspirations were common among the Villa boys, and among my other classmates as well, for that matter. This was not entirely new to me, of course. Friends in Tripoli, like Scott Latham and Bob Bevis, had also talked of getting into the best colleges. But they were the exception. Here, as I soon found out, almost everyone was exceptional. These kids came from the highest levels of the professional class. They were well-traveled, well-oriented, and bright young people who, in the main, intended to do something important with their lives.

If I had anything in common with any of them, it sure wouldn't show in my scholastic record. My grades had been awful for years. It's a wonder, in fact, I was even accepted at AIS, though I was certainly glad to be there. I had my limitations, all right, but I found being around such people exciting. And here I was, at a private boarding school in a brand-new building set among sloping vineyards on the outskirts of Vienna. How could things be much better?

Apparently, though, not everyone shared such feelings. By the end of the first week, I was surprised to learn that Robert had left. He had talked about being homesick, and I guess it was worse for him than I realized. He never said goodbye; instead, he just wasn't there anymore.

Meanwhile, I was beginning to enjoy a great new friendship with Elias. From the start, he and I were taking lengthy walks together after school, sometimes into the Wienerwald, sometimes down to the village of Salmannsdorf. Having friends like Scott and Bob in Tripoli had already taught me what a pleasure it was to be around boys smarter than I was. If anything, Elias was even more gifted than those two boys, and my admiration for him quickly blossomed.

Everywhere he went, Elias took along a book, as though some opportunity to stop and read might suddenly present itself. He liked to talk about the things he read. Of particular interest to him was American political history, and he had a remarkable command of detail. Where I vaguely knew the names of most of the presidents, he would talk knowingly about men who merely served in their cabinets.

It was the same with contemporary politics. He was always versed in the important issues of the day. These matters interested me too, of course. I had long been curious about current events, carefully reading my dad's copy of *Time* magazine every week. But my grasp of issues had barely begun to form by now. It was only on these walks with Elias that I truly began to reflect on such things.

Intellect, however, was not Elias's only gift. As time went on, I would discover in him a deeply felt sympathy for those less fortunate than himself. It was almost as though he felt obligated by his circumstances to show kindness and generosity to others. Things were good for Elias, and he was well aware of it.

For this reason, Elias could only be a Democrat, and in fact, he had just completed a summer volunteering for the campaign of New York's Democratic congressman William Fitts Ryan. Ryan was a strong proponent of the sweeping civil rights legislation President Johnson had just signed in July.

To be honest, at this point in my life, the question of whether black Americans enjoyed full equality or not didn't really matter to me. The best you might say is that I was open-minded about the subject. Elias had personal reasons for the empathy he felt, however. Both his parents had spent most of World War II in a Nazi extermination camp.

He told me how they managed to survive the experience that killed six million Jews. Mr. Menkes, he said, was a talented engineer whose abilities proved too useful to waste. Mrs. Menkes, meanwhile, stayed alive by making dresses for the camp kommandant's wife.

Every time I heard that story, I was moved by it. Who wouldn't be? Nonetheless, sometimes in the evening, after his studies were done, Elias would joke about it, even aping German prison guards to get a laugh from the other guys. Another one of his gifts was his ability to see irony in nearly everything. Years later, I would wonder if this wasn't meant to alleviate some inner pain, but it never occurred to me at the time. I probably laughed louder than anybody.

In addition to the passage of the Civil Rights Bill, another portentous event had occurred that summer in 1964. Under President Kennedy, America had committed itself to aiding South Vietnam in the battle against communism. So far, that hadn't included any active role for American combat troops, but that had changed starting in August. President Johnson told the nation that an American destroyer, the USS *Maddox*, had come under fire from a group of North Vietnamese patrol boats in the Gulf of Tonkin. The *Maddox*, which was not damaged, had responded in kind, apparently damaging some of the boats. In the mind of the president, this was provocation enough for American troops to take to the battlefield. He asked Congress to pass the Tonkin Gulf Resolution, and they did so nearly unanimously.

Whether the attack, or the perception of one, by the North Vietnamese patrol boats was as serious as we were told, or whether it amounted to a trumped-up pretext for military engagement, would be at the heart of nearly all political debate for the next ten years. Like all law-abiding eighteen-year-olds, Elias and I would register with the Selective Service System. Neither of us could have known it, but we were at the threshold of an ugly war resulting in the deaths of more than fifty thousand Americans. One of those who would eventually die was Jim Ward, the gung ho American who lived with us at the Villa.

My friendship with Elias continued to grow as we took those walks together that autumn. Sometimes we would stop in at one of the heurigen down on Hameaustrasse. As young and foolish as I was, I loved being able to order wine in those places, but I never did so when Elias was present. He often said he was a teetotaler, and I respected that. When we could, we would take a table outside in the sunshine and order glasses of *apfelsaft*.

Other times, we stopped at a little grocery, and Elias bought oranges and a mocha chocolate bar to eat along the way. I bought chocolate too, when I had the money. Otherwise, Elias would share.

Money was never a problem for him. Elias was, after all, the only child of a widow who had survived the Holocaust. Even at sixteen, I could see how Elias was influenced by this. As far as Mrs. Menkes was concerned, he was to have everything he wanted, and she had the means to provide it too. According to Elias, she had a generous royalty income from a couple of inventions Mr. Menkes had made while working at John Deere and Company.

There were twenty-eight kids in my junior class. Eleven were boys. Of those, seven were day students who lived in Vienna with their parents. One of them was a skinny kid with horn-rimmed glasses who befriended me in my first-period gym class. His name was Tom Wheeler.

Tom was an outgoing, laugh-a-minute type who had already spent a year at the school. He seemed to know everybody, and since I was trying to find myself socially, I took to him immediately.

One day after school, Tom invited me to ride home with him on his school bus. He wanted me to see where he lived, and he said he would show me how to get back to the school afterward. Along the way, he started jabbering with a pretty girl on the bus, and before long they were laughing and thoroughly enjoying each other. *My gosh*, I thought. *How does he do this? All I can do is sit here stone-faced and envy him.*

The girl was still laughing when we came to her stop. She alighted from the bus and waved goodbye to Tom from the sidewalk.

I could see she was probably a year behind Tom and me in school. With her hair in a ponytail and bangs, she was a picture of innocence. Yet this did not diminish her sex appeal. She had big doe eyes and a nose that turned down just slightly at the end. She looked a lot, in fact, like two other girls I had admired, Linda Sericchio and

Mary Wray. All three were Mediterranean types with dark hair and a grace about them I found intoxicating.

"Who is that?" I asked, feigning nonchalance.

"Oh, that's Dorian Bigalli," said Tom. "She's so cute!"

"Yeah, she really is," I answered. "Do you like her?"

"Oh, yeah, she's great. But we're just friends. I get off at the next stop, so I know her pretty well. Why? Do *you* like her?"

"Oh, no!" I said, lying through my teeth.

Dorian Bigalli, I thought. *Another Italian girl. Hmmm...*

Dad, receiving his Naval commission from his father, 1943.

Nadamar 1944
Back row: Aunt Dorothy Weller, Mom, Nanny
(Dovie Dobson) and a friend.
Front row: Commander Davenport, a friend,
Lt. Commander Dobson, and a friend.

My grandfathers, Nadamar, 1944

Dad in Japan at war's end.

Dec., 1952 - Dana, Ernestine and David cross the
Pacific aboard the SS President Cleveland.

Monkey Forest, Bali, 1953

1955 - Dana and David playing with a baby elephant named Thomasina. She was brought into camp by big game hunter Wimpy Klopp.

Spring, 1959 - aboard the T.S. Hanseatic, sailing from
Southhampton, England to New York City.

November 1959, San Diego

Karlana Carpen, 1965

Graduating with Elias, 1966

Janet Grkovic, 1965

Me at the Senior Prom, 1966

Suzie and her mom, 1950

Suzie and her parents in 1948 with Suzie's step-grandfather,
Toddy Fowler.

Our wedding day, June 17, 1969

Suzie, me, Mary, Cassandra and Jesse, 1988

At the office, c.1990

Suzie, Cassandra, Jesse and Mary, London, 1994

Sophia Kane, Mary, Martin Alder, Stella Gaisford,
Jesse and Cassandra holding Charlotte Gaisford, 2006

With Suzie at Capitol Reef National Park, 2010

Chaco, New Mexico

Suzie and Cheryl, 2010

Raine Martin Siegel, Suzie and Judy Jones, 2014

2018

By now, I had grown very tired of being afraid of pretty girls, but still there wasn't much I could do about it. Even as an eleventh grader, I just didn't have the poise to relax around them. Yet pretty girls were my constant preoccupation. In fact, I'm sure my father would have been disappointed had he realized how much this distracted me from my schoolwork. He was, after all, paying for it.

Too bad I couldn't be more like Elias. He was certainly just as interested in girls as I was, but it didn't keep him from achieving. Obviously, he had a lot more self-discipline than I did. It seems, no matter what I set myself to studying, my mind would quickly wander off the page and onto whatever girl I thought I was in love with at that moment. Right now, that girl was Dorian Bigalli, and like most of my other "girlfriends," she didn't have a clue.

Elias claimed to know a prostitute in Munich who took care of his needs. Maybe he did, but teenage sex was so hard to come by in those days that boys often made up stories. Even at sixteen, not very many guys were happy about being virgins, but I think the condition was nearly universal. I believed Elias's story, but I wouldn't hold it against him if he'd simply made it up. Whether he was getting sex in Munich or not didn't really matter. Like me, he didn't have a girlfriend, and that bothered him immensely.

We always discussed these matters on our walks. From the beginning of the school year, Elias had fallen for a girl named Mary Jane Reynolds. He had no problem talking to her, even expressing his affection, in fact. Mary Jane was pretty, too, but that wasn't what set her apart. What stood her out was her brains. I don't know if she was the smartest girl at AIS, but she was certainly one of them, and that made her and Elias birds of a feather, as far as he was concerned. Alas, she wanted nothing to do with him.

When December approached, talk started about having a Villa Christmas dance. A date was set for the last night of school before the holiday break. Each of the Villa boys was encouraged to invite a girl. At first, I had no idea whom to ask. I certainly wasn't going to ask Dorian Bigalli. After three months of worshipping her, I had never once had the courage to even say hello in the hallway. But there was a smart girl named Jan that I thought of. Like Tom and Dorian, she lived in Vienna with her parents. She was terribly shy, but she was nice, and I didn't think she would turn me down. So I approached her, and sure enough, she accepted.

The night before the party, some of the Villa boys went into the city to visit the annual Christmas bazaar, what the Viennese call the *Christkindlmarkt*. They were going to look for gifts to give their dates the following evening, so I figured I'd better go along. I found a tiny necklace there, a token, really, that cost me very little. The next night, at the party, I presented it to Jan, and she happily put it on. We danced, and I held her tight. I could tell she liked me. In an act of bravery, I kissed her on the neck, and she didn't seem to mind. Later, I took her home in a taxi and kissed her again when we said good night. And then two years went by before I ever spoke to her again.

The next morning, I was driven out to Schwechat for the flight home. I was still excited about my new standing as a young jet-setter, only now I had a new hairstyle to match. This was December 1964, and the Beatles had changed everything for boys like me. No one who gave a damn about fitting in at school was ever going to get another haircut, and that included me, or so I thought.

True to form, my mother went into a tizzy when she saw how I looked. The hair I had managed to grow in three months really didn't amount to that much, but it was a shock to her system. What did I think her friends would say? she demanded to know. What about my father's image in the company? By God, I was going to go right down to the barber in Giorgimpopoli and get a haircut. And so the next morning, that was exactly what I did.

My hair was not the only cause for alarm, however. In a few days, my report card would be coming in the mail. This had been my year to take chemistry, and I was understanding almost nothing of it. Can you imagine? I was the son of a metallurgical engineering graduate from Virginia Tech, and I couldn't comprehend basic chemistry?

By now, though, Dad had seen a lot of lousy report cards, and he didn't quite flip out the way I expected he would. Instead, right after Christmas, we sat down, and he began tutoring me, though I can't say we got very far. Then, it was time to go back to Vienna, where my friend Tom Wheeler cornered me at once.

"Wow!" he said. "What did you do to Jan?"

"What do you mean?" I asked.

"She's got a crush on you, man! Big-time! She's wearing that necklace you gave her, and she hasn't taken it off."

Oh my gosh, I thought. *What have I done?*

I had no romantic interest in Jan. I gave her the necklace just to go along with the other guys, and I kissed her only because I had never kissed a girl before. I was dying to kiss just about anybody. Now, what would I do?

I wish I could have been nice to her. A nicer guy, or a guy with more poise, might have found a gentle way of letting her down, maybe even become friends with her. But not me. Instead, I started hiding. When I saw her coming down the hall at school, I would dart down the stairs or into a classroom, anywhere, just so I wouldn't have to talk to her. As time went on, this only compounded my embarrassment. Finally, at the end of the school year, Jan and her family moved back to the States, and my nightmare was over. Chances are, she had long since become disgusted with me, anyway, and I certainly wouldn't blame her.

In January, there was some kind of problem that resulted in a change at the Villa. I never did learn what it was, but the youngest boy, Michael Shaw, got expelled over it, and the rest of us went through a general reassignment of bedrooms. Now Elias would be down in a quiet basement room with three others who liked to study, and I would share a room on the main floor with Mike Nassie, the boy whose father was the Israeli legate in Prague. This was fine as far as I was concerned. Mike was a practical jokester who could drive me a little nuts at times, but he was very smart and a good friend. Besides, he and I would be the only boys who had a room for just two, and I think we both felt lucky for it.

Elias's friendship still meant a lot to me, though. Often, in the evenings, I would go down to his room. He'd play records on his phonograph, and we would talk about all sorts of things. Steve Remp, the tall Texan and natural leader of the Villa boys, was his roommate now, as was Nick Reynolds, the freshman who happened to be Mary Jane Reynolds's brother. Both of these fellows were scholars, very bright and, I'm sorry to say, a lot more mature than I was.

When March arrived, I had a choice of either going home for spring break or spending a week on the annual AIS ski trip, which this year was to the alpine village of Saalbach. The decision, of course, wasn't mine to make, but thankfully, Dad said he would pay for the skiing, so off I went with many of the other boys. I hadn't skied since I was eight, so I was put with a group of beginners, and I did fine.

A few weeks later, on a gray afternoon, Tom dragged me over to Dorian's house for a visit. I say "dragged" because as much as I was smitten with her, I still didn't have the courage to say anything. How bizarre is that? I had no reason to believe she recognized my feelings, but what if she did know? Wouldn't she think me a geek? Of course, she would! And she probably did know, although, how could she know? And yes, she probably did think me a geek. All this was pulsing through my head.

Dorian's house was an awesome place, very much like the Villa, actually, though not in as good a condition. Inside, the furniture was a little sparse. There was an old couch in the living room and an overstuffed chair likewise showing its age. The only lamp I remember is the one hanging from the ceiling. The Bigallis were an eccentric little threesome, as happy and as much in love with life as they were with one another. There was Dorian, of course. She was the youngest. Then there was Grieg, Dorian's older half-sister, who, at age twenty-something, was a spectacularly beautiful blonde. She, in fact, struck me even dumber than Dorian did. And finally, there was Muriel, their mother, a large blonde-headed woman of about sixty. She was an operatic soprano who, according to Tom, could reach notes high enough to shatter a wineglass. A widow now, Muriel had once been married to Dorian's father, Maestro Dino Bigalli, a noted Italian musician and orchestra conductor.

There, for the first time, at Dorian's house, I heard the record "Walk on By" by Dionne Warwick. Grieg had just bought it, and she was playing it over and over. Soon, I would buy it too and become a big fan. For the rest of my life, every time I heard that song, I would be transported back to the cold and cloudy afternoon in 1964 that I spent in the company of those three marvelously entertaining Bigalli women.

Nearly every aspect of my life was wonderful in Vienna. My extreme self-consciousness around girls was a notable exception. Since day 1, I had taken advantage of Austria's liberal liquor policies by going drinking with my friends on a frequent basis. There was a gasthaus at the bottom of the hill on Hameaustrasse where we went to drink beer, and the various heurigen up and down the street were only too happy to serve us their wine. I probably partook of those establishments more than any of the other Villa boys. Often, I would show up for dinner in a state of mild inebriation, and somehow I kept getting away with it. Then one evening, late in the school year, I pushed my luck too far.

Without my knowledge, Dr. Parsons made contact with Dad and told him what was going on. He said he was going to expel me and needed Dad to make arrangements to get me home. *Oh my gosh,* Dad thought, *we can't have that.* Couldn't they just let me finish the school year? There was little more than a month left.

Apparently, Dr. Parsons equivocated. Sensing an opening, Dad insisted that nothing be done until he could get to Vienna to try to straighten me out. And so it was that my father had to get on an airplane and fly from North Africa to Austria just to talk to me and try to persuade the school not to kick me out. Boy, was I ashamed.

When Dad arrived, he went straight to Dr. Parsons's office, and he got Dr. Parsons to agree to let me finish the year. One proviso applied, however. I was not to leave campus at any time for the rest of the year without specific permission to do so.

When their meeting was finished, Dad came over to the Villa and found me in my room. Despite all I had just put him through, he wasn't upset with me. In fact, he almost seemed pleased. Partly that was because it was never in his nature to be temperamental, and partly, I guess, it was because he had just saved my relationship with AIS from extinction. He told me about the restriction to campus, and of course, I accepted that with no argument. Then, he had a flight to catch back home. There was one other item brought up by Dr. Parsons, though, that he thought he should mention before leaving.

"Oh," I said. "What is that?"

"They wish you wouldn't sing so loud in the shower."

We both laughed, and I hugged him goodbye.

And so it was that, for the last six weeks of my junior year, I was confined to campus. Can you imagine? My parents had spent all that money to educate me in Vienna, and I was practically stuck in my room.

Nonetheless, I did manage to make use of my time. The senior class was in rehearsals to put on the play *Blues for Mr. Charley* by James Baldwin. Late in the process, one of the lead roles opened up when the boy's parents forbade him to participate due to bad grades. No other senior boy was willing to step into the role so late in the process, so I was asked if I would do so. For the next several days, I studied the lines and madly rehearsed with the rest of the cast, and then we put on the play for the student body.

I guess I must have done okay, because I was soon asked to reprise a soliloquy for none other than the author himself. James Baldwin, who was at the height of his fame, had somehow managed to be in Vienna, heard about us, and wanted to see what we were doing.

My first year in Austria was coming to an end. Mom and Dad had decided the family should summer together in Europe, so they brought the Mercedes by ferry across the Mediterranean to Italy. They reached Vienna in time for the last day of classes. My eyes welled up with tears as we pulled away from AIS the next morning. It was a beautiful spring day, just the sort for which the Vienna woods are famous, and I had no desire to leave. Already, I was missing Mike Nassie and Elias and the many other friends I had made. I was convinced I was in love with Dorian Bigalli, a girl I had barely ever spoken to. I figured I would never see her again, and I never did.

We drove clear across Austria that day, stopping for lunch at a roadside restaurant near Innsbruck. We took a table outside, where another group was pouring drinks from a large pitcher of something bright red and loaded with fruit. As soon as the waiter approached, my mother asked what it was, and he told us it was chilled wine with fruit juice. Mom just had to try some, and so it was that we had our first ever experience of sangria.

That afternoon, we crossed through Lichtenstein and drove into Switzerland. We found a place somewhere to spend the night and didn't reach Dana's school in Neufchatel until the next day. She must have been watching for us out a window, because she ran out to greet us before we even got out of the car. She opened the driver door and leaned in to hug Dad. She was crying.

"Oh, Daddy. I am so sorry! They say they're not going to let me graduate!"

"What?" exclaimed our normally unflappable father. "Why not?"

"I didn't do well enough on the exams," said Dana, the tears running down her cheeks.

Dad directed Mom and me to remain with Mark in the car. Then he took Dana back into the school building to see what could be done to salvage the situation. After twenty minutes or so, the two of them emerged carrying Dana's belongings. Neither was smiling.

I never once saw my father lose his temper, but years later, Dad would tell me he was "boiling" that morning. For Dana to spend an entire year at an expensive European boarding school and come away with no credits toward graduation was almost more than even he could take.

NINE

The Kiss

Jenny Kiss'd Me
by Leigh Hunt

Jenny kiss'd me when we met,
Jumping from the chair she sat in;
Time, you thief, who love to get
Sweets into your list, put that in!
Say I'm weary, say I'm sad,
Say that health and wealth have miss'd me,
Say I'm growing old, but add,
Jenny kiss'd me.

We reached Geneva that afternoon, checked in to a hotel, and had dinner at a restaurant nearby. Afterward, we took a drive along the lakeshore, and for the first time, we saw the Jet d'Eau, Geneva's famous giant water fountain.

In the morning, we were off again, driving out of the city and south toward the Riviera. We spent the night in a hotel on the wharf in Marseilles. Then we were back in the car and headed for the Pyrenees. We stopped in Andorra for lunch before driving through the mountains to a village called Molitg-les-Bains. There, in a canyon above the town, we reached our destination.

Le Grand Hotel, as it was called, was indeed grand, but it wasn't what one might expect from the high-sounding name. If anything, Le Grand was more mountain retreat than hotel. Set in a narrow ravine, it had a fabulous natural swimming pool fashioned out of the mountain stream that ran down the back side of the property.

This was a perfect spot to spend a few days, and that was exactly what Dad had in mind. It had an excellent restaurant, so there was no need to go anywhere else. For the next four days, Mom and Dad just relaxed in the mountain air, while Dana, Mark, and I played in the natural swimming pool.

After Molitg, it was only a short drive into Spain, where we would spend the bulk of our summer. Dad had pre-rented a large urban apartment for us in Madrid, a good central location from which to make day trips to such places as Toledo, El Escorial, and Segovia. My favorite spot was the great Prado art museum, right there in Madrid. They had numerous El Grecos there and a large collection by Velazquez that really impressed me.

While at the museum, I wandered away from my family at one point. I was admiring some painting or another when a Catholic priest came up behind me. He started gesturing toward the painting with one hand and saying something in Spanish that I didn't understand. Suddenly, I felt his other hand reaching for my crotch from behind. Thinking this had to be an accident, I took half a step away from him, but he reached for me again. I turned and hurried to catch up with Mom and Dad. For days, I struggled with why this had happened. Was my morality being tested? Was he going to scold me if I hadn't moved away? After all, he was a priest. It would be many years before the widespread sexual abuse of boys, endemic to the catholic clergy, would be exposed.

By now, I was deep into *The Sun Also Rises*, a book I had picked up in Geneva. I hadn't realized when I bought it that it was about a group of expatriates spending their summer in Spain. Was this kismet? Near the end of the book, Jake, the protagonist, winds up in San Sebastian, staying at a beach hotel and swimming in the bay. Amazingly, I read that passage while lying on the very same beach in front of our hotel in San Sebastian. Jake had a war wound that rendered him incapable of romancing Lady Ashley. I was infatuated with a pair of English sisters I had seen one night dining with their parents in the hotel. When I encountered them on the beach the next morning, I parked my towel close to theirs. *Who knows?* I thought. *Maybe they will say something to me.* Thanks to my shyness, I knew I wasn't going to break the ice. In a way, I was just as impotent as Jake.

After a visit to the caves at Altamira (yes, tourists were taken inside the actual caves in those days), we left San Sebastian and drove east, then north, along the Bay of Biscay and back into France. With just a few days left of our trip, we made overnight stops at Biarritz and Lourdes. Then we headed back to Marseilles. There, we drove the Mercedes onto a ferryboat and cast off for Tunisia and the drive back to Tripoli.

By now it was late summer. In Madrid, my father had bought me a guitar that I couldn't wait to start learning to play. To my delight, I discovered that Scott had also had a new guitar. Both of us were now intent upon recreating our folk group experience of the previous summer. Andy Dorman was gone, but in his place appeared a tall, very good-natured, redheaded boy named Mike Anderson. Mike was a year younger than Scott and I. He had a guitar he couldn't play yet, but he also had a good voice and wanted to sing.

Another smart, redheaded boy named Ken Kline wasn't so much into singing, but he had a banjo, and he wanted in. So we were on our way, or at least we thought we were. The fact that Ken was the only one of us who actually knew how to play his instrument, and that we were all soon to be headed back to our various schools, meant there would be no public performances for this group. Nonetheless, we were having fun.

One night, late in the summer, there was a party at the beach club. Midway through the evening, I spied a beautiful young face I had seen only once before, in the Oil School yearbook. She was a year behind me in school, and I didn't know her name, but I could see she must have been away for a while. She wasn't tanned like the other kids.

The next day, when I got together with the rest of our group, Mike Anderson told us he had a good friend who had just returned from vacation. Her name, he said, was Karlana Carpen, and he thought she would want to sing with us. How about if we invited her to join the group?

With that, all four of us, instruments in hand, took off on foot for this new girl's house. When her door opened, I was amazed to see she was the same girl I had seen at the party. Wow! How lucky was that?

Never before could I just be myself around such a pretty girl, but this time I was in the safety of friends. I could just relax and take her in.

That morning, the five of us sat in Karlana's living room. We explained to her what we were trying to do, and she thought the plan sounded great. So we played our guitars, or tried to, and she joined in with us on the singing. Indeed, she had a beautiful voice, and we were all delighted to have her in the group, even though "the group" was never going to amount to anything anyway. With summer nearly over, and our playing skills so pathetic, I wonder now how we thought there was any point to this. Nonetheless, we parted that day having agreed upon a time for our next practice, and on the way out the door, Ken suggested a name for our newly expanded group.

"How 'bout the Wench and the Stench?" he said, and we all laughed.

A lot can go wrong in the social life of a shy teenager, and I certainly was a good example. There was nothing I wanted so much as a girlfriend, yet I seemed incapable of having one. Two days later, though, my salvation finally arrived when Scott Latham presented me with some earth-shaking news.

"Davenport, you dog!" he said.

"What?"

"Karlana has a crush on you, you lucky devil!"

"What? What are you talking about?" I thought he was kidding.

"I'm telling you, she has a crush on you!" he exclaimed.

Could this be true? If so, it would be the greatest news ever. No girl like this had ever shown an interest in me.

"Are you sure?" I asked incredulously.

"Yes, I'm sure! She said so after you left this afternoon."

The implausibility swirled in my brain. When the group reassembled at Karlana's house the next evening, I was apprehensive. Even if she had expressed such a thing, how serious could she be? I didn't know whether to act interested or hold back.

After a while, the others all left, but I stayed behind. Karlana and I sat on her front porch and talked. Then, with the sky darkening, I asked if she'd like to take a stroll on the beach.

We walked until we came to a sandy knoll overlooking the sea, and then we sat. A gentle breeze was coming in off the Mediterranean.

Karlana had an almost childlike voice, befitting her age, I suppose. Yet I could see she was uncommonly smart. I wondered, in fact, if she might find me disappointingly stupid. I didn't know what she expected, but I was getting nervous.

She lay back on the sand and started gazing at the stars. I responded by lowering myself onto one elbow, becoming dangerously close to what I thought was the loveliest face on the planet.

She was only inches away now, her soft voice mingling with the sound of the waves coming ashore. I saw no sign that I was making her uncomfortable. Did she expect me to kiss her? Should I even try? What if she leapt to her feet and indignantly headed back to her house? Then again, what if I made no effort at all? Would she think me a bumbling fool? Maybe not kissing her was just as risky as doing so.

And then, all of a sudden, I just did it. I leaned over the last few inches and kissed her full on the mouth.

Oh, how the gates of heaven flew open! She *liked* it, and of course, so did I. I kissed her again. And again! And again and again. All the unfulfilled passion of my teenage life came pouring out now as I kept kissing her until she finally reminded me that she had to get home. She did have parents, after all.

Jubilantly, I walked her back up to her house. I kissed her one last time and then took off through the dark toward home. Half-skipping as I went, I must have had tears of happiness streaming down my face.

By now, it was late in the month of August. In a little more than a week, I would be headed back to Austria. Karlana would be in Rome at the Marymount School for girls. In the interim, I would spend every moment I could with her, and of course, I would kiss her every chance I got. I did this so much it must have worn thin with her, though she never said so. Every evening after dinner, I went over to her house. We went for walks, and I always found a private place where we could kiss. One day, we took a drive down the coast with the rest of our group to go swimming. I kissed her under the water. I kissed her on the beach. I had no care for what the others might think. I was behaving like a boy starved for affection, and I suppose that was what I was.

TEN

Vienna II

It was the first week of September 1965 when I got back to school. My copy of *Time* magazine was waiting for me on top of my dresser. On the cover was a picture from a race riot that had just taken place in Los Angeles. Buildings were on fire, a burned-out car was overturned, and people were shown running through the streets, carrying looted merchandise. An appalling thirty people had lost their lives. Ironic, I thought. Just recently there had been civil unrest in the streets of Tripoli, and Dad had remarked that rioting was one thing that set America apart from third world countries. We just didn't behave that way. Well, apparently, we did now.

Things were changing at school too. I still occupied the same room at the Villa, and Mike Nassie was still my roommate, but many of the other boys had been replaced by a new group. Gone was the intellectual Mallorcan Alex Mehdevi. Gone, too, was Steve Remp, the natural leader of the Villa boys. Both had graduated. Gone was Jim Ward, the gung ho son of a Marine. In their place was a new group that included a pair of young twins named Jimmy and Tommy Boster. Their father was an American diplomat serving in Moscow. Jim was so smart that he was a year ahead of Tom in school. Tom would be sharing the room next to mine with a boy named Rob Steinhardt. Rob, the son of a University of Kansas music professor, was very talented on the violin and the guitar. Someday, he would be a founding member of the famous rock group Kansas.

Our Villa counselors, the Andersons, had departed. So had Mike's brother Ron. Our new dorm counselor was a tall dark-haired Canadian chemistry teacher who used words sparingly but could say a lot with the expression on his face. His name was Mr. Rattray.

It seemed the first order of business was to schedule some sort of a get-acquainted party for all the boarding students. Someone asked Mr. Rattray for permission, and he obliged. There was a roof garden on the second story of the Villa, and it was agreed that it would be the perfect spot, though I don't think any of us had ever set foot out there before.

We held the party the first Friday night, and we invited the girls from the Heim to join us. The Heim was what they called the house the girls lived in off campus in nearby Sievering.

I remember being so excited when their bus arrived. Of course, I was already madly in love with the girl on the beach, Karlana. Nonetheless, I hadn't lost my interest in other girls. Moreover, my timidity around them seemed suddenly diminished. No longer was I the new boy at school. Now I was the old hand, the upperclassman. It was the girls who were new.

My interest was immediately drawn to the prettiest girl in the group. She was a Norma Jean Baker look-alike with frizzy light-brown hair that was piled on her head and tied up in a ribbon. When the music started, I went right over and asked her to dance.

Her name was Susie Voigt, and what a doll she was! Only, it turned out she was just a freshman. How was that supposed to work, I wondered, with my being a senior? I was three years older than she was. Even so, I kept going back to her to dance, and I enjoyed every minute of it. At the end of the evening, I walked her down to the bus, and amazingly, I kissed her good night.

The following Monday, classes began. My first period was homeroom. The teacher announced that we were supposed to elect our senior class officers, even though half the class members were brand-new and no one had been given any prior notice. Nominations were sought from the floor, and somebody nominated me, of all people, for class president. Two others and I were asked to step into the hallway during the vote, and when it was over, I had been elected.

What? Are you kidding? So far, my grades at AIS were among the worst in my class. What was more, I had just spent the last six weeks of the prior year campused for being frequently intoxicated. By the way, what was a class president supposed to do, anyway? I had no idea.

The following Saturday, a small group of Heim girls came over to hang out at the school. In the afternoon, a couple of other boys and I offered to walk them home. We knew a path through the vineyards, a section of forest and an old cemetery that would get us there.

It was a beautiful September afternoon, and the girls were picking wildflowers as we walked along. One girl in particular caught my eye. To be sure, she was pretty, but there seemed to be a vulnerability about her that I found especially appealing.

Her name was Janet. That night I called her on the phone. We talked for a while, and I got to know her a little. Her last name was Grkovic, which she said was Serbian. Her father, a Navy captain, was the American naval attaché in Moscow, a distinction that would have impressed me a lot had I been mature enough to appreciate what it meant. Janet was a senior now. She had done her first three years of high school in her hometown, the upscale Washington, DC, suburb of McLean, Virginia.

In the days that followed, I received my first letter from Karlana. I remember sitting on the floor in the gym after basketball tryouts and reading each word as though it was precious. So beautiful was her handwriting, and so poetic her language, that I carried the letter around in my pocket for days.

I was never much of an athlete, but I did make the basketball team. No wonder. At six foot three, I was the tallest boy in the school, and there were only twelve boys in the senior class, anyway.

Meanwhile, Janet was doing pretty well herself. She tried out for cheerleader, and not only did she make the squad, but she was also chosen captain. I'm sure that was partly because of how pretty she was, something I was really beginning to appreciate.

In the weeks that followed, I called Janet every night. If there was a party at the school, I would be her date, and soon we began to see ourselves as a couple. From the start, I realized she knew a lot more about clothes than I did. Having spent most of my life outside the United States, and having been the awkward new kid at so many schools, I had little sense of what was stylish and what was not. My clothes were mostly things chosen by my mother out of the Sears catalog. Janet, on the other hand, had all the right stuff, and she always looked smart. Her dresses, as she enjoyed explaining, were Villager, a label that was unknown to me. She had bought them while shopping with her mother at tony northern Virginia department stores like Lord & Taylor. Her shoes were Bass Weejuns, another label that meant nothing to me. I was captivated by it all.

Sometimes, on a Saturday morning, I would gather my laundry and catch the public bus over to Sievering. Near the Heim, there was a Wäscherei, a Laundromat where Janet and I washed our clothes together. If the weather was nice, we would walk around the neighborhood while we waited. Otherwise, we would just sit inside and talk.

She had been born, she said, in Hawaii in 1948. Her birthday was the same as my father's, September 9. Her dad was an Annapolis graduate, a fact that also should have impressed me. When she was born, he was stationed at Pearl Harbor.

When Thanksgiving arrived, Janet took off for Moscow. Mike Nassie asked me if I would like to spend the holiday with him and his family in Prague, and immediately I accepted. There was a number of other students headed that way, and we all caught the same train after classes on Wednesday. I sat next to Susie Voigt the whole way. She was the Norma Jean Baker look-alike I had met at the dance almost three months earlier. We still had an interest in each other, but I would never get past the age difference.

It was dark when we reached the border crossing into Czechoslovakia. Even so, I was able to make out the guard towers on either side of our train and the armed soldiers on the platform. For the first time in my life, I was going behind the iron curtain, and I was mindful of the implications.

Mike's dad picked us up at the station in Prague and drove us to their home. It was a fine, old multistory European house not dissimilar from the Villa. The next morning, Mike and I took off walking into the center of town. Mike showed me Prague Castle. Then we crossed over the famous Charles Bridge, with all its statues, and we walked up to Wenceslas Square. Finally, he took me to the Old Town Square to see the Orloj, a medieval astronomical clock that is a mechanical wonder, if ever there was one.

Despite all these marvels that today attract millions of tourists, I found the city of Prague to be dreary. Partly, perhaps, because it was a cloudy late November day and all the trees were bare. But then, too, there were no other tourists about, unlike nowadays, and shop windows everywhere were utterly bereft of displays. Under Communism, shop windows were only there to be looked out of, not into. I returned to Vienna thinking maybe I didn't get to go to Moscow with Janet, but I still got to witness communism, and I knew I didn't like it.

By the time I got back to Tripoli in December, I felt like I had two and a half girlfriends, and I was feeling pretty sure of myself. As much as I liked Susie Voigt, I had completely fallen for Janet, and now I was excited about seeing Karlana again. She and I had been together only a week during the summer. I didn't really know what to expect, but I was pretty confident I could woo her all over again, if I had to. After dinner on Christmas night, I went over to her house. I was carefully decked out in a new Sears catalog outfit Santa had brought me.

"You look studied," Karlana said almost immediately.

"What do you mean *studied*?" I asked.

"You look like you spent a long time studying your appearance in the mirror."

In an instant, she had pricked my bubble. How could such a young girl deflate my bravado so effortlessly? It was as though she existed on a higher plane than I did. Clearly, Karlana was more perceptive than I was and a lot quicker than other girls I knew. She was more articulate, too, and more direct. If only I had the poise not to care.

Nonetheless, we headed out the door for our usual walk. I still wanted desperately to kiss her, and minutes later, that was exactly what I did.

"Are you trying to debauch me?" she queried.

I hated doing so, but I had to ask, "What do you mean *debauch*?"

"Are you trying to lead me astray?"

This was Karlana, way too pretty to be my girlfriend and way too smart. There was something elusive, maybe even fickle, about this girl. She had written me such beautiful letters throughout the autumn, yet now I wondered if she really even cared about me anymore.

ELEVEN

Yesterday

Now it was January 1966, the year I was going to graduate from high school and go off to college. My grades in the fall had been a little higher than before. I had long been concerned about whether any college might accept me, but now I was really feeling the pressure. Instead of my usual Cs and Ds, I got a report card with Bs and Cs. Still, I was afraid my efforts were too little and too late.

Some of my classmates had already been granted early acceptance at some very good schools. Elias was a prime example. He was going to Columbia University, an Ivy League school. So figuring I'd better get cracking, I now turned my attention to finding someplace that might accept me. After several days poring over what was called *The College Catalogue,* I came up with a plan and sent away for applications. I had chosen three schools: Virginia Tech, where my father went, the University of Connecticut, which was in our former state of residence, and Pennsylvania's Clarion State College. I picked Clarion just to be sure. The catalog said, "Clarion tries to accept everyone."

I knew I didn't really qualify for the first two schools, but I was hoping at least one of them might see I had lived all over the world. Somehow they might think me an interesting addition to their student body. Besides, incongruously, my SAT scores were higher than most.

They didn't fall for it. Both Virginia Tech and Connecticut turned me down. Clarion, though, accepted me. Thank goodness.

Even though I wasn't excited about going there, at least I was going somewhere.

Janet's grades were a lot better than mine. Nonetheless, she chose to go to Sullins, a junior college for women, coincidentally just 120 miles or so from Virginia Tech. How propitious that would have been had I been accepted there, and how different our futures might have been. Sullins was 430 miles from Clarion, a distance, I'm afraid, that was just too great for maintaining a romance. Janet would be seeing a lot more of other young men than she ever would of me. Nevertheless, I managed to convince myself that she and I would one day marry. I would simply have to find ways to see her as often as I could.

Every year for spring break, AIS sent students off on a week-long ski trip in mid-March. This year the boys were going to the Schmittenhöhe, a ski mountain at Zell-am-See, which is not far from Salzburg. I got permission from my folks and signed up. When we arrived, Tom Wheeler, a boy named Dwight Magnusen, and another boy named Guido Gale were assigned to a room in the chalet with two sets of bunk beds.

Unfortunately, with Janet nowhere in sight, I fell right back into my adolescent ways. One night, I somehow managed to get ahold of a liter of Slivovitz, a Czechoslovakian plum brandy, and sneak it into our room. When nobody else would even taste it, I said, "All right, I'll just drink it myself." With that, I chugged the whole thing down, like some moron trying to kill himself. My three friends were astonished, but I just laughed the whole thing off. Laughed it off, that is, until about five minutes later, when I suddenly vomited a gusher of dinner-laden booze all over the room. Now it wasn't so funny to anybody, least of all me. I spent the next hour and all of the next morning cleaning up while my friends went skiing.

Apparently, having a girlfriend around was the only way I was able to behave. With my college future established, and with the clock running out on our time together, I now focused all my attention on Janet. Thanks to my father, I had enough allowance, barely, to take her out on dates. Once, we went with a group of friends picnicking in the Wienerwald on a Saturday. She and I were lying on a blanket near the bottom of a twenty-five-foot cliff when our friend Dwight Magnusen and a girl lost their footing and spilled over the edge of the cliff. The girl was unhurt, because she had landed on top of Dwight, but he landed on rocks and badly broke his leg. The bone was poking through the skin.

Looking over Janet's shoulder, I had watched the entire incident and was horrified. So was everyone else in the group. I quickly took off running toward a nearby village to get some help.

Of course, my other dates with Janet were far less dramatic, but all were wonderful experiences, at least as far as I was concerned. In those days, every taxi in Vienna was a black Mercedes, and taxis were often how we got around. Once on a Sunday, I picked her up early in the morning and took her to breakfast on the Ringstraße at the Intercontinental Hotel. While we were enjoying our meal, Dan Blocker, one of the stars of the very popular American TV show *Bonanza*, walked through the dining room.

For our senior prom, our class chartered a riverboat for a dinner cruise down the Danube with live music and dancing. I wore a white dinner jacket that belonged to my father, and I picked up Janet at the Heim in the usual black Mercedes taxi. When she came down the stairs, she was wearing a powder-blue satin gown with a matching ribbon in her hair. She was easily the prettiest girl at school, and this night she was dressed to prove it.

So much of my attention was focused on Janet that I barely noticed we were on a river cruise. We danced every song together, and when the band took a break, I asked if I could use one of the band's guitars. I performed "Summertime" from *Porgy and Bess*, which was an odd choice, I guess, but it was a song I knew.

There was no curfew at the Villa, but that wasn't true for the girls. I got Janet back to the Heim by midnight. I shared the cab with Tom Wheeler, and we dropped his date off too. Then Tom and I went to his place so he could change into more comfortable clothing. We both wanted to stay out and continue the fun.

There had been a light rain, little more than a mist, really, falling all night, but we had umbrellas. We walked the couple of miles back to the school, clowning around as we went from streetlamp to streetlamp. I changed my clothes, and then we made our way down the hill into Salmannsdorf to await the morning's first bus into the city.

We had no specific destination in mind; we just felt the need somehow to keep the party going. By the time we reached the city, we were both hungry, so we headed over to the Intercontinental to get an early breakfast. After that, we went exploring through the hotel. We came to a lobby on one of the upper floors, and there we sat down to figure out what we were going to do next. In no time at all, both of us were stretched out sleeping. Sometime later, we were jarred awake by a man in a suit. He told us we had to leave, and so we did.

Our time in Vienna was running out. As always, I looked forward to the end of the school year, but this time I was living a dream that I didn't want to end. I was an eighteen-year-old who had spent the better part of high school out from under parental supervision. My emotional commitment was greater to Janet than to anyone else. She had become my de facto family. True, I was immature. None of my life in this fabulous city was paid for by me. None of my dates with Janet were paid for by me. Everything was the product of a monthly allowance provided by my father. But in Vienna I had acquired a sense of happiness and well-being greater than at any other time in my life.

Dad didn't make it to my graduation, but Mom did. She took a room at the Schild, a nice little hotel on Hameaustraße, where she stayed three nights. Janet's mother was in town too. The four of us took a lunch together at the Golden Dragon, a local Chinese restaurant. To my great satisfaction, the two mothers took to each other right off. Both had lived much of their lives in Navy families and both had been all over the world, even lived in Shanghai at about the same time. They had a lot to talk about.

At the ceremony, the graduating seniors were marched in to the recorded sound of "Pomp and Circumstance." There were no caps and gowns, so the boys wore jackets and ties. Elias and I walked in side by side. Of the thirty-nine kids in our class, Elias graduated second. I graduated twenty-sixth, barely out of the bottom third.

Afterward, I accompanied Janet on the tram back to the Heim. When we reached her stoop, I held her close and I kissed her good-bye. I didn't know how I was ever going to see her again, but I promised I would. Then, I turned and descended the steps down to the sidewalk. It was a beautiful June afternoon. On my way back to the tram, I passed in front of a handsome three-story villa. There was piano music coming from an upstairs window. Someone was playing "Yesterday."

TWELVE

Alone Again, Naturally

Throughout my senior year, Dana had been living with Nanny in Miami. Mom and Dad had sent her there to repeat the twelfth grade at a public high school, but it didn't work out. Being free to make her own decisions had become more important to Dana than finishing her education. In short order, she fell for a guy named Robert Camp, and the two of them eloped right under Nanny's nose. For a time, none of the rest of us knew where they were.

For me, though, back in Libya, things were pretty quiet. By now, Karlana and her family had been relocated back to the States. So had Scott Latham and his family. Mike Anderson was still around. He and I hung out together, mostly in the evenings. Mike was now learning to play guitar, but the rest of the group was gone, so we gave up trying to be a combo.

I remember reading *Catch-22* that summer and laughing out loud at nearly every page. The rest of my time I spent writing letters to Janet, who was still in Moscow, and reading the letters that came in from her almost daily. I don't know what we had to say that was so important, but it meant a lot to me that we were staying in touch.

Then, September arrived, and I was on my way again. My parents flew me to Pittsburgh, Pennsylvania, via Rome and New York. While waiting for my connection in Rome, I was astonished to see Elizabeth Taylor and Richard Burton very close up. They were undoubtedly the biggest Hollywood superstars of the 1960s, yet they passed by me so closely I could have whispered to them. Burton had a full beard. I found out later they were in Italy filming *The Taming of the Shrew.*

At Kennedy Airport in New York, I took a helicopter over to LaGuardia for the flight to Pittsburgh. That was something new to me. When I finally boarded my next plane, it was already dark outside. Sometime during the flight, I asked the stewardess if I could have a beer. "Not while we are in Pennsylvania airspace," she said. "You have to be twenty-one." That was new to me too.

Dad had told me to catch a cab at the Pittsburgh Airport and have the driver take me to the downtown Hilton, which was what I did. We drove through the dark for a while until we entered a long, brightly lit tunnel. When we emerged, we were thrust into a phantasmagoria of lights and bridges and skyscrapers. My cabbie explained that this was where the Allegheny and the Monongahela Rivers meet to form the mighty Ohio. Near the point of confluence, what they call the Golden Triangle, was my hotel.

It was late when I checked in. The handsome young man at the front desk appeared to be my age. He was curious how a contemporary of his was staying alone at such a nice hotel. I explained that I was headed for college, Clarion State College to be exact, and he lit up a smile.

"That's where I'm going!" he said. "Only I have to wait until spring. That's why I'm working here, to save up some money."

I told him I would keep an eye out for him. As I rode up in the elevator, I thought about how much better I was than that fellow, not better off, just better! He might be better-looking than I was, but I never had to get a job. I was a young globe-trotter from a family that could afford to send their kid to college, while he obviously wasn't. Someday, I am happy to say, this attitude of mine would be completely reversed.

The next morning, I got directions to the bus depot and started a ten-block trek up Penn Avenue, carrying my suitcase and guitar. I bought my ticket, but having a couple of hours to kill, I took off walking again, this time down Liberty Avenue. By happenstance, I came to a music store, and I went in. I found the music to the Beatles' latest album, *Revolver*, there, and I bought it. Now all I wanted to do was try playing it, so I walked back to the bus depot, found a seat, and got out my guitar.

It was a beautiful, sunny afternoon when I arrived in Clarion. On the way into town, my bus took me past the college. The first thing I saw was an incongruous, bright red-and-white water tower sticking straight up into the sky from the campus's highest point. It looked just like a hot-air balloon ready for liftoff. Otherwise, the campus appeared to be pretty much what I expected, a cluster of buildings, mostly quite old, plenty of ivy, and an expanse of trees and lawn.

One block later, the bus turned left and proceeded down what was clearly the main street in town. It wasn't seedy, by any means, but clearly, Clarion was no gleaming gem. All the storefronts were from a bygone era. I noticed a diner, a five-and-dime, a drab-looking furniture store, an old hotel, and a couple of diminutive movie theaters. One was playing *Who's Afraid of Virginia Wolf*, the other *Fantastic Voyage*. After only three blocks, we were at the end of the downtown area, and the bus pulled over to the curb next door to the county courthouse. My ride was over.

It was afternoon now, and I was hungry. Right in front of me was something called the Dairy Store. Despite its name, it was really a very small lunch counter, so I went in. I ordered a BLT and a chocolate shake, two American classics I hadn't eaten, or even seen on a menu, in my three years out of the country. When they arrived, I was delighted. In a way, I thought, I was finally home, and I was liking it. Afterward, I grabbed my things and I started walking back toward the college.

The first person I came to when I reached the campus was a middle-aged man in a jacket and tie whom I presumed to be a professor. I asked him if he could direct me to Shafer Hall, my assigned dormitory. Looking down at my baggage, he said, "Sure, but it's a pretty good trek from here. You'd better let me give you a ride."

So he led me over to a parking lot, helped me put my suitcase and guitar into the trunk of his car, and off we went. It turned out that Shafer Hall was a brand-new building not even entirely finished yet, and it was a mile away from the rest of the campus. I was greeted at the entrance by two people at a table who were giving room assignments and passing out keys. My room was on the third floor, and they told me how to find it.

Shafer Hall was a pair of halls, really, two big cubes, each with a lifeless interior courtyard. One side was for women, the other side for men. The two buildings were connected only on the ground floor by a space that had been intended as a cafeteria but would never be completed. The whole complex probably had enough rooms for six hundred students, and though it was brand-new, it afforded no residential feel at all. It was as if one wasn't there to be housed so much as warehoused.

I found my room. Having arrived before my roommate, I quickly claimed the bed by the window and started unpacking. I could already hear the sounds of commotion coming from the hallway, a foreshadowing of how things were going to be for a while. Unlike me, pretty much every young man out there was experiencing his first day free of his parents, and the mood was celebratory.

Soon my roommate arrived. He was a skinny, bespectacled, callow sort of a fellow who was nonetheless unpretentious and pleasant. He asked me where I was from, and he appeared quite surprised when I struggled to answer. He had lived his whole life, he said, in the same house in a northern suburb of Pittsburgh. His name was Jim Huber, and I decided I liked him immediately, despite the difference in our backgrounds.

That evening, Jim and I walked up to the campus together to get dinner at the college dining hall. For the first time, I was seeing some of the girls who would be part of the scenery for a while, and despite missing Janet, I was very excited by what I saw. The prettiest of these girls were a lot flashier than the adolescent high-schoolers I was used to. Mostly, they were decked out in miniskirts and wore giant dangling earrings. Some of them sported asymmetrical hairdos, cut short on one side, longer on the other. I was, of course, spellbound.

The boys of Clarion, on the other hand, weren't impressing me nearly so much. Almost all of them were still wearing the short hair my high school friends had abandoned when the Beatles came in. Among the returning students, fraternity jackets seemed to be a must, and a lot of the new freshmen already wanted them. Soon, they would be going to pledge parties, seeking the sort of inclusion I knew I didn't want.

Back at the dorm that night, and every night for the first few weeks, boys were hollering at one another and running up and down the hallways, slamming doors. I was dealing with jet lag, so I appreciated none of it. I remember lying in bed wondering if this was because I didn't get into a better school. Was Elias experiencing the same thing at Columbia? I didn't think so.

The next morning, the entire freshman class attended an orientation session in the gymnasium. During his presentation, the college president, Dr. Gimmel, made a point of spotlighting the "great" variety of student backgrounds. He asked all those who were from Clarion County to stand up. Then he called upon those from Allegheny County, Beaver County, and so on, all the Pennsylvania counties in turn, to stand up. He asked if anyone was from out of state. Two stood up. One was from New Jersey, the other from Ohio.

Clear in the back of the hall, I could see what was coming, and it was making me uncomfortable. "How about anyone from a foreign country?" President Gimmel called out.

I didn't flinch.

He waited.

"I know we have someone," he said. "Where are you?"

Now, Jim Huber was elbowing me in my side. "That's you! Get up!"

The kids around us started looking our way to see what was going on. To avoid attracting even more attention, I was forced to rise.

"Where are you from?" asked the president into the microphone.

Practically shouting so I could be heard up in the front, I responded, "Austria!" Then I retook my seat.

"Oh," he said, his tone revealing just a hint of disbelief. Then he paused. "I was under the impression we had a student from South Africa. Is he not here?"

Now I was full-on embarrassed. "That might be me, too!" I said, rising again. "I attended boarding school in Austria, but my family lives in Libya, which is actually in North Africa."

Well, there it was. If Clarion thought they had two foreign students that year, I was both of them. I had wanted anonymity as a way of fitting in, and here I had been exposed practically from the outset. I guess the shyness I thought I had overcome at AIS was still very much with me, for I was embarrassed. I should have had better sense. A lot of people would have welcomed attention of this sort. They might have found it to their advantage. But not me. Years later, people would sometimes still recognize me as the foreign student. "Oh, yeah, I know you," they might say. "You're the guy from Australia." Or "Aren't you the guy from South Africa?" More often than not, they would get the country wrong, and I would just say yes.

By the end of the first month, my parents came to town. They were due for a stateside leave, anyway, and I guess they wanted to get a sense of where I was and what I was doing. Besides, back in June they had promised me a motorbike as a high school graduation gift. It was time to make good.

The nearest Honda dealer to Clarion was twenty-five miles away near Oil City. Dad got them on the phone and arranged the purchase and delivery of a 90cc Sport model. It was trailered down that evening and brought straight to my dormitory.

Whoa, was I excited! Sure, it was pretty small, particularly for my six foot four frame. The Gileras I had craved in Tripoli had been 125ccs. But like every one of those Gileras, my brand-new Honda was bright red, and of course, it was still a *motorcycle*! As I recall, it set Dad back less than $300, but to me it was priceless.

After my parents left, I was free to ride my new bike all I wanted. Thereafter, and throughout the autumn, I kept going to my classes, all right, but my attention to my studies was abysmal. Virtually all my free time was spent on that little motorcycle.

Even as many of my contemporaries were hooting it up and enjoying their newfound freedom, some, I'm sure, were already planning a future in teaching or lawyering or who-knows-what. Clearly, I wasn't in that group. Despite my virginity, or perhaps because of it, I only dreamed of being loved. Always on my mind were Janet Grkovic and Karlana Carpen and how I might ever see either one of them again.

Nonetheless, I was now surrounded by a whole new panoply of females, and believe me, some of them were very tempting. Hanging out at the student union, I had already decided which ones I liked best. Many were sorority girls. There was Trish Sexton, a Sigma Sigma Sigma. She was a statuesque blonde with an angelic face that was simply luminous. There was Sandy McKenna, the slender but athletic drum majorette. She marched out in front of the band at all the football games. She was a Delta Zeta, which, for my money, was the best-looking sorority on campus. Two other Delta Zetas were Cassie Kelly and Kathy Farrell. Either one of them could have been a movie star. Cassie was a blonde, Kathy a brunette.

Then there were two standouts who didn't belong to any sorority, and they might have been the most popular girls of the lot. More often than not, I would see them together, and they were always having a good time. I took them to be roommates, and in fact they were. The more animated one was a fast-talking explosion of personality, a beautiful, blond Barbara Streisand look-alike. Her name was Raine Martin. Her friend was a striking Italian American girl whose appearance reminded me of Suzanne Pleshette, the actress I had admired so as an adolescent. This girl was a classic Mediterranean beauty with dark curly hair, an olive complexion, and a figure to turn a man's head. Her name was Suzie Albanesi.

These young women, and a few others, were the ones who really impressed me among the 1,500 co-eds at Clarion. Not one of them had the faintest idea who I was, of course. Each was a dream girl, and for that reason, each was well-known to every other heterosexual male on campus. For a daydreaming introvert like me, all were completely out of reach. Or so I thought.

And so yes, I lusted after what I was seeing all around me at Clarion, but my romantic intentions remained focused on the two girlfriends who were far away, the ones I'd had in high school. Using a pay phone in my dormitory, I was calling Janet every week. She was still, after all, the girl I thought I was going to marry. I knew she had grandparents living near Washington, DC, and it was there she would be spending Thanksgiving. Having no place else I would rather be, I arranged to meet her there.

As it happened, Tom Wheeler's parents also lived near DC, in Silver Spring, Maryland. He had already dropped out of Babson College up in Boston, and he was living with them. On Thanksgiving Day, I caught the bus to Pittsburgh, and I flew out standby that night. By the time I reached National Airport (now Reagan National Airport), it was after midnight, too late to call Tom to pick me up. But I had seen the skyline of our nation's capital out the airplane window, and now, standing in the terminal, I could see the Washington Monument and the Capitol dome. Both were brilliantly illuminated, and I couldn't wait to get closer.

As usual, I had very little money, so I set off on foot, carrying my bag. I walked out of the terminal and then northward toward the Fourteenth Street Bridge. There, I crossed the Potomac, and then I walked the few remaining blocks to the Mall. By the time I got there, it was so late that I felt as though I had the whole city to myself. I turned and started heading toward the Capitol. On my right, as I walked, I spied a cluster of rockets coming into view. All were standing straight up as though to threaten some distant foe. Was I dreaming? Then, as I drew closer, I could see the sign indicating I had reached the Smithsonian. Slowly turning 360 degrees, I marveled at the entire panorama. What an amazing sight, all of it fully lit up and laid out in front of just me. It was as though I had somehow been left behind after closing at Disneyland and I had the whole park to myself.

By now, though, I figured my day had been long enough. Exhausted, I found a bush near the entrance to one of the museum buildings, and I crawled under it, curled up on the ground, and went to sleep.

It was well after sunup when I was awakened by the sound of people arriving for work. Having no other apparent choice, I relieved myself on the very spot where I had just lain for several hours. Then I crawled out into the sunshine and went off to find a pay phone.

Tom came to pick me up with Jim Ward in a baby-blue VW. Jim was one of the Villa boys, the gung ho American son of a Marine. He was about to become a Marine himself and had already signed to go to Vietnam. His parents were out of town, and he was in the mood to party, but first he had to get back to the gas station where he worked. Tom had gotten a job at a bank, and he was due back too, so I agreed to hang out at the gas station for a few hours until both of them got off.

For a while I just stood around. Then I went out and took a seat on the curb in front of the station. Soon, Mike Valunas showed up. He was another kid from Vienna. He and Jim had been best friends for a long time, and in fact they had signed up to go to Vietnam together. He sat down beside me, and before long, he brought up the subject of Janet. He told me he had always had a terrible crush on her and had been jealous of me because of it. I wasn't very worried. Mike wasn't the best-looking kid. He had a crooked nose and lantern jaw that made him look like a boxer who had lost too many fights. Besides, he was very timid, and he was easily the nerdiest boy in our class. Nonetheless, I admired him for his willingness to expose his feelings in this way, particularly since he and I had never been much more than acquaintances. I didn't know it, of course, but he had little more than a year left to live. Mike and Jim both were going to die in Vietnam.

The four of us spent that evening downstairs in the family room at Jim's parents' house. We drank some of his father's beer and turned the stereo up loud. After a while, we went joyriding in Tom's Volkswagen. We laughed about some of the great times we had in Vienna. Then, Tom dropped the other two off and took me back to his parents' house, where I would sleep on a sofa.

The next day was Saturday, November 26, 1966. That afternoon, Tom took me over to see Janet. She answered the door looking beautiful, of course. She was wearing her hair shorter now but otherwise looked about the same. We hugged, and I kissed her, and then she led me into the house, past the den, where Mr. and Mrs. Varn were watching the Army-Navy football game. Like Janet's father, Mr. Varn was a career Naval officer, and like my Bumpa, he had been stationed in Shanghai in the 1930s. Mr. Varn hardly looked up when Janet announced who had come to the door. Navy was losing.

I was ecstatic to be in Janet's presence again after so many months. To be fair, she seemed happy to see me too, although she was never the type to gush her affections. If anything, she seemed more excited about being back in the company of her brother, who was also in town. I wasn't going to be discouraged, though. Somehow, her feelings about me didn't seem to matter as much as how I felt about her.

We spent a couple of hours talking, but then, as evening began to fall, Tom showed up, and it was time for me to go. That was it. That was all I got to see of her. The next day, I was on the plane back to Pennsylvania. All I could think about was Christmas break and getting back to see more of Janet Grkovic. I knew the next visit would be a little more complicated. My parents had already arranged for me to spend the holidays with Gamma at Nadamar. There was no way I could be in two places at once.

When the time came, I decided to take the train down from Pittsburgh to DC. It would cost me less, and since the Pittsburgh bus depot was at the train station, it would save me having to hire a cab to the airport. Unfortunately, I didn't have a clue what I was doing. I should have paid more attention to the math. The distance from Pittsburgh to Washington is only 250 miles, yet the train took all night. I thought I would just pass the time sleeping. As it turned out, I might have been the only passenger on the entire train. Certainly, I was the only one in my car. And no wonder. This was a good, old-fashioned milk run. We must have stopped two dozen times, and one of the stops was a two-hour delay to unload freight. Sleeping was utterly out of the question.

We reached Union Station the next day, some thirteen hours after departure. I called Tom, and he arranged to have Jim Ward's sister, Maryann, pick me up. By now, Jim was in boot camp, and I guess Tom was at work. But the next day, Tom took me over to Janet's grandparents' house, and I spent the whole day with her. I would have held her in my arms the entire time had she let me, but I could tell something wasn't right. Rather than talking about us, she wanted to effuse about her family, and particularly her brother. He was so handsome. He was so well-proportioned physically and so smart. It got so bad my face started to twitch. I was getting the message. There was nothing particularly special about me.

Late in the day, I called Tom, and while I waited for him to pick me up, Janet lowered the boom. It was time for us to break it off, she said.

Many years of reflection would transpire before I would understand how sensible Janet was being. Yes, we had been very close in Vienna. In the absence of our parents, we had been like family to each other, but even now, we were only eighteen. And we were separated into two different worlds, different colleges in different states, hundreds of miles apart. Were we really supposed to remain frozen in time for four years, denying ourselves the experience of dating other people or even growing into our separate social settings? It didn't make sense to Janet, and it shouldn't have made sense to me either.

Nonetheless, I was hurt. I had lived in outer orbit from my parents for two years now. Yes, they were still supporting me financially, but I no longer depended on them emotionally. For that, I had turned to Janet, and now she was pushing me away. I kept asking myself why. What kind of love is it that can be so easily discarded? If she tired of her mother or her brother or her grandparents, would she just break off those relationships too?

The next day, I had to leave for Nadamar, but before I did, I called Janet and told her I wanted my high school ring back. I had given it to her in Vienna, and I didn't want her to keep it anymore. When I got to her house, she brought it to the door, and I tersely said goodbye.

As Tom drove me away, I rolled down the car window and threw the ring out.

I spent the rest of that Christmas break at Nadamar with Gamma and my cousins. Gamma took me into Norfolk to see *The Sound of Music*, a big hit of a movie that had been filmed in Austria while I was living there. She also took me down to test for a Virginia driver's license, which would make me street-legal for the first time. Christmas Day, we did a progression party to the various households of my cousins' extended family. By the time I got back to Clarion, I was satisfied that I had managed to have a good time despite Janet. Besides, there was always Karlana.

In January, grades came out. My starting grade point average was a 1.82. This meant I had almost as many Ds as I did Cs and no As or Bs at all. Scholastically, I hadn't changed a bit, except that now, instead of daydreaming in class, I frequently wasn't even there.

I wasn't hearing from Janet anymore, but Elias was still calling me from New York. As it turned out, Columbia's spring break didn't align with Clarion's, and he thought it would be great if I could come stay in the dorm with him for a few days. He would still have some classes to attend, but otherwise we could hang out together in Manhattan. I agreed, and when I told Karlana what I was doing, she asked me to come see her too. She was still a high school senior, but her family lived in Princeton, barely fifty miles from the city.

It was great seeing Elias again. Despite my constant preoccupation with girls, I still considered him to be the best friend I ever had. Just like in old times, he and I took off on walks together, and he filled my imagination with his thoughts. He told me he was tutoring a black kid once a week in Harlem, which is right next to the Columbia campus. One night, he said, he was walking to the boy's apartment when a man in the shadows said to him, "You're out here kind of late tonight, aren't you, *whitey?*" This frightened him a little, he said, but it wasn't going to stop him from helping the kid.

It would sure stop me! I thought.

Elias also told me that he was concerned about what Americans were doing to the environment. Nowadays, a statement like that would be utterly mundane, but this was 1967, and I had never heard anyone say such a thing. Nor had I ever seen anything in print on the subject, although I'm sure Elias had.

Then Elias told me something that really surprised me. He said he was thinking about becoming a doctor. I had always known him to be brilliant on the subjects of history and politics. Likewise, he had always impressed me with his interest in literature and with how philosophical he was. The sciences were something, on the other hand, that had almost never come up.

Finally, Elias wanted me to know he had a love interest. He took me over to Barnard, hoping he could introduce us, but it had to be impromptu, because, as usual, his affections were unrequited. Fortunately, we did run into her in the lobby at her dorm, and I must say, there was no criticizing his taste. The girl was a beautiful brunette, one who would have caught my eye immediately. *He'll never get her,* I thought.

We took in a Simon and Garfunkel concert at the Lincoln Center while I was there. Elias paid, of course, since he was the one who always seemed to have the money. The next day, Elias tried to convince me that I needed to get out of Clarion and go to school in New York. I told him the obvious, that I would never be admitted to a place like Columbia. He said I should apply to Hofstra, but, with my 1.82 average, I doubted that could happen either. I greatly appreciated his desire to help me, but I had pretty much shut the door on going anywhere other than where I already was. With that, we said goodbye and I headed for the Port Authority terminal and the bus to Princeton.

I was really hoping my visit with Karlana would revitalize her affection for me. While walking in Greenwich Village one day, I had caught a glimpse of a girl who looked astonishingly like Janet. In fact, I had followed her just long enough to make sure she wasn't Janet. But Janet was gone now. Like it or not, she had vanished into my past. The brilliant and beautiful Karlana was all that remained, and the more I thought about her, the more convinced I was that she was my last chance of ever having a girlfriend.

When the bus let me out at Princeton University, I had an hour to kill, so I walked around the campus admiring the collegiate Gothic style of some of the buildings. As at Columbia, I was, of course, surrounded by kids my own age, and I was jealous of every one of them. These were the kids who, like Elias and Karlana, were just plain smarter than I was. I not only couldn't get into one of these schools, but from the way things were going, I might also not even survive at Clarion.

At an appointed time and place, Karlana and her father pulled up in their family car. After a warm greeting, they took me to their home in a gently rolling suburban neighborhood. There I would spend the night. As was our custom, Karlana and I went walking and talking before dinner. I kissed her a couple of times, but then she resisted me. *Maybe she thinks I'm moving too quickly,* I thought, so I backed off. The next morning, after breakfast, we went for a second walk. We talked, and she was as insightful as ever, so much to say and so good at expressing it. Then, when I thought I saw an opening, I tried to kiss her again, and she pulled away.

Later in the morning, we climbed into the car with her parents to go visit a pair of friends they had in Orange, New Jersey. We spent that afternoon at the friends' apartment and then returned to Princeton in time for me to catch my bus back to Manhattan.

THIRTEEN

Roustabout

I returned to Clarion believing what now seemed obvious. Whatever power I thought I had to attract girls in high school had somehow vanished. I had gained a few pounds in college. Could that be the reason? Or was it my hairline, which was already starting to recede? Maybe, with so much competition in the States, I just didn't stack up so well.

That spring, a letter arrived from Dad. He said he and Mom had finally heard from Dana. She and her new husband, Bob Camp, had relocated to Portland, Oregon, where Bob was working as a rep for Bunker Ramo, a technology company. Dana wanted to reconcile. Consequently, Mom and Dad were going to fly from Libya to New York and buy a car. From there, they would drive to Clarion to pick me up. The four of us, including Mark, would make a cross-country trip to visit the newlyweds. Finally, the letter said that Dad had arranged a summer job for me working on an offshore oil-drilling platform in Alaska.

The next time I talked to Elias on the phone, I told him about our plan, and he said he would try to meet up with us. He had been accepted for summer school at Stanford, and he thought it would be an easy jog up to Portland on his way to California. All this sounded great to me. After all, I had no other plans.

One thing, though: my parents wanted me to sell the motorcycle. Having had second thoughts about my safety, they had come up with a better idea. After Portland, they would drive all the way to New England, where they wanted to look at vacation property. Then, they would turn their new car over to me before going back to Libya.

Unfortunately, my motorbike was a mess. The first and only time I ever let a friend borrow it, he had gotten into an accident almost immediately. He wasn't damaged, but the bike was, and I didn't have the money to get it repaired. So I sold it, but not for what it should have been worth.

Soon, Mom, Dad, and Mark arrived in a brand-new Oldsmobile Cutlass, and we were off on our transcontinental adventure. One of the things I remember best about that journey is eating my first ever Reuben sandwich somewhere near Omaha, the city where it was invented. I guess I must have liked it. I also recall a disappointing stop at Mt. Rushmore. There was fog so thick that day we were unable to see even the faintest outline of the four presidents.

The trip took about a week. Happily for me, Dad was letting me do some of the driving. I was not to go over sixty-five miles per hour, regardless of the legal limit. Most of the time, we were on the interstate system, which was still pretty new in those days, but we traveled two-way roads a lot too. Our last night found us in The Dalles, Oregon. We awoke in our hotel room the next morning and heard the news on the television. Israel had just invaded the Sinai. It was June 5, 1967. The Six-Day War had begun.

That day, we stopped for lunch at a coffee shop, what now would be called a family restaurant. At one point during the meal, I saw an antique car driving through the parking lot. Not wanting anyone to miss it, I pointed out the window with my fork still in my hand. "Look!" I exclaimed.

My mother had just spent an entire week riding in an automobile with Mark and me. Never in her life had she enjoyed the company of children, least of all now. And so, she unloaded on me. Where on earth were my manners, pointing out the window with a fork in my hand like that? Of course, it was no matter that at every meal our family ever ate together, she had lit up a cigarette at the table. I didn't bring that up, but it sure occurred to me.

Sadly, there was nothing unusual about this episode. It was the sort of thing that happens when parents run out of patience with their kids. With Mom, it happened all the time, but I had been out on my own for almost three years now, and I was no longer used to being treated this way.

We arrived at Dana's that afternoon. She and her husband had a nice unit on the ground floor of a small apartment building. It was decently furnished. Dana had lost a little weight, and she was nicely dressed. She was a stay-at-home housewife now, had even acquired a little Chihuahua to keep her company. In short, she was everything her mother might approve of—by all appearances, light-years away from being the troubled teenager of her recent past.

Bob Camp was somewhat older than Dana, and he was a quiet, serious type. At least that was the way he came across to me. Maybe he just wasn't comfortable meeting Dana's family for the first time. Or maybe, by now, he was disillusioned with his marriage altogether. In any event, he made little attempt to ingratiate himself.

This was 1967. The baby boomers were entering college. The era of the hippie had just begun, and the American zeitgeist was shifting into something more open to alternatives. Bob Dylan had sung about how the times, they were a changin', and *The Graduate*, a movie about a college guy who spurns the values of his parents, was a huge box office success. Yet here was twenty-year-old Dana, having abandoned her youth and taken up the life of a middle-aged woman. I wondered if, for all Dana's defiance, she was now trying to adopt a life worthy of our mother's approval. If so, I wondered how happy she could really be.

Mom, who had spent years grousing about Dana's behavior, now decided to break from character and try to make the best of things. She put on an effusive, though, to me at least, transparent, display of warmth toward her only daughter and her new son-in-law. I'm sure it wasn't easy.

Our second day there, Elias called on Dana's phone. He was in town and ready to get together. He came over in a taxi and joined us for lunch. Afterward, he and I took off walking, as usual. Elias had heard about Reed College, a challenging liberal arts school where students lived and studied under what was apparently a pretty relaxed atmosphere. The school was a couple of miles away, so getting there and back, as well as exploring the campus, would consume the afternoon.

Elias always had a lot to say, and I was always an appreciative audience. We covered the usual subjects: historical stuff he had read, what he thought about the political situation, the Vietnam War, and so on. And as always, we talked about girls. There was no doubt in my mind that his libido was every bit as powerful as mine, and his luck no better.

Late in the afternoon, we got back to Dana's apartment, and he called a taxi. When it arrived, I walked him out to the sidewalk to say goodbye. Then, I watched as he was driven away. Elias was a very important friend to me. In Vienna, and in the US, we had shared an awful lot together and at a very formative stage in our lives. What he offered me in terms of insight and character, I had never encountered in a friend before and seldom since. If only I had known that day I was never going to see or hear from Elias Menkes again.

Three days later, it was my turn to leave. The money from the sale of my motorcycle had run out, so Dad gave me a plane ticket and $35 in cash. This, he thought, was all I would need to get to Alaska and start my new job. Not knowing any better, I put up no protest.

As it turned out, I should have. It was a Saturday, and when I reached the address in Anchorage where I was supposed to report, it was closed for the weekend. Even in those days, thirty-five dollars was not enough to provide me with lodging and meals for two days, especially not in a place as expensive as Alaska. Yet that was what was needed if I was to survive until Monday. I walked miles looking for a decent hotel, and the only one I encountered was a place called the Captain Cook. They wanted twenty-eight dollars for just one night, so I kept walking. Finally, I gave up, returned to the Captain Cook, gave them their twenty-eight dollars for the first night, and then went up in the elevator to go to bed. I would figure out later what to do about the second night.

In the morning, I got up, skipped breakfast, and headed out onto the street. I spent my whole day without food, just walking around the city, carrying my small suitcase. I say "city," but really, Anchorage was hardly more than a frontier town. Many of the streets were still unpaved, and sidewalks were often boardwalks, just like in the Old West. Some people, I'm sure, would think such a rugged environment stimulating, but having very little money and facing so many unknowns, I found the whole place just too remote and foreboding.

I slept that second night, a Sunday, on the ground. Walking past a vacant lot during the day, I had seen a large sheet of cardboard and decided it might do for a bed. Only seven months earlier, in front of the Smithsonian, I had endured just such a night on the ground, only this was going to be much more unpleasant. In DC, I had found privacy in the shadows under a large bush. But this was Alaska in summer. I was going to sleep all night in an open field under a sunlit sky. I felt very exposed.

The next morning, probably looking like a bum, I showed up at the office of the Santa Fe Drilling Company. I found the man I was supposed to see, and though he appeared not to be expecting me, he gave me a job. I would be a roustabout, making $4.20 an hour, almost three times the national minimum wage. The only problem was, I had to get myself to the site. This, he explained, required flying by commercial aircraft out to a place called Kenai. From there, I would fly by company helicopter across the Cook Inlet and land on a drilling platform.

As I had practically no funds, I asked if the company would provide my plane ticket, and he said no. So I agreed to follow his instructions, even though I didn't know how I very well could.

I did have my checkbook from my bank in Clarion, but the account was empty. I wondered if I could get the airline to take a check that I knew was bad. If they did, I could write to Dad, in Portland, and ask him to wire the funds to my bank in time to keep me out of trouble. After taking the long walk out to the airport, that was exactly what I did. That night, I slept on an offshore drilling platform off the coast of Alaska.

A roustabout's job is to do what you might call the grunt work. Not much training or expertise is required, although, I confess, I never really had much of a handle on what I was supposed to be doing. There was one other college kid on board. He was from New Jersey. He and I both worked under the same foreman, a roughhewn man well into middle age who resented us both. He never came right out and said so, but it was pretty clear he faulted us for taking these lucrative paychecks away from local working men who had families to support.

Instead of showing us, or even telling us, what he wanted, he would just start working and expect us to fill in the blanks. Neither of us, though, had ever been on a drilling rig before, so we were often confused about what to do. When that happened, he would get angry, and it didn't matter how hard we tried to please him. "You f—— worms are all alike!" he would say, using oil field vernacular.

The shifts were twelve hours on and twelve hours off for ten days in a row. Then you got five days ashore. As it happened, the kid from New Jersey was college roommates with one of Walter Hickel's sons. Walter Hickel was the sitting governor of Alaska and would eventually be Richard Nixon's secretary of interior. So when our first five days came around, he took off for Anchorage to stay at the governor's residence. No such fate awaited me, however. Having no place else to go, I rented half a room at a dingy Kenai hotel and just hung out there.

Half a room means sharing with a stranger, but the guy I shared with was only there the first night. He was a fat, gray-headed old guy in a scruffy T-shirt, and I didn't really want to talk to him, so I pretended to be asleep when he came in. I lay there thinking about Moby Dick and Ishmael's night at the Spouter Inn. *Thank goodness,* I thought, *this isn't two to a bed.*

Near the end of my second ten-day tour, our resentful foreman suddenly told the other kid and me to run up to the control room and report to the drilling supervisor. As usual, we had no clue what we were doing, but we soon found out. The drilling supervisor told us he was laying us off. Just didn't need us, he said, which we knew was baloney. We had been marked for failure from day 1. No one, it seemed, wanted two "worms" around.

The New Jersey kid (whose name I don't recall) and I were off the platform that morning and back in Anchorage. We got our final paychecks cashed, bought plane tickets, and then at his suggestion, walked to the governor's residence. Only, there was no one there but the housekeeper. Recognizing my companion, she led us into a large family room and invited us to wait until somebody showed up. After a half hour or so, nobody did, so we thanked her and took off.

Next, we walked to a movie theater and saw *The Dirty Dozen*. After that, we wandered. When we came to a music store, we went in. I had about $800 in my wallet, more money than I'd ever seen before. I saw a beautiful Gibson twelve-string guitar there. At $350, it probably cost a lot more than I would have paid a day later in the lower forty-eight, but you know what they say about a fool and his money. Between the guitar and the plane ticket, I had already gone through most of my summer's wages. Nonetheless, that guitar would be a prize possession for the rest of my life.

After a brief visit with Tom Wheeler in DC, I managed to locate Mom and Mark. My parents had bought a lot at the Bolton Valley Ski Resort in Vermont. Mom was staying at a lakeside vacation village near Burlington so as to be on hand to get construction started on a house. Dad, meanwhile, was back at work in Tripoli. I caught a plane to Burlington and spent the rest of my summer at the vacation cottage with Mom.

I managed to make it up to Bolton only once while I was there, but I must say, I was impressed. What Dad had planned was a ski chalet right at the resort, a family retreat where he and Mom could eventually retire. By the time I got there, work was already underway, and I could tell I was going to like it.

By now, Mark was eleven. As much as I had always loved him and enjoyed doing things with him, he and I had never been able to share our feelings the way brothers who are closer in age can do. Staying at the vacation village might have been an opportunity to work on that. After all, neither of us had any friends around. Nor were we in school or having to go to jobs. I did take him to a drive-in movie one night, but mostly I spent my days reading. *Valley of the Dolls* was a best seller that summer, and I tried to read it, though I soon lost interest. Mark, meanwhile, never seemed to be around. At mealtimes, Mom would send me out to find him. I would go searching for him, calling his name, and then suddenly he would appear as if from nowhere. Years later, he would tell me he had been breaking into cottages.

FOURTEEN

Under Arrest

At the end of summer, I saw Mom and Mark off at the Burlington Airport. They were headed back to Tripoli. I was about to drive the Oldsmobile down to Clarion to start my sophomore year. Per our agreement, the car would be mine to use and care for as long as Mom and Dad were out of the country.

One of my classes that fall was a three-hour, one-evening-per-week art history class. There was a kid I recognized from my dorm who was also in the class. His name was Dylan Smith. He and I would fall in, talking to each other on the long walk back to the residence hall, and I got to liking him. For one thing, he was a lot smarter than most of the other boys, and he had a lot to say. His favorite activities, it seemed, were rock climbing and spelunking. One night, he asked me if I would like to join him on a weekend caving excursion down to West Virginia.

At six feet four inches tall, and weighing 220 pounds, I was a little big to be crawling around in caves, but Dylan assured me I would have no problem. The one thing I did have that I am sure made me valuable was transportation, something Dylan lacked.

Of course, we would need money for gasoline, but Dylan had a quick solution for that problem. He knew of a site several miles northeast of town where a new road was going in. There was a fuel tank there for construction equipment, and if we went late that night, we could fill my tank for free. I should have been appalled, but I wasn't.

We waited until almost midnight before heading out the door. When we got to the construction site, we drove several hundred yards beyond it to make sure no one was around. Then, I turned my headlights off and circled back until we reached the tank. While I left the motor running, Dylan jumped out of the car and started pumping the gas. I am sure he acted quickly, but it didn't feel that way. We were a good two hundred yards from the paved highway, but I was unnerved by the lights of every passing vehicle. As far as I was concerned, every car that appeared was a police cruiser. "Hurry up!" I kept saying in a loud whisper.

There was a popular TV series in those days called *Mission Impossible*. It was about a group of undercover espionage agents who used highly creative means to foil bad guys in exotic fictional places. Every episode involved a lot of sneaking around, and that greatly appealed to my sense of adventure. Every week, when the show was on, I made a point of watching it in the TV room at the dorm. In fact, *Mission Impossible* was the only program, other than *60 Minutes*, that I ever watched.

Of course, there was no way an immature nineteen-year-old student getting bad grades at a little-known state college in Pennsylvania was ever going to be selected for important secret-agent work. But I was about to learn how thin the line between good and evil can really be. Like the guys in the TV show, Dylan and I had just outsmarted somebody, or so we thought, and I had a free tank of gas as my reward. And yes, the fear of being caught had been great, but so was the exhilaration of getting away with it.

The following Friday, Dylan and I set off for West Virginia and a cave called Overholt's Blowing. Dylan had rope and headlamps and whatever other equipment we needed, so all I had to do was let him take over. Our one tank of gas wasn't going to be enough to get us there and back, but Dylan knew how to take care of that problem. As I drove the car, he kept a keen watch out the window, and well after dark, with the tank running low, he spied our first opportunity. We had just passed a group of dump trucks all parked in a row, and he asked me to turn the car around and go back. When we got to the line of trucks, he told me to pull in next to one and stop where we couldn't be seen from the road. That night I learned how to siphon gas using my mouth and a rubber tube that my forward-thinking friend had brought along.

We drove on for a while longer and found a place to park where we could sleep in the car without being disturbed. The next morning, we went off to find the cave.

Overholt's Blowing runs for some seven miles under the earth, but we never got anywhere near that far. Early on, we came to a crawl space so narrow that I was afraid of getting stuck, so I refused to go any farther. By midday, we were in the car again, headed back to Clarion. As much as I enjoyed the experience, I guess I must have pretty much ruined it for Dylan. Nonetheless, he made no complaint.

Near the Clarion campus was a snack food distributor we passed on our weekly walks back to the dorm from art history class. On one of these nights, Dylan noticed that a window had been left open. It was too high for a man to climb through unaided, but he thought he could do it if I gave him a boost. The next thing I knew, he was tossing bags of potato chips out the window, and I was gleefully catching them. From that week on, the snack food building would be a regular stop on our way back to the dorm.

It would be easy to blame all this larceny on Dylan, but it would be wrong. Clearly, he was well practiced at it before I came along. He also had a quick mind and a body capable of all sorts of contortions I could never manage. So yes, in a sense, he was the Artful Dodger, but that doesn't mean I was Oliver Twist. Far from it. In fact, every theft we committed gave me an adrenaline rush that left me wanting to do something even bigger the next time.

Of course, there was more going on for me at Clarion that fall than just carrying out burglaries. Since my high school days, I'd had an interest in theater. In college, I was finding it very difficult to get a serious part in a play, but I did perform secondary roles in a few campus productions. I was in Thornton Wilder's *Our Town*, and I had a part in Tennessee Williams's *Cat on a Hot Tin Roof*. It was during rehearsals for the latter that I got to know a fellow named Jim

Canelos. He had a bigger role than mine, and no wonder. A dapper Greek American with a handsome head of slick black hair, he was a director's favorite. He was also a very self-confident and well-known young man around campus.

One day, late in the fall, Jim approached me for a favor. The Clarion football team was having a banner season. They were set to play West Chester State College, some three hundred miles away near Philadelphia, for the state championship. Since I was one of the few kids around who had a car, he wanted to know if I would take him and a couple of his girlfriends.

"Who are the girls?" I wanted to know.

"Raine Martin and Suzie Albanesi."

Raine Martin and Suzie Albanesi! My heart leaped! "Yes, I'll take you!" I said, making the decision right then and there. (Are you kidding? I'd take those two girls anywhere.)

The next day, I was parking my car on Main Street when I saw Jim in my rearview mirror. He was walking in my direction, and he had Raine and Suzie with him. I was so excited I reached down onto the seat beside me and picked up my new reading glasses. They were wire rims, a style suddenly popularized by John Lennon. *Maybe,* I thought, *I'll make a better impression if I'm wearing them.*

Jumping out of my car, I greeted Jim, and he introduced me to the girls. Of course, thanks to my reading glasses, both of them were out of focus, but I was having a moment I would remember the rest of my life.

That Friday, Jim, Raine, Suzie, Dylan, and I took off on our drive across the state of Pennsylvania. We had to cram some of our baggage in with us because my trunk was so full of stolen pretzels and potato chips.

We took a hotel room in King of Prussia that night. We shared it between the five of us. The next morning, we sneaked out on the bill. Then we went off to watch Clarion defeat West Chester for the state championship.

After a while, a diet of pretzels and potato chips gets pretty old. So does the intrigue of sneaking into the same building over and over. Dylan and I both started wanting to take on a greater challenge. One night we investigated a produce warehouse not far from campus, and sure enough, we found a way to get in. We never wanted to actually break in anywhere; instead, we thought it was smarter to gain access without damaging anything. That way, we'd go undetected and be able to hit a place again, if we wanted.

Sure enough, as with the snack food distributor, we found an entrance that wasn't locked. This time, it was a delivery bay. It consisted of an unlocked garage door behind a locked wire screen, but there was just room for someone strong and nimble enough to climb over the screen and then open the door. Once again, in our case, that was going to be Dylan.

We returned to the dorm that night with a large box full of fresh fruit. Now we had two stops on our midnight grocery run. Soon, it would be three, and then four. Within a few weeks, we were drinking stolen beer and eating stolen lobster tails.

By the middle of January, Dylan and I were going out almost every night. We had also acquired a third accomplice. He was a really good-natured kid named Larry Withrow. Then a fourth, named Mike Maloney, joined in, although he was never more than just a lookout. Our confidence was growing, but we realized, so were the chances of being caught. So we decided to move in to a cheap basement apartment in town. There were just too many potential witnesses living at the dorm.

We decorated our new place with posters we had stolen in one of our burglaries. When we thought it was ready to show off, we invited some girls over for an evening of beer drinking and making out, hopefully. I invited Raine Martin, and I was amazed when she accepted.

At Clarion, if you referred to the girl who looked like Barbra Streisand, it wouldn't matter whom you said it to; they would know you meant Raine Martin. But Raine's look also reminded me of Janet Grkovic. So I was pretty stoked.

I picked her up at her dorm that night, and we walked the half-mile or so to the apartment. She was the first girl I ever asked out in college, and I fully appreciated how very popular she was. Of course, I was nervous as all get out and just praying she wouldn't notice.

Unfortunately, when we reached the party, everyone else was already there, and they were already demonstrating their affection for one another.

This was awkward. Was a girl who was such a favorite on campus supposed to start passionately kissing me at the very outset of our first date? Had she ever even shown the slightest interest in me before? Was this the impression I was trying to make? Of course not. Even so, I kissed her, and as good as it felt, I really did so because I was embarrassed not to. Then I kissed her again, several more times, in fact. And she was a good sport about it, too, although I'm sure she must have felt set up. Finally, I just stopped and I asked her if we could go for a walk. She agreed.

What a relief. It was a cold night, but the sky was clear and the stars were out. Now I could relax and just enjoy being with this special girl. We made our way back to the college, and I kept thinking, *Man, would I ever like to be her boyfriend!* The more we talked, the more I realized what an exceptional person she was. Smart, outgoing, earnest, good student—she was all these things. No wonder she was so popular. She liked everyone, and everyone liked her right back.

Eventually, we reached her dorm. I tried to kiss her good night, but she just laughed and turned away. She thanked me for the date and went inside. I probably never had a chance with Raine Martin, anyway, but if I did, I knew I had just blown it.

And then, a day or so later, Dylan and I were planning our next hit. I forget whose idea it was, but we both thought it would be fun to try to get into Ben Franklin's five-and-dime up on Main Street. There was renovation going on up on the second floor, and it was enclosed by nothing more than a large sheet of polyethylene. Getting in ought to be easy. Once you ducked under the plastic, you would be invisible from the outside. Then you could climb the scaffolding and enter the building on the second floor. And what were we after? God only knows. It was all just part of the ride.

As usual, we waited until very late at night to make our approach. Just as we had planned, we ducked under the polyethylene and climbed the scaffold. On the second floor, we discovered that a stretch of the exterior wall had indeed been removed, but the opening had a temporary cover over it of random boards that had been nailed in place. No problem. Expecting this to be the case, we had brought a few tools, burglar tools, if you like, and we quickly gained access.

The sales floor only occupied the ground floor of the building. We were on the second floor, and we quickly discovered that to get down the stairs into the customer area would require leaving behind evidence of damage, something we were unwilling to do. So we rooted around in what was obviously a storeroom and found nothing more than a few stuffed animals.

Not wanting to leave empty-handed, we picked up a large cardboard box, threw a few of the animals into it, and then headed back out the way we came in. Once outside, we took off on foot, leaving our loot behind. This was a typical ploy. As long as we left the stuff behind, we were not yet guilty of stealing it. If we encountered any police, we had nothing to explain. In an hour or so, we could pull up in my car, throw the stuff in the trunk, and be gone in seconds.

As we began our walk back to the apartment, a light snow began to fall. We still had our burglar tools in hand, but they would be easy to toss aside in the dark if we encountered anyone. We got several blocks away before, lo and behold, some headlights appeared. Just as planned, we ditched our tools by the side of the road, and sure enough, we soon recognized a police cruiser coming toward us.

I don't know how many police officers were employed by the Clarion Borough in January 1968—probably not very many—but the night of the Ben Franklin job, it was the chief of police himself who was out patrolling. Like any good cop who encounters young men wandering the streets late at night, he was suspicious. Emerging from his car, he began quizzing us. Who were we? What were we up to? He shone his flashlight back and forth between our faces and the weeds at the side of the road. Had he just seen us throwing something away? he asked.

"No," we said in unison.

"Well, I think you better come with me," he said, opening the back door of his cruiser. We were on our way to the police station.

At this point, I think Dylan and I both were still pretty relaxed about the whole thing. Thankfully, the chief had not gone into the weeds in search of our tools. Nor were there any stolen goods in our possession. What on earth could he charge us with?

Unfortunately, there was more to the chief's suspicions than Dylan and I were counting on. We had always taken care not to do damage, and we never stole more than enough food to eat ourselves, so we thought our burglaries were clean. In other words, we thought nobody was reporting them. But we were wrong. People had reported them, and the police had been looking for us for weeks.

After more questions at the station, the chief said he was going to hold us. He wanted to do some investigating. I thought he meant we would wait at his office while he went looking for whatever it was we had thrown into the weeds. *I hope it's still snowing,* I thought. *Maybe our tools will be buried by now.*

Instead, he took us back out to the patrol car, and in a few minutes, we were walking up the steps to the Clarion County Jail. There, we were separated from our belts and the contents of our pockets and locked up in separate cells for the rest of the night.

The light in the jail was pretty dim, but I could easily make out the large rectangular dayroom on the main floor. There were a table and benches maybe fifteen feet long that ran down the center of it. At the far end of the table was an iron stairway that led up to a second-floor catwalk. On each of the two floors were ten cells, five to a side. It was too dark to make out any occupants. Except for the iron doors, stairs, and catwalk, all the construction was concrete.

I only sat on the bunk, as I dared not lie down or go to sleep. Doing so might be tantamount to moving in, something I had no intention of doing. In my adolescent mind, I kept going over the situation. Without any actual evidence, how could the chief keep us here for more than a few hours? Even if he located our tools, how could he connect them to a crime? We had replaced the boards covering our entrance at Ben Franklin's, and we were carrying nothing in the way of loot. Surely, a box of stuffed animals sitting next to a building wouldn't prove anything.

By the time the first rays of sunlight appeared through my tiny slot of a window, the jail lights had already come on. I heard the clatter of cell doors being opened one at a time, and then a fellow came around to open mine. He was, he said, the trustee, a prisoner chosen to do the jailer's work inside the cellblock.

Stepping out onto the hard tile floor of the dayroom, I got my first glimpse of the prisoners. There was a dozen or so. All were immediately curious about Dylan and me. They had heard us coming in during the night, and they wanted to know our story. Some were even younger than we were. There were no college kids among them.

We lined up in what might have been a kitchen had it not lacked appliances. What it did have was a big stainless steel sink, which, I would soon find out, was for hand-washing stainless steel food trays, stainless steel coffee cups, and stainless steel tablespoons. One by one, we grabbed our breakfast bowls as they were passed through a slot in the wall. This morning we were having hot cereal and coffee.

Dylan and I appeared to be something of a curiosity to these men, and I must say, they were just as interesting to us. Sixteen months earlier, on first arrival in Clarion, I had been surprised by the degree of provinciality I saw among the students. The distinctive Western Pennsylvania accent, which was so new to me, had contributed to that impression. So too had the ubiquitous small talk about the Pittsburgh Steelers and the Pittsburgh Pirates. Now, however, I found myself in a group that really was provincial, a rustic bunch of Appalachians, local rogues, if you will, to whom a town as small as Clarion must be the center of the universe.

Over breakfast, we got to know a little about one another. I wouldn't say they were hardened people, though some certainly looked that way. There were plenty of homemade tattoos among them and lots of facial hair. Some employed profanity quite liberally in their speech. Then, after the meal, all who didn't tuck snuff into their jaws rolled cigarettes using tobacco and papers supplied by the county.

By now, I was really suffering from lack of sleep. Nonetheless, I was still awake late in the morning when the chief suddenly reappeared. He was, he said, bringing charges against us for "attempted" burglary at Ben Franklin's five-and-dime. And that wasn't all. He was also going to charge us with several other burglaries, including those at the Clarion Fruit Company and the Wise Potato Chip distributor.

My heart sank. How on earth did he know about these things, and where did he get his evidence? I saw my answer quickly enough when our friend Mike Maloney was brought in. Poor Mike Maloney. He had enjoyed the fruits of our thievery but had never wanted to be involved in the actual crimes. The few times he participated, he acted only as a lookout. And now, here he was, rousted from his bed, his college career perhaps ruined, largely because of my and Dylan's selfish stupidity.

Obviously, the chief had gone to our apartment, awakened Maloney, and grilled him. Mike, whose primary emotion throughout our exploits had been fear, must have spilled his gut immediately. I can't say I blamed him. He had resisted involvement from the very outset. Why should he put himself at risk to save our skins?

All three of us were fingerprinted and photographed. Then we were sent back into the cellblock. Our bail, we were told, would not be set until after our arraignment, which hadn't even been scheduled yet. So according to the chief, we were just going to have to relax for a couple of days. We weren't going anywhere.

This was one of the lowest points in my life. I went straight back to my cell, and this time I stretched out on the bunk. All I could think about was what a loser I was. My father was such an accomplished man. He had taken me all over the world. We had visited so many important landmarks, eaten in beautiful restaurants, stayed in famous hotels. He had such an important job at such a big company. Yet here I was, locked up in jail. My grades were awful. My girlfriends had dumped me. I had been fired from the only job I'd ever had. As I thought about these things, my mind began to drift, and soon I was sleeping for the first time in twenty-four hours.

Two days later, the three of us were taken to the police station for our arraignment. This was sort of a preliminary trial to consider the evidence before setting bail. Only one of our victims was on hand. He was the owner of the Clarion Fruit Company, a gregarious man who, if anything, seemed to feel bad about the trouble we were in. He was there to testify about what had been stolen. He said we couldn't have taken more than a few hundred dollars' worth of produce. In fact, he said, he might never have noticed had we not stolen his thirty-six frozen lobster tails.

Listening to such a nice man talk about the things we had done to him made our crimes sink in for me even more now than before, and I was feeling pretty foolish. But the arraignment wasn't over yet. There was still one more witness, a younger man. He said he had been driving by the scene of one of our burglaries late one night when he saw several boys crossing the street.

"Do you recognize anyone here today who was in that group of boys?" the prosecutor asked.

"Yes, I do," the young man answered.

"Would you point him out, please?"

The young man raised his arm and extended his index finger directly at me. *No wonder,* I thought. *I am six inches taller and fifty pounds heavier than either of my accomplices. Plus, I am the only one who is fair-haired and prematurely balding.*

We were remanded for trial. Our bail was set at $6,000 apiece. This was money, we were told, that would be returned to us when and if we showed up in court. If we were unable to come up with $6,000, then a bondsman would be the alternative.

As soon as we got back to the jail, a bondsman was somehow already waiting for us. For $300, he said he would get us out, but the $300 was a fee, not just a deposit, and it would not be refunded. Neither Dylan nor Mike had any money at the jail, but amazingly, I did. I, who rarely ever carried more than a few bucks, just happened to have more than $300 in my wallet, though that had been taken from me by the jailer for safekeeping.

My immediate thought was to bail myself out. Then I could call whomever Dylan and Mike asked me to and get them bailed out. But Mike had what he thought was a better idea. He said he had the money in his bank account to spring two of us. If he could just use my money to get himself out first, he could go to his bank and pick up the funds for Dylan and me.

I quickly agreed. It wasn't that I was a such a trusting soul. In truth, I found it hard giving Mike the money I could have used to spring myself, but under the circumstances, I felt I owed it to him. An hour later, Mike was free, and we were eagerly awaiting his return.

Only, he didn't return, not that day, nor the next, and I soon realized I had been had. Given no alternative, Dylan contacted his parents and arranged for his release, but my parents were on the opposite side of the planet, and my own money was entirely gone.

You might think I was stuck, but I did have one other option. As much as I dreaded doing so, I could call Nanny, my poor old grandmother. Tired of being alone, she had just driven all the way up from Miami in her little Chevy Corvair to visit me in Clarion for the first and only time in her life. It being winter, she was staying in her room at the Clarion Motel, chain-smoking cigarettes and drinking beer all day. I dreaded having her find out what was going on, but I didn't really have a choice. Reluctantly, I gave the jailer her name and location, and he called her for me.

Soon, I was back on the street, headed straight for Nanny's hotel to try to explain things to her. She was surprisingly calm. She told me she had sent a telegram to my parents, and my heart sank yet again. The jig was certainly up for me at this point, but I had hoped somehow Mom and Dad wouldn't have to know.

Days later, our family would have two rooms at the Clarion Motel. One was Nanny's. The other was for Mom and me. Mom's first priority was to hire an attorney. Having no confidence she might find a good one in a town as small as Clarion, she located one fifty miles away in the town of Butler. To be sure, Clarion did have attorneys, and we probably didn't need a very special one anyway. Dylan and I had already discussed what we wanted to do, and we intended to plead guilty. We thought doing otherwise would be a waste of everyone's time. By now, there were simply too many people who knew what we had been up to. Besides, we thought the judge might go easier on us if we confessed.

When my lawyer arrived from Butler, he, Mom, and I went to lunch at the Captain Loomis, downtown Clarion's only dinner house restaurant. He asked me about my case, and I assured him I was guilty. He made no bones about my intention to plead that way. I gave him my trial date, which was in late May, almost four months away. He said he would be in touch.

A couple of days later, Mom got a telegram from Dad. Something had come up and she needed to hurry back to Tripoli. I didn't know what it was, but I was going to have to handle things on my own from this point on. Wasting no time, Mom got Nanny turned around and headed back to Miami. Then she gave me enough money to rent a room at a cheaper hotel. As quickly as she had come, she was gone.

It would be a while before I would be told what had happened back in Libya. Almost unbelievably, my twelve-year-old brother, Mark, was in legal trouble too.

FIFTEEN

1968

I didn't know it at that time, and neither did Mark, but he had just done me the biggest favor. When you have one son charged with burglary in the United States and another son charged with the same crime in an Arab country like Libya, the latter offense is the one that's going to keep you up at night. That was the way it was for Mom and Dad. Thanks to Mark, my problem had been moved right off the front page, so to speak, and I would now have the luxury of being under my own recognizance.

I was out of school now. I had missed too many classes to finish the semester. My trial date wouldn't allow me to do so, anyway. With nothing better to occupy me, I started hanging around the campus and enjoying what I could of the social life.

One evening, I was in the library when I ran into Suzie Albanesi. As always, she was beautifully dressed and smiling. We had a brief and completely inane conversation about pimples, of all things, but I happily would have talked about anything with her. I was sure I was being flirted with, but I wondered how that could be. Suzie was a favorite of all the boys on campus. She was even in a relationship already with a college senior, a fraternity guy named Jack Wall, an athlete who played on the varsity basketball team. Where in this picture was I supposed to fit? I was a jailbird, for crying out loud, a jailbird who hadn't found a girlfriend in almost two years.

The next time I ran into her, Suzie flirted with me again, so I started keeping an eye out for her. At lunchtime I would wait around the cafeteria until she showed up, and sure enough, I got to eat with her a few times. Some of the prettiest and most popular girls at Clarion were her friends, so I was getting to eat with them too. Before long, I was laughing and joking along with all of them, and I could hardly believe my good fortune.

There were serious problems in the world. This was the winter of the Tet Offensive in Vietnam. Throughout the war, US Defense Department progress reports had been consistently optimistic. So much so that skeptics had begun to suspect the Johnson administration of inflating the enemy's casualty numbers. How else could such a small war be taking so long to win? Now, all of a sudden, communist soldiers, who were supposedly losing badly, were pulling off well-coordinated and ferocious attacks all over the country. What was more, they were taking the battle to areas previously thought to be safe, such as the American Embassy in Saigon. This was bad news for the US, and as far as I was concerned, it was bad news for Vietnam too.

It was just the sort of thing to encourage the antiwar movement. America had long been debating the morality of the war, and the clash of opinions was largely divided along generational lines. The baby boomers were unhappy with the status quo. Student demonstrators were shutting down college campuses. So-called flower children had flooded into the Haight-Ashbury district of San Francisco to engage in something called the Summer of Love. The Beatles were singing "All You Need Is Love." Timothy Leary was advising young people to "tune in, turn on, and drop out." At the box office, *Bonnie and Clyde* and *Cool Hand Luke* were smash hits. Both romanticized contempt for authority. I could go on.

This was America in 1968, and unfortunately, I was inspired by some of its worst aspects. What resounded with me was, you don't need to go to war, you don't need to go to class, and you don't need to go to work. All you need to do is *act up*!

We didn't need those potato chips and bananas we were stealing; they were snack foods, for crying out loud. We weren't selling them. We couldn't even make a meal out of them. Besides, we all had cafeteria cards. The whole thing had been for sport, and now we had a price to pay.

Suzie and I hung out together the rest of that winter and into the spring. Fool that I was, I would try to get her to cut class, but she only did once. Her conscience was too powerful, but then, so was her enthusiasm for learning. She had always had good grades, and she wasn't going to let up now.

Our conversations frequently dealt with the subjects she was studying. She was an elementary education major. When I entered her life, she was reading Maurice Sendak's book *Higglety Pigglety Pop! or There Must Be More to Life*. She was so excited about it that she read the whole thing to me one afternoon while we sat out on the campus lawn. Her positivity and her beauty mesmerized me.

Never far from my mind, though, was the realization that Suzie already had a boyfriend. She and I were able to see each other only because he was student-teaching in another town. He did have a car, though, and they had a standing date every Tuesday night. So if I wanted her to be mine, I had a lot of work to do.

One of those Tuesdays was March 19, Suzie's twenty-first birthday. I went to see her in the afternoon and reached her dorm just as a package was arriving from her mother. The weather was nice, and the box was large, so we went outside and sat on the lawn to open it. Inside was a frilly pink dress and a pink wristwatch to match. Suzie was delighted, and so was I. She couldn't linger, though. Her boyfriend was coming to take her out, and she had to get ready for him.

I hid behind some bushes and waited so I could see them take off together. Sure enough, he showed up. He was driving a Chevy Corvair with a straightened wire hanger for a radio antenna. I watched him enter the building and then come out with Suzie on his arm. Like a gentleman, he opened her car door for her. Then he got in the other side, and off they went.

I knew now that Suzie was what I had always wanted. She was Lorna Doone. She was Linda Sericchio. She was Mary Wray. She was every Alitalia stewardess I had ever admired. Her perfect features, her dark hair and olive skin, her beautiful figure, all were perfection to me.

And then one day, I kissed her. We were sitting in a big chair at her dorm, enjoying each other's company. When she got a little close, it just seemed to happen. I think I was as surprised as she was. Years later, she would tell me she loved that first kiss and wondered why it took so long for me to get around to it. But to me, there was something awkward about it. It felt like I had crossed the line with someone else's girlfriend.

What I really had crossed, though, was the great divide. No longer was I just Suzie's friend. From now on, I was her sweetheart, and there would be no going back. After that day, she never went out with Jack Wall again.

I hate to break the mood, but this same week, President Johnson was preparing to make an announcement. On March 30, at the end of a televised speech from the White House, he said he would neither seek nor accept his party's nomination for re-election in the fall. Later, it would be said that his health and the fatigue of five years in office were the culprits, but it seemed obvious to me that he was afraid of being defeated. The antiwar candidate, Senator Eugene McCarthy, had done well enough in the New Hampshire primary to deny Johnson getting a majority of the vote. Encouraged by this, Robert Kennedy was now in the race. It was already clear that defending Johnson's handling of the war would have been a real dogfight.

Six days later, on April 4, Martin Luther King Jr. was assassinated in Memphis, Tennessee. We were barely three months into the year, but 1968 was going to be one for the history books.

The week King was assassinated, I was approached by Dylan Smith with a proposition. His lawyer had advised him that things might go easier for both of us if we showed up in court already having paid restitution. By his reckoning, as well as mine, not much money would be necessary, maybe $1,000 at most. Neither of us had that much, of course, and there were few opportunities to earn it in a town as small as Clarion. Dylan thought we should both move in with his parents down near Pittsburgh, where temporary jobs would be easier to find. I had no desire to leave Suzie so early in our relationship, nor did I particularly want to move in with Dylan's parents. Nonetheless, I knew he had a point, and I agreed to go along.

As soon as we got to Pittsburgh, Dylan found a job working in the service department at a Porsche dealer. I went to work delivering free samples of Tab, the original sugar-free Coca-Cola, door to door. It was only the second job I ever had, and I was paid $1.75 an hour. By the time we returned to Clarion for our trial, we had enough cash to take care of things. Surprisingly, our victims would accept our funds only reluctantly. None of them felt we had taken that much, but we assured them we had.

Our trial came on May 30, a Friday. Mike Maloney was there, the guy who double-crossed me out of my bail money. I didn't even make eye contact with him. We waited our turn as half a dozen or so other cases were taken first. Amazingly, every one of them was for fornication and bastardy, a crime I didn't even know existed.

When our case was called, the judge asked how we wanted to plead. All three of us responded, "Guilty, Your Honor!" This was Judge Weaver, an elderly man who had been on the bench for decades. We had been warned he would give us six- to fifteen-month sentences. Such was his custom in first-time burglary cases, and our being clean-cut college students would make no difference. In fact, our case just might be a useful example to other students thinking of committing such crimes.

Sure enough, six to fifteen months was what Dylan and I got. Mike, though, got three to six, largely thanks to our having vouched for his limited involvement. The three of us were taken away immediately and marched out the back door of the courthouse and across the street to the jail.

To me, at age twenty, six months seemed like a very long time. How lucky I was to have Dylan there with me. No, the Clarion County Jail wasn't a dungeon. Nobody was going to beat me or put me in solitary confinement. None of the other prisoners would ever attack me physically or threaten me with homemade weapons. This was just a small county jail where, for the most part, everyone could be expected to get along. Most were in for nonviolent crimes like burglary or passing bad checks, though there were two murderers. One was an older man, by appearances a harmless fellow who had just completed ten years at the state penitentiary. He had been moved to Clarion pending release. His crime? Having caught his wife drinking with her boyfriend at the VFW club, he pulled out a gun and shot the guy dead.

The other murder was by a habitual criminal who had spent most of his life behind bars. He was just in Clarion to be tried for some crime or other that he had committed there. He was good-natured, but the other inmates were careful to give him his space. One night, while everyone slept, he was going to bend the bars out of a window and take off running. None of us knew that kind of strength was humanly possible, but somehow he did it. Several weeks later, the jailer told us the guy had been recaptured somewhere in West Virginia, but he was never brought back, at least not while I was there.

Of course, I would have loved to escape, too, and who knows, maybe I could have found a way. But as far as I could see, escape was for lifers. A six-monther like me would have to be an idiot to do such a thing.

So I was stuck there, locked up every night in a cell, never seeing the outdoors and existing amid people with whom I had little in common. There was no TV, no access to a telephone, and in my case, little chance of receiving visitors. Visits were mostly limited to immediate family members, and mine were nowhere near Pennsylvania.

One day, though, someone did show up at the jail to drop off some books for me. It was Kathy Byrne, a smart and beautiful girl I knew mostly through Suzie. She had checked out the books at the college using her own library card, and she did so without even asking if I wanted them. I set to work reading them immediately, and two weeks later, she returned with even more books.

Suzie, meanwhile, was spending the summer living with her family and working as a waitress at the Chartiers Country Club near Pittsburgh. She was a busgirl at first, but then they put her to work as a waitress down by the swimming pool. Because her parents didn't have the means to help, she had been going to college out of her own pocket and with student loans.

There was a lot going on in America that summer in 1968. On June 6, just two months after Martin Luther King's death, Bobby Kennedy was assassinated. He had just won the important democratic presidential primary in California. In July, Benjamin Spock, the famous baby doctor, was convicted for promoting draft evasion. In August, the Republicans nominated Richard Nixon for president in Miami. He had succeeded in resurrecting his political career by campaigning around the country for other candidates and by promising "peace with honor" for Vietnam. Two weeks after Miami, Hubert Humphrey won the democratic nomination in Chicago, but massive demonstrations and police overreaction created a distasteful spectacle that would severely hurt his chances.

All this and more I learned about each night listening to a transistor radio I was allowed to have. I would read my books until lights-out, and then I would lie there, catching what news I could in the dark with the volume turned down low. Afterward, I would tune into a music station and listen to the same popular songs every night. "Hey Jude" by the Beatles, "This Guy's in Love with You" by Herb Alpert, "Classical Gas" by Mason Williams, "Mrs. Robinson" by Simon and Garfunkel, and "MacArthur Park" by Richard Harris were some of the most frequently played. I heard them over and over.

At the end of three months, Mike Maloney was released. I was glad to see him go. He and I had never spoken the entire time he was there. With autumn coming on, I now turned my attention to Suzie, and I wondered if she would come around. Kathy Byrne was still bringing me books, and I knew the two of them were good friends. Then, one day, it happened. They came together to pick up my finished books and drop off some new ones. I knew they had been there, because they walked around the outside of the jail afterward, and I could see them out the window. When the jailer brought in my books, I noticed one of them, *David Copperfield*, was quite a bit fatter than the others, and I decided to read it first. It quickly became my favorite book and has remained so throughout my life.

Not long after that, Kathy and Suzie found out that church groups were coming to the jail to conduct Sunday services with the inmates. One Sunday morning, the two of them showed up out front wearing their most conservative dresses. They asked the minister if they could join in, and without consulting the jailer, the minister consented. That morning, I sat next to Suzie on a bench in the heart of the Clarion County Jail, holding hands and praising Jesus like I'd never done before or since. She was so tanned from working out by the pool that summer. She had never looked more beautiful.

Before the congregation parted, I let Suzie know about an upcoming appointment I had at the dentist. If she happened to be in the waiting room at the right time, she could see me there too. I really didn't have a toothache, but I had put in a request weeks earlier because I knew it could be a rare opportunity to step out into the sunlight.

When the day arrived, I was put in handcuffs and escorted by two officers down Main Street. Sure enough, when we reached the dentist's office, Suzie was sitting there in the waiting room, anticipating my arrival. She knew better than to speak to me with the officers watching, but the smile on her face said everything. I might have lost some weight, and I might be pale as a ghost, but thank goodness, I was still her boyfriend.

The only other time I got out of doors during the entire six months was a few weeks later, when help was needed unloading a dead deer out of a pickup truck. I was only outside for two or three minutes, but I savored every second of it. Roadkill venison is plentiful in northwestern Pennsylvania, and it was the only red meat we were ever given at the jail.

Not long after that, I received my first official visitor when a tall dark-haired man of about fifty came to see me. He was wearing a black suit and a clerical collar, so I knew at once he was a Catholic priest. Standing in the visitor's cage at the cellblock entrance, he introduced himself to me as Father Somers. "I am not here to proselytize you," he promised, and surely he wasn't. Instead, he was there just out of caring for his fellow man.

I liked Somers immediately. He had a natural kindness about him and a gift for the English language that made him both endearing and fascinating to me. He quickly made it apparent that he was no ordinary clergy. Mostly, he explained, he was an academic serving on the faculty at the college. How he came to hear about me, he didn't say, but he called on me twice, and both visits meant a lot.

My other visitor, believe it or not, was Dad. Having some business in New York, he had decided to tack on a side trip to Clarion. That was going to be a lot of trouble for a one-hour visit, but he must have thought it important. Meanwhile, I still remembered the time he went all the way to Austria to keep me from being expelled at AIS, so I felt pretty humble about the whole thing. While he was there, he told me that the house in Vermont was finished. He and Mom were going to spend the Christmas holidays there, and they wanted me to join them. He explained that the key to the house would be available for me in the offices at the Bolton Valley Ski Lodge. Then, for the first time, I learned about the trouble Mark was in, which explained Mom's sudden departure before my trial.

Then it was October, and the presidential race was in its final weeks. The polls were indicating another close one for Richard Nixon, but this time he was going to win. When the time came, I was able to hear the election returns on my transistor radio, just as I had followed the Olympic results from Mexico City two months earlier. That was how I learned that two black American medalists had raised their fists at the playing of the "Star Spangled Banner."

One Saturday afternoon in November, I heard voices calling me from the dayroom. When I went to investigate, I saw that some of the inmates were looking out one of the windows. Outside on the sidewalk, which was some fifty feet away, were Suzie and Raine dressed in eagle costumes. They had volunteered to act as mascots at the college football game, and they wanted me to see how they looked. Suzie had bleached her hair blond, and the cap on one of her front teeth had fallen out. For the first time ever, I had no desire for her to come any closer. Afterward, though, I thought about how her life had continued while mine was frozen in place. I wondered how long our relationship would last after my release.

In the middle of November, Dylan and I both sent handwritten notes to Judge Weaver. We knew our eligibility for release wasn't until the day after Thanksgiving, and we wondered if he might let us out a couple of days prior.

On Tuesday, November 26, four days before the completion of our six-month sentence, the jailer called out Dylan Smith's name and told him he was going to see the judge. Dylan was gone about twenty minutes. When he came back, he was very happy. He had been told to gather his things. He was free to go.

Then it was my turn. I was led into the courthouse and up the stairs to the judge's chambers. In a few minutes, the judge was explaining to me the conditions for my release. For the next nine months, I was to notify him of any changes I made in location, and if I got caught committing any crimes, I would have to come back to the jail immediately and serve an additional nine months. I asked if I was free to go up to Vermont to spend Christmas with my parents, and he said I was.

I returned to the jail and collected my things, including what the jailer had been holding for me. He handed me the envelope containing, among other things, my own $190 and my belt. I thanked him and headed out the door.

Perhaps fittingly, the walk back to the college was the very same walk I had taken little more than two years earlier when I first got off that bus from Pittsburgh. At that time, my life was a clean sheet of paper, but now I knew things would be different. Even so, I chose not to think of the mistakes I had made. All I wanted was to find Suzie.

SIXTEEN

The Wedding

Suzie and I spent that night together in the apartment of a friend. The next day, she shared a ride with some other girls down to Pittsburgh for Thanksgiving. I caught a ride with Dylan, whose father had driven up to get him. On Thursday, using Suzie's instructions, I caught a city bus out to McKees Rocks, where her family lived. I got off at Kenmawr Plaza Shopping Center and called her from a phone booth. She told me to start walking up Fairhaven Road. She would walk in my direction and meet me halfway.

I started up the hill, and after several minutes, I spied her coming toward me. It was one of those rare autumn days in western Pennsylvania when the sun shines brightly, the sky is brilliant blue, and just a few giant white clouds are floating by. Suzie was dressed in jeans and a tight pullover sweater that showed off her extraordinary figure. At twenty-one, she really was a young woman and not a teenager anymore. Her exotic Italian looks were so striking. I marveled at how she could still consider me her boyfriend.

We stood there hugging on the side of the road, and of course, I kissed her. Over and over, I told her how pretty she was. It was all I could think to say. I took her hand, and then we started in the direction of her parents' home at 131 Connie Park Drive.

When we reached the front door of the modest split-level house, we were greeted by a young woman who looked a lot like Suzie and was every bit as beautiful. "David, this is my sister, Audrey," Suzie said.

Hardly were we inside on the landing before another stunning brunette, their mother, appeared at the top of the stairs. Suzie hadn't prepared me for this. Mrs. Albanesi, who was only thirty-nine years old, looked for all the world like a movie star. I knew I must be blushing, and I fought hard to conceal it.

Their Thanksgiving dinner had already been cleared from the table, but Suzie asked me if I was hungry. I said I was, and she took me to the kitchen. She said she would make me a turkey sandwich, and she asked me how I wanted it.

"Just mayonnaise and cranberry sauce," I said.

"Cranberry sauce? Really? In your sandwich?" She had never heard of such a thing.

Having been locked up for six months, I had sorely missed being in the company of females. Yet here I was, free for only two days and already surrounded by three gorgeous ones. One of them was even feeding me. That was new! Had I died and gone to heaven? As I sat there watching Suzie make my sandwich, I thought, *This is the girl I'm going to marry.*

Of course, there were other members of Suzie's family. There was Vince, her father, and her younger brother, Vincie. Suzie had told me a little about them before. Both were quiet, serious types, introverts, really. Vince was a hardworking TV repairman who never took a day off. When he wasn't at the shop doing service work, he was making house calls or repairing sets in his garage. Vincie, on the other hand, was an aspiring rocker who, at seventeen, already played guitar in a band and hung out with his long-haired bandmates. He'd always been a good kid, according to Suzie, but lately he had become rebellious.

Then there was Mary Ann. At twelve, she was the youngest member of the family. She was very good-humored and outgoing, just as Suzie had described her. She was just learning to play chess, and she wanted to take me on that very night.

Finally, there was Grandma, Suzie's maternal grandmother, who, sadly, had none of the beauty of the other women in the family. Grandma had led an impoverished life, having her babies out of wedlock and surviving the Depression by a combination of running numbers and bootlegging. Her live-in boyfriend had killed himself by asphyxiation in the garage one day while they were still in their thirties. Nearly toothless now, Grandma spent her days in the basement, chain-smoking cigarettes and doing the family ironing to a constant stream of TV soap operas and game shows.

It would have been nice if I could have just stayed there with Suzie and her family forever, but that simply couldn't be. My parents were planning to spend Christmas at their new ski lodge at 407 Thatcher Road in Bolton, and they expected me to join them. After all my mistakes, I was determined not to fail them. They wanted me to spend December getting the house ready for their arrival. This really just meant shoveling the snow off the driveway every day, which would turn out to be a surprisingly big undertaking.

I did spend that Christmas with them. Afterward, Mom and Dad were ready to leave again. I wanted to return to Clarion to finish my degree, but they thought that would be a mistake. Better I should get a room at the YMCA in Burlington, enroll at the University of Vermont and leave my past behind. This didn't appeal to me, of course. I would miss Suzie a lot. I knew that for sure. But I felt it important to please Mom and Dad, so I agreed.

Mom, meanwhile, enrolled Mark at Cardigan Mountain, a private boarding school for boys in New Hampshire. Having had plenty of behavior problems of his own, Mark wouldn't be going back to Libya this time.

My parents did return to Tripoli that winter, first Dad, and then Mom. After I dropped Mom off at the Burlington Airport, I drove into the city and looked at a room in the YMCA, but I couldn't go through with it. I didn't know a soul in that town. What's more, given my track record, I doubted the university would ever accept me.

Mom had told me to forget about those "silly girls" back in Pennsylvania, but I was obsessed with getting back to Suzie. So I left the car at the house in Bolton and hitchhiked my way back to

Clarion. I knew how my parents would feel about this, but I couldn't let that matter. I had to do what I had to do.

As soon as I found Suzie, I asked her to marry me. Yes, I only had a year and a half of college, but I had lived away from my parents for almost five years now, and I longed for companionship. My parents were in Libya, a place I knew I would probably never see again. My siblings, my friends all were spread out around the world in places I didn't even know. Yet here was Suzie, whom I adored. She was kind. She was caring. She was smart. She was everything I wanted.

Of course, neither of us had any money. Nor did we have jobs or even an idea how we might support ourselves. It was foolish even contemplating marriage under the circumstances. But I was too young and too motivated to care.

Suzie was still going to church on Sundays. Often, she was up on the altar, playing the tambourine while hymns were being sung. She didn't really believe the doctrine anymore, but she enjoyed the liturgy and liked being among the parishioners.

There were three priests in town. Father Somers was one of them. He was the fiftyish intellectual whose visits had meant so much to me when I was in jail. Father Zeitler was another, a much younger man of thirty or so. He counseled students at the campus Newman Center with a cheerfulness and enthusiasm that made him a favorite with the kids. And finally, there was Father Meizinger, an older man who was the parish priest. If Suzie was going to marry me, she wanted to consult at least one of these three men first. For some reason, she chose Father Meizinger.

When we met, I guess I expected the good pastor to approve of our plans right away, but he didn't. How could he? It takes more than love to sustain a marriage, he explained, and he suggested we put off our plans until later.

Rats! I thought. *That's not what I want to hear.*

Disappointed, I let things go for a few weeks. Then one day, I approached Suzie again. I reminded her that I was not a Catholic, and I suggested we get a second opinion by going to see Judge Weaver at the county courthouse. She agreed, and I made the phone call.

Judge Weaver was probably just as old as Father Meizinger, maybe older. He looked across his enormous desk at the two of us huddled before him, and then spoke.

"Hold off," he said, "until you are ready!"

After that, I dropped the subject for a while. Summer was approaching, so I started working on my next brainstorm. Why couldn't we, I wondered, hitchhike to a seaside resort, get jobs, save up some money, and then take off for a happy life of wandering in Europe? Already, we had done some serious hitchhiking around the East Coast with our friends Kathy Byrne and Rick Sherbondy. Why couldn't we do the same thing in Germany or France?

Suzie, bless her heart, thought this was a wonderful idea. When I told Kathy and Rick about it, they agreed. In fact, they said they would go too. Then another friend, Linda Loxterman, said she wanted to go. My goodness, this was getting more interesting by the hour.

For some reason, we selected Ocean City, Maryland. Just to be sure we could find work and a place to stay, Rick and I decided to go on ahead of the girls and check it out. Early one morning, we loaded our sleeping bags, our backpacks, and our guitars into the trunk of friend's car and got a lift down to the Pennsylvania Turnpike at Swissvale.

With so much baggage, we thought it might be a challenge getting someone to pick us up, and sure enough, it was. So agreeing to meet the next day in front of the Ocean City post office, wherever that was, we split up.

It took me only two rides to get all the way to Ocean City. My first driver was a young airman headed for Dover, Delaware. He was pleasant enough, though neither of us did much talking. Outside of Dover, I was picked up by a very talkative Jewish man from New York City. He was nice enough, too, at first, but when he saw the German camera I was carrying, my father's Rolleiflex, he became irritated.

"Do you know what that camera cost?" he asked, raising his voice. "Two Jewish lives, that's what. Two Jewish lives!" Then he launched into a lecture about the Germans and the Holocaust.

I completely sympathized with his point of view, but sitting there in his car with no possible way to conceal my blond hair and blue eyes, and clutching my father's Rolleiflex, I confess, I was pretty anxious to get to Maryland.

Ocean City sits on a narrow ten-mile stretch of sandbar connected to the coastline by a bridge. We crossed that bridge just as the sun was going down, and then he stopped to let me out. Lights were already coming up along the Boardwalk, so I slipped on my backpack, picked up my guitar and sleeping bag, and headed in that direction. Soon, I was standing on the boards, gazing down at the people on the beach and the surging ocean behind them. All around me, folks were strolling in the evening air, taking in the sights and sounds of the boardwalk.

I knew I was going to sleep on the beach that night. There was no other choice, if I was going to conserve what little money I had. But the smell of caramel corn in the air was reminding me that I needed to eat. So I chose a direction and started walking. Before long, I reached a man selling hot dogs, and I bought one.

I felt so free and happy that night, walking among the tourists and the vendors with their saltwater taffy and souvenirs. I came upon a head shop selling psychedelic T-shirts. I couldn't afford to buy one, but the shirts were displayed under a black light, and I marveled at how it made them look.

By now, my day had been a long one. I noticed that people were mostly gone from the beach, so I began to look for a restroom and a place to roll out my sleeping bag. That night, I slept under the boardwalk with the sound of the ocean in my ears.

When I awoke, the beach was nearly deserted, but seagulls were soaring and screeching in the wind. I ate a piece of chocolate I had in my pack, and then I went off to use the restroom. My first order of business now was to try to locate Rick. I wasn't expecting any difficulty. In fact, I was half-surprised I hadn't already seen him walking up and down the beach. After getting directions from a vendor just opening his stall, I made off in the direction of the post office.

There was a problem, though, of which neither Rick nor I had been aware. Ocean City, Maryland, is not the only Ocean City on the East Coast. In fact, there is another Ocean City only eighty miles away in New Jersey. And while I was at the one we had intended, Rick's ride had taken him to the other one. I still didn't know this as I walked back and forth between the post office and the boardwalk all day, so I was getting worried. Thankfully, though, Rick had figured things out and was on his way. We found each other late that afternoon, down at the beach.

Ocean City turned out to be just what we were looking for. We both managed to score jobs right away at a hotel called the George Washington. I told our interviewer I had enough short-order experience to be a cook in the downstairs café. This, of course, was total nonsense, but I thought I could fake it. Rick, on the other hand, was a little more honest. He was hired to do pretty much anything and everything. What really clinched the deal, however, was when they offered us free living space in a dormitory behind the hotel.

Delighted with our good fortune, we dropped off most of our things at the dormitory and headed back to Pennsylvania to collect the girls. When all five of us returned to Ocean City a few days later, the girls were hired on the spot, and they were also given rooms in the dormitory. Suzie and Kathy would be waitresses in the dining room, Linda a waitress in the café.

In the meantime, another short-order cook had been hired, and this one actually had some experience. So by copying everything I saw him doing, I could learn to manage. As it turned out, though, the hotel was under new owners. Things were so disorganized that within days all five of us were talking about finding someplace else to go.

Throughout all this, I was still thinking about marriage. So I broached the subject again, and once again, Suzie thought we should talk to a priest. We found one down the boardwalk, a ruddy-complexioned, stocky man with a broad smile and a pleasant disposition. His name was Father Mack. But of course, once he heard our story, he, like the others, advised us to wait.

I was tired of putting it off, and frankly, so was Suzie. She was beginning to have doubts about the propriety of our hitchhiking around the country together as singles. So on June 16, a Monday, we thumbed a ride into Snow Hill, the county seat of Worcester County. We located the courthouse and went in to apply for a marriage license. We were told we had to wait a day before the law would allow us to get married, so we caught another ride back to Ocean City.

The next morning, June 17, 1969, was sunny and beautiful. Linda was scheduled to work, but Kathy, Rick, Suzie, and I all had the day off. So the four of us got dressed, had some breakfast in the hotel kitchen, and then headed out to the highway to hitch a ride to Snow Hill.

You never know who is going to pick you up when you are hitchhiking. One day you get a driver who is fascinating or friendly or both. The next day you find yourself in the company of someone who scares you. You just never know. But the ride we caught on this most memorable of days was one of those marvelous encounters in life that just happens to come along at the perfect moment. Hardly had we gotten our thumbs out before a thin middle-aged man in a blue-and-white sedan pulled over and asked us where we were going.

"Snow Hill," we all said in unison.

And then Kathy gleefully offered, "We are going to a wedding!"

"Wonderful," he said. "Hop in!"

We all climbed into the car.

"Whose wedding is it?" he asked.

"They're sitting right next to you!" said Kathy from the back seat. "David and Suzie!"

At this point, just about any other middle-aged person on the planet might have thought himself in the company of idiots. After all, none of us looked anything like members of a wedding party. Rick and I both had our guitars, and all of us were wearing blue jeans. Suzie had on a very loud yellow-and-red paisley dashiki, and as hard as it is to imagine, she was out hitchhiking with no shoes on. Yet to this man, running into us was a cause for celebration!

As we continued down the highway, he told us his name was Bill Gale. He said he was from Wilmington, Delaware. He had just been released from Johns Hopkins in Baltimore, where he had been receiving psychiatric treatment. He explained that he and his wife

220

had a tradition of vacationing separately every year. Only, this year, he hadn't planned anything in advance. We had caught him wandering down the Maryland coast, simply looking for something to do.

"My wife told me I could spend $1,000," he said, "and until you guys came along, I had no idea what I was going to do. But I do now!"

So now there were five of us. We arrived in Snow Hill and pulled up in front of the courthouse. I went inside, but the clerk was away at lunch. Bill parked the car, and everyone got out. We chatted for a while. Rick and I played our guitars. Then, after a time, I went back inside and picked up our marriage license.

Next, Bill insisted we get the bride some flowers, so we walked a couple of blocks over to where we were told there was a gift shop. We waited inside while Bill had a white bouquet made up for Suzie. He picked up a roll of film for his camera, and he bought Suzie a little makeup compact as a gift. Suzie, meanwhile, read poems to us all from an E. E. Cummings book she had taken down from the shelf.

Then it was time to find a church. We had noticed a couple of them in the center of town, so we headed in that direction. We reached the first one but found no one there, so we walked down the street to the second one.

It was the First Presbyterian Church, and for us, nothing in particular distinguished it from any other, except, that is, at this one a pastor was present. We asked him if he would marry us, and he said he would. His wife and daughter might like to be present, though. Could we wait just a bit while he ran to get them?

There were scaffolds set up behind the altar. The church was being renovated. But with its stained glass windows and vaulted ceiling, I thought it a fine setting for our ceremony. After several minutes, the pastor appeared with his wife and daughter. You could see in their faces they were excited. With so much joy in the room, you'd have thought we were all getting married!

Suzie and I stood side by side that Tuesday afternoon as the pastor led us through our vows. When he was nearly finished, he looked up at me and asked if there was a ring. I produced a little rose ring I had bought Suzie months ago on Main Street in Clarion, and I slipped it on her finger.

After the ceremony, we paused to take a couple of pictures. We were all smiles, but I remember thinking the pastor and his wife must not expect this one to last very long.

Then we exited the church and headed back to Bill's car. Bill remembered a secluded stretch of beach, and he wanted to take us there so we, as he said, "could commune with nature." For an hour or so, we did just that. Then we drove back to Ocean City.

We found Linda, and then Bill took all five of us to the Phillips Crab House for an early dinner. When we arrived, I saw the large round opening in the brick facade of the building, and I asked Suzie to climb up into it with her bouquet so I could take her picture. She still wasn't wearing any shoes.

Later, Bill took us back to the George Washington. He was going to leave us now, but we exchanged addresses so we could get copies of the pictures he had taken.

Then, Suzie and I walked down the boardwalk in the pink light of evening until we reached a nearby phone booth. She wanted to call her mom.

"Mum…hi," she said when her mother answered. "Guess what!"

What I remember next is Suzie saying over and over, "But, Mum, it's my wedding day. You should be happy. Aren't you happy? It's my wedding day!"

Then she handed me the phone, and did I ever feel awkward. Here was this wonderful woman being treated almost thoughtlessly by someone she hardly knew. Why couldn't I have waited just long enough for her to be at her daughter's wedding? How foolish this all must seem, and how guilty I suddenly felt.

But my new mother-in-law had just the right thing to say, more so, in fact, than I could have expected. "Welcome to the family, David. I want you to call me Mom."

SEVENTEEN

Back to College

The George Washington had been purchased by a private family, none of whose members appeared to have the slightest idea how to run a hotel. The café, where I was just learning to short-order-cook, was staffed entirely by students on summer break who had no more experience than I did. This could have been made to work, but unfortunately, the manager was incompetent. He knew nothing of how to cook or serve food. Nor did he have any grasp of how to motivate his people. Instead, he continuously insulted everyone.

The hotel's main dining room, where the girls worked, was no better. The chef was a hopeless alcoholic who couldn't put out an edible meal. By the time Suzie and I got married, it was clear to all five of us we were going to have to move on. We had just enough dollars between us to hitchhike up to Rhode Island. The Newport Folk Festival was a month away, and we wanted to experience it.

To celebrate the wedding and our departure, Rick announced he had a special treat to share. He had acquired some LSD from a stranger on the beach. Wouldn't we all like to give it a go? Well, the girls wanted nothing to do with the stuff, but callow fellow that I was, I jumped on the idea. By now, all of us had a notion of what tripping was about. We had certainly heard plenty about it. It was supposed to be a wonderful, mind-bending experience, a sort of journey through storybook land. Shapes and colors were supposed to come to life as though they were living organisms.

That day, the first one of my new marriage, Kathy, Rick, Suzie, and I went down onto the beach and found a place to sit in the sand. Then, Rick took out two small scraps of paper with what looked like little inkblots on them. Without hesitation, he and I each swallowed one.

I cannot say I have ever been proud of having started out my marriage in this manner, and I won't go into detail about what I experienced. I will say, though, that for me, LSD was everything it was cracked up to be and a whole lot more. I enjoyed it immensely! Nonetheless, I knew there would be no place for illicit drugs in my life.

A day later, our senses had recovered; we packed our things and headed out the door. Faced again with the problem of finding someone willing to pick up four people carrying backpacks and guitars, we split into two couples. Rick and Kathy would meet up with Suzie and me that night, if possible, at the main post office in Newport, some four hundred miles from our starting point. We were, of course, assuming there was a main post office, and fortunately, there was. But we didn't find one another there until the following morning.

We spent our first day looking for employment. How preposterous it seems to me now that we thought we could get jobs when we didn't even have an address. We intended to sleep in a city park until we had earned enough to rent something. Anyway, it didn't matter, because we quickly found the Newport job market had nothing to offer.

Next, we went to Greenwich, Connecticut, a town that, of course, was familiar to me. Right away, we found a rental room the four of us could share on Greenwich Avenue. At the bottom of the street, down at the waterfront, there was a hotel and restaurant called the Showboat Inn. It was at the wharf, and tied up alongside of it was an old steamboat. By now, Rick and I were confident the girls could get employment just about anywhere. Both were pretty, and both had a lot of personal charm. So we tried the Showboat Inn first, and sure enough, they got hired as waitresses. "Oh, and by the way," the boss said, "the steamboat could use a fresh coat of paint." Would Rick and I be interested? You bet we would.

After two weeks, though, we had painted that boat stem to stern, and we were back out on the street. Furthermore, having been barely squeezed into the schedule, the girls couldn't possibly get the hours in the dining room to make enough money. I think it was Kathy who suggested we move on again and try our luck in New Haven. Thanks to Yale University, it was a prominent college town, and I guess she thought we might find it a more exciting place to be.

As soon as we got there, the four of us pooled our money again, and this time, we managed to rent the third-floor apartment of a pleasant townhouse. Within a few days, the girls were working as waitresses at a nearby restaurant, and I managed to get on as a trainee cook in the kitchen at Saint Raphael's hospital. We bought some used bicycles to get around on, and for the first time all summer, things were seeming tenable.

All four of us helped with the meals, even though I was the only one who had even a vague notion of how to cook. Suzie specialized in making ice tea, partly because she loved the stuff, but also because it was the only thing she knew how to do. Because we were married, she and I were accorded the only bedroom. Kathy and Rick slept on the kitchen floor in their sleeping bags.

I didn't know it at that time, but on the eleventh of July, my friend Jim Ward died in Vietnam. Likewise, I hadn't heard of the death of my other friend, Mike Valunas, which had occurred on March 24, also in Vietnam.

There were big things about to happen, though, that I would know about. On July 20, 1969, the four of us spent the evening in front of our little black-and-white TV set, watching Neil Armstrong take man's first steps on the moon. In August, news came of the gruesome Tate-LaBianca murders in Los Angeles. In little more than two weeks, we had gone from mankind's crowning technological achievement to one of the most heinous crimes in American history.

In our personal lives, though, something even bigger was about to take place. Having missed a period, Suzie made an appointment to see a doctor. We were about to become parents.

What an awakening this was. In an instant, my silly notion of earning enough money to take a group of friends hitchhiking around

Europe was gone. Suddenly, tuning in, turning on, and dropping out held no appeal for me at all. Instead, images of my own father began taking over in my brain. Just as he had provided so responsibly for me and my siblings, so must I now face up to the responsibilities of parenthood.

It was clear to me that getting back into college had to be my first priority. I needed five more semesters to obtain a degree, and it was not going to be easy. After all, I could no longer call upon my parents to pay my expenses. What was more, with a baby to care for, Suzie wouldn't really be able to work. So we would have to make do with whatever I could earn, likely no more than part-time income at minimum wage.

Fortunately, student loans were a possibility. So were food stamps, if necessary. Clearly, if I set my mind to it, we could make this work.

So we explained the situation to Kathy and Rick. They were understanding, maybe even happy. Perhaps they, too, had been thinking of going back to school. If so, our circumstances presented a pretty good rationale. All four of us began packing. We said good-bye to our landlady and made the trip back to Pittsburgh in a modest Ford Falcon that Rick's parents provided. By the time we got to Pittsburgh, Suzie's mother had prepared a bedroom for Suzie and me.

I figured my best bet for immediate income was to stick with cooking. I had learned enough already that I figured I could manage. I went into downtown Pittsburgh and joined the culinary workers' union, which, in turn, referred me to a job opening at Point Park College. They needed a cook in their student cafeteria, so I went down to apply. I was hired at $2.50 an hour.

It wasn't much. Hell, it was hardly anything. Even so, in a few weeks, Suzie and I, with her mother's help, found an affordable first-floor apartment in a run-down old house at 3 Lawson Avenue in nearby Crafton. There wouldn't be enough money for a car, of course. But that would be okay. I could take the bus to work. Our food budget, we figured, couldn't exceed $13 a week. Even in those days, that was a pittance.

Suzie's grandparents provided us with a bed, an old chair, and an even older couch. For a dining room table, Suzie found a used desk and several chairs advertised in the paper. They were free to a good home, so we snatched them up.

By December, Point Park College had let me go. They never said why. Maybe they figured out I wasn't any good, I don't know, though it wouldn't have been for lack of effort on my part. Next, I managed to get hired at the Pick Roosevelt Hotel, where I would be working as a broiler man through lunch and dinner. I caught on quickly there and was soon pretty happy with the work. I found it a lot more pleasant than making cafeteria food.

At home, Suzie and I were eating chicken livers, the only meat we could afford. We were hopelessly poor. On March 8, 1970, our little daughter, Jesse, was born at St. Francis Hospital. We chose *Mary* for her middle name, after Suzie's mom.

It would be difficult to overstate what an important event Jesse's birth was in my life. She arrived in the middle of the night after Suzie had spent many hours in labor. In those days, husbands were not allowed in the delivery room, so I had to wait until they brought her out. Standing there in the hallway with Suzie's mother and father, I felt the mantle of fatherhood for the very first time descend upon my shoulders. That was my daughter I was looking at, *my daughter*. Her eyes opened for just a moment, and then she started to bawl.

Getting back into Clarion was now more important to me than ever before. Within days, I sent a handwritten letter to the dean of admissions, and I described my situation. Would he please overlook my abysmal history and give me a second chance?

When the response came, I was almost afraid to open it. But to my relief, it said I was welcome to come back starting with the summer semester. Many years later, I can say that the success I have had in my life has been due in part to a handful of kind gestures, and this was one of the most important. The dean of admissions might so easily have turned me away. He didn't know me personally, and I can't imagine how he thought any good could come from reaccepting me to the college. Yet that was what he did. Forty-five years later, I still remember his name. It was Walter Hart. Funny, neither he nor his family would ever know what an important difference his kindness would make in my life or in the lives of my wife and children. Without Clarion, I seriously doubt I would have ever finished college.

In early June 1970, I quit my job. Suzie, Jesse, and I rode the bus up to Clarion. Through a real estate office, we located a little house at 415 Pine Street, and we moved in the next day. The rent was $85 a month, which seemed like a lot of money at that time, but I was expecting a student loan, and I had already lined up a campus job doing janitorial work. What was more, Raine said she would subrent one of two tiny bedrooms from us, so we figured we could pull it off.

I took three courses that summer and got an A in each one. There would be plenty more As to come. Of that I was certain.

Money was such a critical issue at this moment in our lives. I could not afford for college to take any longer than necessary. Normally, a bachelor's degree requires four years to complete. I only had a year and a half under my belt, so I had two and a half more to go. I figured, though, that if I took the maximum number of allowable credits each semester, and if I included two full summer sessions, I could graduate in just eighteen months. I knew it wouldn't be easy carrying such a heavy course load and working a campus job at the same time, but it was what I felt I had to do.

Clarion was such a small college. It had always specialized in teacher education, something that didn't really interest me. Liberal arts degrees were offered, however, so that was what I pursued. Before, I had majored in political science, thinking it might somehow apply to a career in diplomacy. Now, though, I dropped that idea. Nobody with a felony record is going to get hired at the State Department, I reasoned. So now I decided to major in English. This might be good preparation for law school or maybe something in advertising.

Meanwhile, Suzie got hired to wait tables at Johnny Garneau's Golden Spike Restaurant. She would be working only at night while I stayed home taking care of Jesse. Without Suzie's tips, we wouldn't survive. My memories of this explain why I have been a generous tipper ever since. If only everyone were so considerate when dining out. The work is hard, and the people who do it often live day to day on just what they take home in their pockets.

By the time I finished school in December of 1971, my parents had figured out where we were. They came down to Clarion to meet their new daughter-in-law and their first grandchild. I guess I should be ashamed of having abandoned them the way I did. My father had always been such a good dad, but my mother was so negative about anything her children ever said or did. Her constant criticism had already driven Dana to run off, and before long, Mark would do the same. So no, I am not ashamed. Mom never would have been in favor of my marrying Suzie, even though doing so turned out to be the best decision I ever made.

Dad was only forty-eight years old at this time, yet unbeknownst to me, he had retired from the company a couple of years earlier. He would tell me one day that the problems he was having with his kids were a part of that decision, but dealing with corporate politics had been the biggest factor. This was a continuous emotional burden he felt he could finally afford to unload. Afterward, he had taken a job teaching high school physics and chemistry in Bolton, but he had soon tired of dealing with disinterested students and dropped that too.

So my parents sold the house in Bolton. Long, freezing-cold winters spent on a Vermont ski mountain hadn't turned out to be such a great retirement idea, after all. Instead, they now planned to relocate to San Francisco and were in the process of doing so when the dreadful news arrived that Nanny had suddenly died of a heart attack.

EIGHTEEN

The Restaurant Business

My father would later say that Nanny was always unhappy, and I do remember her being depressed a lot. She was born in tiny Coal City, Alabama, where her father, Miles Morton Sanders, died from tuberculosis when he was just thirty-three. The family was destitute. Seeking work, Nanny's mother, Elizabeth Electra Seals Sanders, left the little girls behind and took off for Charleston, South Carolina. Nanny (Dovie) was seven then, and her sister Blanche was even younger. In time, Elizabeth got a job managing a boardinghouse and was able to send for her children.

Nanny was a teenager, working in that boardinghouse, when Bumpa (Ernest) came around looking for a room. That was how they met. Nanny couldn't foresee that he would one day rise to the rank of lieutenant commander or that the two of them, with a daughter, would travel the world and be stationed in places like China or the Philippines. She just knew she wanted a better life, and this optimistic sailor seemed like a good prospect. For one thing, he was twenty-two. She was only seventeen.

And so on April 2, 1920, the two of them, known to each other as Dobie and Dovie, were married. Their union would produce just one child, Bumpa's namesake, my mother, Ernestine, who was born on September 16, 1924, in San Pedro, California. With Bumpa gone to sea so much of the time, mother and daughter would be very close. One can imagine how spoiled a child little Ernestine must have been.

Indeed, years later, when Mom was grown and raising a family of her own in Indonesia, Nanny practically grieved over our absence. When Bumpa died in 1960, things got no better. That was why Nanny sold her house in San Diego and moved to be near us in Connecticut.

With no husband around to control her drinking, Nanny quickly started making my mother miserable. At first, she wanted to move in with us, but under the circumstances, Mom wouldn't hear of it. After a couple of years living nearby, Nanny contacted some distant relative in Miami and quickly decided that was the place to be. She called a moving company and headed for the Sunshine State. I remember Mom and Dad thinking this was way too impulsive, but they didn't try to stop her.

Poor Nanny. She died November 10, 1971, at the age of sixty-nine. I don't know what became of her "distant relative," but my grandmother spent the last decade of her life living alone, sitting in front of her black-and-white TV, chain-smoking Parliament cigarettes and drinking one Pabst Blue Ribbon beer after another.

As soon as the news came, Mom and Dad made haste down to Florida. They settled her modest affairs and then flew, with her casket, to San Diego, where she could be buried in Bumpa's grave at Fort Rosecrans.

It's funny how unexpected events can become such important inflection points in life. That was certainly the case in December, when my parents arrived in San Diego. The sudden reminder of how nice the Southern California weather is was enough for them to abandon their plans for San Francisco. They realized now that where they really belonged was in San Diego, the closest thing our family had ever known to a hometown, anyway.

That same December in 1971, I graduated from college. After a two-and-a-half-year absence, I had managed to finish only three semesters behind the rest of my class. I felt pretty good about that. Mom and Dad were already packing their things for the move West, but Suzie and I intended to stay in Clarion long enough for her to get her degree. She had completed the academic requirements already; all that remained were a few gym classes and a semester of student-teaching. But then, within weeks of her starting back, we discovered she was pregnant again.

How was Suzie going to do a bunch of gym classes and go student-teaching while she was having, and then caring for, a new baby? And by the way, how much more of our poverty could we take, anyway? We discussed these things, and then we talked about how much better life was likely to be for my parents in California. Dad was encouraging us to follow them out there, and his point of view suddenly made a lot of sense.

For the rest of Suzie's life, I would feel responsible for letting her drop out so near the end of her college career. She had been an excellent student her entire childhood, and her degree would have been something to make her working-class parents proud. I was reassuring her that we would live in California for just a while and then we would move back to Pittsburgh. That way, she could eventually finish and even spend her life living near her family, if she wished.

What on earth was I thinking? Was I going to be so successful that we could just move around the country at will? Seems pretty silly now, but I believed it.

On March 8, 1972, Jesse's second birthday, we were down at Greater Pittsburgh Airport, saying a tearful goodbye to Suzie's parents and boarding a plane. This was long before cell phones, and given how expensive long-distance calls were at that time, both Suzie and her mother knew what was being lost. I did, too, of course, but I kept comparing Pittsburgh to San Diego in my mind and thinking how good an idea this really was.

"You're taking away my baby," Suzie's mother kept saying as she cried and clung to our little Jesse. But it was too late. We were on our way.

Pittsburgh in early March was all brown and white and freezing cold. San Diego, on the other hand, was pure Technicolor served up at room temperature. We knew the minute we got off the plane that we had made the right decision. My parents were in a rented luxury condo near Mission Bay, where it seemed everyone was either in a swimsuit or Bermuda shorts. Palm trees and bougainvillea were all over the place. This was the life for me.

Mom and Dad had already put down earnest money on a beautiful home, at 4430 Brindisi Street, in the Sunset Cliffs section of town, one of San Diego's most desired neighborhoods. The house was nearly new and had a good view of the ocean, which was just two blocks down the hill. They would be moving in soon, and they would live there for the next forty years.

Suzie and I, meanwhile, had managed to sell our few possessions before leaving Pennsylvania. Providing I got a job fairly quickly, we might have enough money to rent a place of our own. Dad, God bless him, gave us his car, and we went looking. We found a furnished second-floor apartment at 2966 Kalmia Street, and we moved in.

The car was ours to keep. Dad wanted a new one, anyway, and he could see we would be nowhere without it.

Armed with my English degree and a brown double-knit suit I had just bought at Sears Roebuck, I somehow thought employers all over town would be dying to talk to me. I soon discovered that not to be the case.

My greatest interest in college had been creative writing, so I saw myself either in advertising or journalism. First, I checked out the only two ad agencies I could find in the phone book. They turned out to be tiny one- and two-man operations that couldn't possibly use an inexperienced walk-in like me. I didn't even bother asking for an interview. Next, I went downtown to the *San Diego Union* newspaper, but without an appointment, I couldn't get past the security guard.

That night, though, I found a help-wanted ad in the paper. The Zoo had an opening in their advertising department. I couldn't believe my luck! Was it possible that after only one day out looking, I might have a chance at a job in my chosen profession at the world famous San Diego Zoo?

The next morning, I was there when the office opened. They weren't ready to give me an interview, but they did ask me to fill out an application. They would call me, if they were interested.

Out of ideas, I next turned to an employment agency. I thought they would be impressed by my education (can you imagine?), but all they cared about was my work experience, which, of course, had nothing to do with advertising. So they sent me out on a couple of restaurant interviews. Afterward, they told me the employer feedback on me was very poor. One of the employers said I had acted like I didn't even want the job. I had to admit, I remember being asked what I would do if I suddenly came into a lot of money. Without thinking, I had blurted out that I would build a cabin deep in the woods and live off the land. Boy, was I naive!

To be fair, though, I really didn't want those jobs. In fact, I held them in such low regard that I was more concerned about appearing overeager than I was about getting hired. After all, I was an executive! I was Mr. College Graduate! I hadn't put in all that hard work getting my degree just so I could cook hamburgers.

And yet I had a sweet little daughter at home and a beautiful young wife who happened to be pregnant for the second time. Both were counting on Daddy to bring home the bacon, and with what little money we had, Daddy wasn't doing too well.

That night, I called my father and asked for his advice. He said, "Son, you will have opportunities coming at you all your life. When you see them, you will grab them. Right now, though, all you have to do is get started at something, *anything*! It really doesn't matter what."

Years later, I would look back and realize how good Dad's advice had been. The following day, I was sent out on another interview. This time, I was at the Royal Inns of America, a San Diego–based hotel-restaurant chain. Somehow, I got ushered in to talk to the president, and I made sure he knew I wanted the job, *no matter what it was*. I had spent my childhood staying in hotels and eating in restaurants all over the world, and by golly, whatever this job was that he had, it was exactly what I was seeking!

Well, it worked. It turned out there was, in fact, an opening at a freestanding company coffee shop called the Jolly King, in Covina, California, a suburb of Los Angeles. There was a cocktail lounge attached, and they needed a manager-trainee to learn the whole operation. Alas, I would be starting at absolute bottom, and we would already have to leave San Diego, but it was a job, and I took it!

That afternoon, the Zoo called. They had filled the advertising position but wondered if I would be interested in working at one of their fast-food concessions.

Restaurant work is hard. Particularly for a manager-trainee. In college, I had only worked as a cook. Now I was all of it. I washed dishes. I bussed tables. I worked the cash register. I waited on customers. To top it off, the Jolly King was open twenty-four hours a day. I would relieve the manager just before dinner so he could go home, and then I would be there all night supervising cleanup and doing the day's paperwork. Occasionally, we would get a rowdy customer after the bar closed, and I would have to deal with that too. If you broke my salary down by the hour, I was easily the lowest-paid employee in the whole place.

Within a few months, though, the company needed a manager at another store, and they took my boss. I was given my first promotion, becoming full manager of the Covina bar and coffee shop combined.

At about the same time, on October 6, 1972, Suzie went into labor, and our second daughter, Cassandra Elizabeth, was born at the Glendale Adventist Hospital.

We were living in an unfurnished apartment in nearby Azusa, where Suzie was already making friends, but it wouldn't last. Unbeknownst to me, Royal Inns was already failing. Before the year was out, they asked me to transfer to a better location. They were offering me the restaurant manager's job at the Royal Inn in La Jolla, which seemed to me to be as plum an assignment as I could get. La Jolla is San Diego's wealthiest community, and working there would put us a lot closer to where my parents lived. So I accepted.

Within weeks of taking on my new position, I was set upon by something entirely unforeseen. My gallbladder started acting up, and soon I was in too much pain to work.

In those days, removing a gallbladder meant opening up the abdomen, and that entailed weeks of patient recovery. How would my employers be able to save my job for me that long, and for that matter, why would they? I wondered.

In the end, though, the question was moot. By the time I was back on my feet, the restaurant had been turned over to a new operating company. Royal Inns of America was going into bankruptcy.

Just one year out of college, with a wife and two children, I found myself unemployed. It was Christmas. We had moved to another unfurnished apartment, and we were pretty much out of money again.

Fortunately, Suzie had been saving S&H Green Stamps. We were able to cash them in for a couple of meager gifts for little Jesse. We were going to do without a tree, but after dinner, on Christmas Eve, I went down the street to where there were some for sale. I thought maybe, at the last minute, I might just get one for free.

The man there was closing up when I arrived. I asked him for his cheapest tree, and he showed me one that was "only" six dollars, a price that would take most of what Suzie and I had between us.

As I was paying, I asked him, "What do you do with the ones that didn't sell?"

"Tomorrow, we take them around and donate them to the poor," he responded.

I didn't say a thing.

I have come to a few brick walls in my life. This Christmas in 1972 was certainly one of them. Completing college with a near 4.0 average while managing to eke out a living for my little family had been a challenge. So had working long graveyard shifts learning the restaurant business. Somehow, I had expected the world to open up its arms to me, but it just wasn't happening.

Memories like these remind me of how important it is to choose the right life partner. A lesser woman than Suzie might have been completely disillusioned by now. In college, she had been one of the prettiest and most popular girls around. She had plenty of suitors, believe me. Why she didn't view marrying me as a mistake by this point, I don't know. But at times like this, her belief in me, as well as her consistent optimism, is largely what sustained us as a family.

God bless Suzie. She saw the loss of my job as an opportunity for me to find something more rewarding than the work I was doing. And I might have done so, too, but I didn't have the time. I had to find something immediately! When I saw in the paper that an outfit called Colony Kitchens wanted a manager-trainee, I made an appointment for an interview, and I got the job.

I was in training for several months in early 1973, first at the Rancho Bernardo store, then at Oceanside, and finally at San Ysidro. San Ysidro is the southwesternmost San Diego community, sitting on the American side of the border with Tijuana. By summer, I was promoted to manager of that store, and I worked my heart out.

Tourists by the thousands make the drive down to Tijuana in the summer, and at times I think every one of them must have stopped to eat at our restaurant. But I learned an important lesson working there. A really busy restaurant can be even busier, a lot busier, in fact, if it is well managed. A cleaner, better-organized kitchen will be a faster kitchen. A faster kitchen will turn tables faster. This results in more tips for servers and frees up more spaces in the parking lot.

By the end of summer 1974, our sales were up 25 percent over the year before, which, in itself, had been a good year. During the winter, the tourist business had slowed, but we still put up great comparable sales numbers, something that was being noticed at the main office. Now, when the company needed to replace the manager at our flagship operation in San Juan Capistrano, I was the man they called. It was August, the same month Richard Nixon resigned from the presidency. Coincidentally, his home at Casa Pacifica was only three miles from where we would be living.

The Mission San Juan Capistrano is where the swallows return every year. They always do this on the same day, March 19, which happens to be Suzie's birthday. The town is a tourist destination, but it's also a natural stopping point on Interstate 5, because it is located roughly halfway between San Diego and Los Angeles. When the freeway was first completed, a man named Bruce Demeers, who already owned a tiny coffee shop on the Coast Highway in Laguna Beach, saw the opportunity. He built a restaurant and bar near the Mission and became an immediate success.

When I arrived, the place was ten years old. Supposedly, it was the second busiest restaurant in California, after Coke Terrace at Disneyland. Its enormous sales volume, in fact, accounted for the development of the chain of seventy or so other Colony Kitchens throughout the southwestern US. I considered getting this assignment, after little more than a year with the company, a real feather in my cap.

Suzie quickly located a furnished house for rent that was right on the beach, a big deal for someone who grew up in Pittsburgh. She was going to love it, and so would our little girls. Already, we had purchased a new Ford Pinto station wagon, and now I bought a used Honda 350 motorcycle. For the first time, the two of us had the means to get around separately.

Suzie found part-time evening work as an occasional banquet waitress. I, meanwhile, jumped into my new responsibilities with the same urgent determination I had displayed before. Once again, sales comparisons grew rapidly.

To be fair, 1974 and 1975 were years of high inflation. We must have raised our menu prices by a good 10 percent during that period. But my sales in San Juan would grow by 25 percent, just as they had in San Ysidro. In less than a year, we were doing $25,000 a week, pretty darn good, considering we only got $1.75 for a cheeseburger and fries. Coffee was just twenty cents a cup. Once again, I attributed my success to being highly organized. It seemed obvious to me that my predecessors had let business slip through their fingers.

One day in late summer 1975, my boss, a man named Jim O'Halloran, showed up at the restaurant and gave me some very welcome news. At age twenty-seven, with only two and a half years at the company, I was being promoted to district manager.

As excited as I had been about taking on San Juan Capistrano, I was even more excited about my new position in the company. Obviously, I would be getting a bigger paycheck now and more responsibility, but I would also have much more freedom to pick and choose where I wanted to work each day. Instead of putting out fires myself, I would be building a management team to do that for me.

My first step was to report to company headquarters, which was in nearby Costa Mesa. There, I was ushered into Bruce Demeers's office. He asked me a few questions about myself and my family, then he told me what was expected of me in my new role. He wanted to know if I had confidence in my assistant manager, a fellow named Jack Sessions, to take over the store. I said I did, which was true. Jack had been my best assistant at the company, and there had been several.

Next, Mr. Demeers talked about the area I was going to be supervising. The company's newest district, it was also the most far-flung. It included one existing location in Golden, Colorado, and a second property that was about to begin construction in nearby Denver. There were two restaurants in Nebraska, one in Omaha, the other in Grand Island, and two more in the Salt Lake area. Soon, he told me, construction would begin on stores in Provo and Orem, Utah. It would be a challenge, for sure, but he was confident I could handle it. So was I.

I was provided with a brand-new baby-blue Chevy Monte Carlo for both company and personal use, and I was given a credit card to handle all business expenses. "We want you to live in Denver," Mr. Demeers said, "but you will be out of town a lot, so feel free to take your wife to dinner on this card when you are in town. It will be good for both of you."

By now, Suzie and I had been married six years. Never before had we had a spare penny, so I knew Suzie would be excited, and she was. Soon, we were saying goodbye to our new life at the beach and heading for an even newer one by the mountains in Colorado.

Already, in 1973, Israel and her Arab neighbors had fought in what was called the Yom Kippur War. Thanks to America's having aided Israel in the conflict, the Arab nations were now punishing us, and the rest of the world, with an oil embargo. Our government responded by imposing a fifty-mile-per-hour national speed limit to conserve gasoline. It was hard to say how long these conditions might last, but the Colony Kitchen management had decided to take them as a sign of things to come. Even though the company owed its success to people driving on the interstate highway system, Mr. Demeers deemed it necessary to pivot toward serving local customers nearer to where they lived. Most of our new restaurants, therefore, would be constructed within communities instead of out on the highways. My district, being new, was primarily made up of such locations.

Of course, none of these economics really mattered to a twenty-seven-year-old like me. I was just glad to be moving up in the world. I would be flying to most of my stores. After all, if I had to drive between Nebraska, Utah, and Colorado every week, I would have had little time for anything but riding in the car. Flying meant I would be staying in hotels most nights and taking most of my meals in restaurants. All the more exciting, I thought. Boy, after years of struggle, I was feeling important again.

My salary was only $1,400 a month, but Suzie and I had enough money to put down on a building lot in a suburban housing development. By the following spring 1976, I carried her across the threshold of our very own home. The address was 10750 North Parfet Street, Broomfield, Colorado. To come up with the down payment, which was $2,700, we had practically starved ourselves and the kids all winter. It took the sale of my motorcycle for $650 to finally put us over the top. The total purchase price for the house was $37,000.

In the months ahead, I would discover new challenges I hadn't met before. In California, I had succeeded by improving our ability to handle business that was already there. Now, though, the business simply wasn't there. The Omaha store, which was on the second floor of a gas station, was called Mr. Up. It had the same menu as a regular Colony Kitchen, but it almost never had any customers. The only time people showed any interest in dining above a gas station was late on Friday and Saturday nights after the bars closed. Then we would get packed. So we had to employ people willing to work at just those particular times, which was nearly impossible. The store was doomed, and it didn't take me long to figure that out.

The Grand Island store was a Hobo Joe's restaurant. Again, it was essentially the same menu as a Colony Kitchen, and it actually did a good business, but the health department was already trying to shut it down. It was located on Interstate 80, twelve miles south of town, in an area where there was no sewer. It was equipped with a septic tank that didn't function because of its proximity to a wetland. As it turned out, the Grand Island store was doomed, too!

The existing Denver store, actually in Golden, was another failed Mr. Up concept. It did somewhat better than Omaha, but soon after I arrived, the company put it up for sale. They had learned the hard way that nice restaurants didn't do very well when located above gas stations. Meanwhile, construction on a second Denver area store had kept getting delayed over legal problems with the landlord. It never would be finished.

Clearly, I was not the fair-haired boy anymore. Within months of my having taken it over, most of my district, new as it was, was being shut down. Already, I was left with just the two existing, and two more planned, stores in Utah. Why was I living in Colorado?

And so after twelve months in our new home, we sold out and headed for the Beehive State. We took a small loss on the house, but the company graciously made it up to us.

Having already made frequent business trips to Salt Lake, I was able to buy a house before Suzie's arrival. Leaving my company car there, I flew back to Denver to get Suzie and the kids, and we made the long drive together. How well I remember our arrival late that night. Driving down Interstate 80 through Wyoming, we descended the Wasatch Mountains through Parley's Canyon and burst out into the sudden panorama of lights that blanket the Salt Lake Valley at night. Wow! What a sight!

NINETEEN

This Is the Place

It was January 1977. Our new home, the second one we ever bought, was at 9431 South 1335 East in Sandy Utah. It cost $45,000, eight thousand more than our first house a year earlier. My agent, a Mrs. Ballard, was a sixty-five-ish hausfrau of a woman, heavyset, quite cheerful, and always out of breath. She was referred to me by her nephew-in-law, one of my managers, so I had her come around to his restaurant to meet me. I showed her to a booth and immediately offered her a cup of coffee.

"Oh," she said, "no, thank you, David. I'm a Mormon, and we don't drink coffee."

"Oops! I know that," I said. "I just forgot. Let me bring you a cup of tea."

Obviously, I had some learning to do when it came to the Mormons. I knew they didn't drink coffee, but no one told me they didn't drink tea. I must say, rules such as these didn't make a lot of sense to me, but I was eager to learn.

Mrs. Ballard drove me around some of the newer neighborhoods at the southern end of what Salt Lakers refer to as the East Bench. Because of its closer proximity to the spectacular Wasatch Mountain scenery, this was more desirable than the homes down in the valley. Of course, that meant the homes here would cost more too. After a couple hours looking, I realized there was nothing I could afford.

Sensing my disappointment, Mrs. Ballard finally asked, "Well, which house did you like best?"

I told her I liked a bi-level with yellow siding, partly because it was similar to the house we had just given up in Colorado, but also because it was the cheapest.

"Let's call the builder," she said, "and see what we can work out."

A day later, I had the house under contract, but only because Mrs. Ballard reduced her commission substantially. Otherwise, there would have been no deal, not in that neighborhood, anyway.

Once again, someone I barely knew had stepped into my life at just the right moment and given me a boost that would make a lasting difference. After we closed on the home, I never saw or spoke to Mrs. Ballard again, but I would remember her name the rest of my life.

Jesse, meanwhile, was halfway through the first grade. Already we would be enrolling her in her second elementary school. Was her childhood going to wind up like mine, going from school to school? I wondered. Would my company soon be transferring me to yet another location? I wondered about that too. At this point, we barely had a toehold in the middle class. We were still living paycheck to paycheck with no assurance we would ever really prosper. I'm sure I must have had a permanent worried look on my face.

At least I would have better hours now as a district manager, or so I thought. I expected to be spending a few evenings and weekends with my family now, too, but it wasn't going to turn out that way. There were still responsibilities to keep me on the road. I had only been with Colony Kitchens four years, and I had done very well as far as promotions were concerned. But I was making $17,000 a year, a paltry sum, considering my education and how big my job was.

After only a couple of months living in Utah, I was creating a résumé and perusing the help-wanted ads in the *Salt Lake Tribune*. I was hoping there might be some really good opportunity outside of food service that I was qualified for. One Sunday, I found something that piqued my interest. Merrill Lynch was seeking female candidates to train as stockbrokers. That wouldn't include me, of course, but I remembered they had recently lost a court case involving gender discrimination. Maybe their ad was part of an effort to atone. Whatever was going on, they apparently had room for new recruits, and that struck me as an opportunity.

The next day, I called Merrill Lynch and got an appointment to come down into the city and apply. When I got there, my head swirled. I was a coffee shop guy, accustomed to bussing tables and helping out in the kitchen. Suzie was always telling me when I got home that I smelled like food. I did usually wear a tie, but I didn't even own a suit, and my five-year-old car was a bright-orange Ford Pinto, for which I had paid $2,600.

Merrill Lynch was on the third floor of a modern glass building on South Temple Street, adjacent to what was called the ZCMI Mall. Through the windows was a spectacular view of the Mormon Church Headquarters across the street, with its beautiful grounds below by the famous Hotel Utah. Next door was the Kennecott Copper building. I couldn't imagine a more impressive address than this one being anywhere between Denver and Los Angeles.

The Merrill Lynch office was mostly an expanse of forty or so desks equipped with quotation machines. Here, attractive secretaries and brokers in impeccable business suits sat, busily talking to clients on the phone and writing up orders to buy and sell stocks. In the center of the room was a bullpen with theater seating for a dozen or more clients, mostly men, who sat watching stock quotes go by on a large electronic sign. There was money here. You could almost smell it.

I was ushered into a quiet room and given what amounted to an IQ test. When I was done, I was told I would get a call if my score was high enough. A day or so later, the call came, and I was given an appointment to come in for an interview.

I had hired a lot of people myself since my own clumsy attempts at getting a job after college. By now, I knew exactly what attitude to strike. I was interviewed by the sales manager, a man named Steve Cochran, whose dark-haired good looks were the very image of what one might expect on Wall Street. I wasn't intimidated, though. I felt I had enough success under my belt to qualify for an opportunity like this. I told him that, given a chance, I would work hard to make him glad he hired me. I'd be there early in the morning and late into the evening building my business to support my family. If he didn't hire me, I said, I would talk to E. F. Hutton. Hutton, of course, was the competition. The next day, Mr. Cochran called and offered me the job.

Despite my brave face at the interview, I knew I was taking a risk. Suzie and I still had no savings to speak of, and I was going to quit a solid job to become a trainee at something I knew little about. What if I couldn't sell? All those guys in suits might have looked like corporate executives, but they were salespeople! This was a job working for commissions, not salary.

And there was another problem. The application clearly asked if I had ever been convicted of a felony, and I indicated "no," even though it said my background would be checked by the FBI. My father had once told me, "Son, just lie about it. Otherwise, it will hold you back all your life." I knew he was right about that. How could a big-name financial services firm like Merrill afford to put felons to work managing other people's money? They couldn't. And what would happen to me when they found out? The answer to that seemed obvious.

Suzie and I had talked about this. She probably believed in me even more than I did, and she thought a better life was just waiting for us. She urged me to go for it.

I kept recalling the words of my father. "Opportunities will come at you all your life. When you see them, you will grab them!" I thought about Dad's father, a man I never met. He had died when Dad was twenty-five. What a lost resource his death must have been. Throughout my career, my own father, along with Suzie, of course, would be my most important source of wisdom.

I took the job. I started in May of 1977. I was twenty-nine years old. My monthly draw would be $1,200 to start, some $200/month less than I had been making at the old job.

My first day, I was wearing a new suit. One suit was all I could afford, so it was going to get pretty familiar. After a brief get-acquainted meeting with the office manager, I was shown to a desk and given a three-inch-thick loose-leaf binder full of study material. This was to be a correspondence course conducted by the corporate head-quarters in New York. By rule of the New York York Stock Exchange, I would have five months of branch office study, with periodic tests given along the way. If I completed the course successfully, I would be sent to New York for five weeks of training on Wall Street. In addition to that, I would sit for a six-hour exam conducted at the American Stock Exchange. If I passed, I would be licensed as a registered representative, what most people simply called a broker.

That first morning at the Salt Lake office, my study was interrupted when someone announced over the public-address system that the Trans-Alaska Pipeline had just been temporarily shut down. Wow, I thought, announcements like that never happened at the Colony Kitchen. Suddenly, I felt like I was at the nerve center of the universe, and I loved it!

Mostly that summer, I just sat at my desk and studied, but at times, I was called upon to answer phones or help with routine office work. Every day there were news stories about a serial killer on the loose in New York. In a taunting letter to the police, he had called himself the Son of Sam. Using a handgun, he was shooting young women out on the street late at night. I was reading the *Wall Street Journal* regularly now, and I followed the story day by day. Soon, I would be in New York myself, and I wondered if he would be caught before then. Thankfully, he was.

That September, I arrived in the Big Apple, and if anything, I found I was overprepared for the test. Good thing, too, because I came down with appendicitis and needed surgery while I was there. I can't say I enjoyed the experience, but I was happy about missing some of the five weeks of sales training. It surprised me when a few of the other candidates failed the exam and were sent home by Merrill Lynch. Whew. Thank goodness I wasn't in that category.

Back in Salt Lake, I was assigned a desk and an assistant to share with three other brokers. My challenge now was to get on the phone, start calling people who likely had money, and try to drum up some business. Yikes! This might be easy for some, but I knew it wouldn't be for me.

And it wasn't. I discovered immediately that I had a real problem with rejection. At that time, in early 1978, the Dow Jones Industrial Average was trading around 800, almost 20 percent below where it had peaked twelve years earlier in 1966. People I talked to were already so disillusioned with stocks that they had no interest anymore.

There are ways to make money in both up and down markets, however. One way to do so was to trade options. I won't explain them here in detail, but an *option* is a means of using just a little money to control a block of shares. Some options are a bet on the stock going up, others a bet on a stock going down. All are highly leveraged, so if you are as smart as I thought I was, you can achieve a very high return without putting up much cash. One thing, though, it all better happen pretty fast, because options expire, and once they do, they are worthless.

It wasn't until the 1970s that options had been listed on exchanges and traded in an organized way. For that reason, relatively few of the older brokers bothered with them. With their well-established businesses, there was little reason for them to do so. For me, though, options seemed a godsend. First, because they didn't require a large investment, I could show them to just about anybody. In fact, I could even buy them myself with my limited means! Second, because they had an expiration date, they represented a built-in sale to be executed soon, which meant I would get a second commission. Then, presumably, the proceeds would be reinvested in another option with yet another commission. Because of the leverage, little guys, which was what my small handful of clients were at first, could get bigger in a hurry. It seemed obvious to me. If I was going to struggle to find new clients, I was going to have to be very good at pleasing the few I already had. Growing their wealth, I figured, would result in growing mine too. Options were the way to go. Or so I thought.

My first few months in the business, I didn't even cover my $1,200/month draw. I showed up every day in the same suit and read the *Wall Street Journal* front to back. Other brokers were on the phone all day long. I barely ever dialed out. As I write this, many years later, I still don't know why I found it so hard to pick up the phone.

As a new broker, however, I did get the floor duty once or twice a month. On these days, I would take all incoming calls from people who wanted to open an account. I would also receive any walk-ins who didn't already have a broker. Thanks to this, I did slowly start to have a little activity. I would discuss options with almost everyone, and those who were interested became my trading accounts.

By the end of the first year, 1978, I had my production up to a respectable level. Suzie and I felt confident enough to have another baby, and so our daughter Mary was born on February 7, 1979. We named her after Suzie's mother, mostly because I wanted to.

There were probably thirty-five or forty brokers in that Merrill Lynch office. Most of them were experienced men with solid businesses and ample client assets to tend to. I had nothing of the sort. Instead, I had a handful of clients for whom I traded options in a very aggressive way. Yet by the end of the second year, I was one of the top five producers in the office. Can you imagine? The gains I was making for people were so big that some were finding more money to bring me. Others were introducing me to their friends. I was on a roll! In February 1980, Suzie and I sold our house for $68,000 and spent $137,000 on a new one at 3016 Dimple Dell Lane in Sandy. We bought a shiny, new bright-red Audi, and Suzie was wearing a fur coat I gave her for Christmas.

We had finally made it. Or so I thought.

TWENTY

A New Beginning

It seemed like every trade I made for my clients in 1980 went bad. If I bet a stock would rise, it went down. If I bet a stock would go down, it would rise. And because I was using options, most of our positions were winding up worthless. The loss was 100 percent. Two or three trades like that, and my hard-earned clients would be gone, and that was exactly what happened. One by one they left, and I was going home every night a beaten man.

But I wasn't going to let that stop me. No, I was much too smart for that. I had always been good at parlor games. Whether it was chess or Monopoly, or just a game of cards, I always seemed to win. I did well on intelligence tests too. So my bad luck was just temporary. Right?

Wrong. Things got worse.

By the end of 1980, I had good production numbers, but I had very few clients left. Due to historically high interest rates, the monthly mortgage payment on our new house was $1,127. If I didn't do something, we were going to wind up on the street.

As it happened, EF Hutton had just opened a new office in the Sugarhouse section of town. It was strictly for big hitters, and they were offering signup bonuses to brokers from other firms. With few clients left to serve, I really didn't qualify, but I did have the production record, however misleading that might be. Maybe a signup bonus could buy me enough time to get things going again.

I called Nick Bapis and got an appointment. Nick, a man of about forty, was the most successful broker in Utah. While top producers at other firms in town were generating maybe two or three hundred thousand dollars a year in commissions, Nick was producing over a million. He was so big that Hutton had built this new office just for him and anyone he wanted to invite along. After a brief interview, Nick offered me $35,000 cash to come over, which, even in those days, wasn't a lot, but I was in trouble, and I took it.

So once again, I was the new man at the office, and once again, I had no clients, at least not to speak of. My first challenge, obviously, was to start finding investors willing to give a young broker a try. I already knew I was hopeless at making cold calls, but ever since my college days, I had enjoyed public speaking. Now, I decided, was the time to start promoting and conducting investment seminars. I could mass mail invitations, maybe even put an ad in the paper. Somebody was bound to show up.

Great, I had a plan to get new clients, but what was I going to show these people? Surely, I wasn't going to talk about options anymore.

At a loss, I turned to the local library. Despite my training at Merrill Lynch, I felt I was missing something. Maybe among the finance books I might get some ideas. I checked out a skinny book called *The Richest Man in Babylon* by George S. Clayson, and I took it home.

What I read that day set me on a new course that would change my life. *The Richest Man in Babylon* is a series of parables explaining how easy it is to become wealthy and why some people have so much more money than the rest of us. The first and most important tenet of the book is that one must habitually keep one-tenth of his earnings for himself. Spend nine-tenths on food, clothes, whatever, but keep one-tenth for yourself.

"But we don't have enough to live on as it is," a character in the book points out.

"Then why are all your purses equally lean, even though all of you have different incomes?" is the response. The truth is, people tend to adjust their spending to use up their earnings no matter what they are. To avoid this, one must pay himself first. Follow this simple rule, and while others may struggle, you will always have money!

Reading this reminded me of one of my favorite literary characters, Wilkins Micawber, the perennial debtor who says in a letter to David Copperfield, "Annual income twenty pounds, annual expenditure nineteen (pounds) nineteen (shillings) and six (pence), *result happiness.* Annual income twenty pounds, annual expenditure twenty pounds ought and six, *result misery.*"

In other words, pennies a year, one way or another, was the difference between the man who always had money and the man who was headed for debtor's prison.

Okay, so the first thing I had to do was get out of debt. My mortgage was one thing. It put a roof over our heads, and we could expect it to produce a return on investment over time. But what about our credit card debt? And how about the fancy, new automobile I was driving that had car payments to match?

In truth, the 1970s had been a decade of ever-increasing inflation in the United States. With prices rising at a rate faster than the cost of borrowing money, maybe it wasn't all that foolhardy for a needy young family to buy now and pay later. But that was the seventies. Now it was 1981. Interest rates were dramatically higher precisely because a man named Paul Volcker had taken over as chairman of the Federal Reserve Board, and he was determined to stop inflation cold. Our new president, Ronald Reagan, had promised to join the battle, and he was about to prove he meant it. That August, he audaciously fired eleven thousand air traffic controllers who were striking for higher wages.

I don't think there ever was a more underestimated president than Ronald Reagan. Partly this was because he was a movie actor. But what a lot of people didn't realize was that he had a college degree in economics, something that made him unique among prior presidents.

Eight days after he fired the air traffic controllers, Reagan signed into law the Kemp-Roth Tax Cut, which included a provision making tax-deferred individual retirement accounts (IRAs) available to all Americans. I might mention he accomplished both of these things just four and a half months after being shot in the chest by a would-be assassin.

At thirty-three, I still held many of the same liberal attitudes I had developed in college. But now my ideas were changing fast. A government's most important function is to keep its citizens safe, but second to that is to promote the general prosperity. Between Volcker and Reagan, America now had a team in place that understood the importance of investments in creating jobs and a higher standard of living. Volcker knew, if inflation were brought low, interest rates would go down. If interest rates went down, the economy would improve. People would be more likely to invest in productive assets rather than just buying such things as collectables or gold and silver. Meanwhile, Reagan understood what an investment boom it would cause if everyone put money aside for retirement. He also understood that people who are investors make more responsible citizens and smarter voters.

So the writing was on the wall for me. I started playing with the numbers. Somewhere, I discovered the following nugget of wisdom. Given a choice between receiving $1 million as a gift or a penny today followed by two pennies tomorrow, four pennies the next day, and so on for thirty days, which gift should one choose? If you do the math, you will choose the latter, because astonishingly, those pennies compound to over $10 million!

This is a terrific lesson in what is called the miracle of compound interest. But of course, no investor doubles his money every day. So I wondered, What sort of result might one get using more realistic rates of return?

There is a mathematical trick I read about in my training called the rule of 72. Whatever your annual rate of return on investment is, if you divide it into the number 72, your answer will roughly be how many years it will take to double your money.

I started plugging in numbers. I was thirty-one. Suppose I opened a $2,000 IRA for myself and I earned 9 percent per year on it, which is pretty close to what the American stock market has returned over the long run: 9 divided into 72 tells me I would double my money in eight years.

This would give me $4,000 at age thirty-nine, $8,000 at forty-seven, $16,000 at fifty-five, and $32,000 at age sixty-three. That is sixteen times my investment. At 9 percent! Can you imagine?

Then I did the same exercise using 12 percent as a rate of return. After all, I was a professional stockbroker. Maybe it wasn't so far-fetched to think I might outperform the market by 3 percent per year. You can figure it out yourself. At 12 percent, I would have $64,000 by the age of sixty-one. Wow, that's thirty-two times my investment. And herein lies an important discovery: 12 percent isn't just a little better than 9 percent; it's more than twice as good, and I realized, if I could live long enough, it would be a thousand times better!

All these numbers, of course, are based on a single $2,000 investment at age thirty-one. Put aside a little more than that and keep adding to it over time, and you will accumulate millions of dollars over the course of your lifetime.

One thing was obvious, though. No savings account was going to give me results like these. If I wanted to succeed, I would need to take some risk, not high risk, mind you, just *some* risk. After all, the numbers demonstrate that even small increases in rate of return produce an exponentially higher result.

Okay. So now I knew I was going to be an investor, no matter how many needs I had to postpone to get started. First, of course, I would have to get rid of my debts. After that, I knew exactly what I wanted to do. As I saw it, the various investment categories had returned the following results over the past century or so:

Savings Accounts:	2–3%	Treasury Bills:	2–3%
Long-Term Gov't Bonds:	4–5%	Real Estate:	4–5%
Gold and Silver:	3–4%	Collectables:	?
Stocks:	9.5%		

A lot of fortunes have been made in real estate, but how can that be if the average return is only 4.5 percent? The answer is that most real estate is bought with borrowed money. If you only put up twenty thousand to buy a one-hundred-thousand-dollar house, then your 4.5 percent ($4,500) gain gives your down payment a return of 22.5 percent. Alternatively, though, if the house goes down by 4.5 percent, your loss is 22.5 percent. That's the power of leverage. It can make you rich, and it can wipe you out.

Having been burned so badly in options, I didn't want leverage. So for me, stocks were the obvious choice. And because I could see what an enormous difference a few extra percentage points would make, it was critical to buy my stocks in an account that was either tax-free or at least tax-deferred.

For the first time, I recognized what a stockbroker's job really ought to be. No longer would I focus on speculating for my clients; instead, I would show them how to set reasonable long-term goals for themselves. Then I would set their plans in motion by helping them buy good stocks. While I was at it, I would do the same thing for myself. Together, we would get rich—patiently, yes, but predictably!

All this was great, of course. I knew exactly what I wanted and just how I was going to achieve it. But there was one more hurdle in my way.

One afternoon, I got a call from Don Stevens, manager of the downtown EF Hutton office. Don had responsibility over our location as well, and he wanted to come out and talk to me. "Sure," I said cheerfully. "I'll be here."

My cheerfulness was a put-on. I figured I knew what this was about. In three years, Merrill Lynch had never uncovered my past. I knew when I switched to Hutton that my record would be examined again and I might not be so lucky a second time. If this were about anything else, wouldn't we just discuss it over the phone?

When Don arrived, he suggested we go outside to the parking lot, and I knew in an instant I was toast. I had a beautiful young family to support, and I was an honest and dedicated employee. But leading Wall Street firms like Hutton don't put their clients' money in the hands of convicted felons. In fact, the New York Stock Exchange had a policy against even licensing people like me.

"Dave," he said, with a serious look on his face, "did you get in some trouble with the law in your past? I've been notified that you have an arrest record."

The blood must have drained from my face. "It's true, Don. When I was in college, I was taking food from a warehouse, and I was caught."

"But weren't there several felonies, not just one?"

Oh, boy, it had just gotten worse. "That's right," I said nervously. "My friends and I sneaked into a couple of warehouses, but it was always to take food to eat. They were pranks, really, and it was all very foolish."

"Why didn't you come clean on your application?"

"Don," I said, "that happened twelve years ago, when I was still a teenager. I was nineteen. My dad told me, if I admitted to it, I'd never get a job, and I believed him. I'm really sorry."

Don Stevens was as solid as your favorite grandfather. I didn't think I could ask for a better man than he to decide my fate.

"Well, Dave, I'll talk to Dale Frey and see what he wants to do, and I'll get back to you."

Don Stevens barely knew me. Dale Frey, meanwhile, was our regional vice president. He lived in Denver and had met me only once. So I figured my chances of surviving were pretty much zero. Nonetheless, I got a call from Dale the next day. Where Don Stevens was a soft-spoken, unassuming type, Dale was a big handsome man who commanded the room with an almost boyish enthusiasm.

"Dave, Don tells me you didn't put your record on the application because your father told you not to. Is that right?"

"That's right," I responded.

"Well, I respect that," he said. "So we're going to go to bat for you."

Oh my gosh, I thought. *Was I going to be okay?*

"Of course, it isn't up to me. It isn't even up to the firm. The New York Stock Exchange uncovered this, and they are going to need some convincing not to revoke your license. But we are going to put our legal department to work on it and see what we can do."

"Thank you so *much*, Dale!" I said. "I will work hard to deserve this."

"Marvelous! You just keep doing your job. I'll get back to you."

I couldn't ask for more. Dale had said it wasn't up to him. It wasn't even up to the firm. But I knew better. If he or Don Stevens or Nick Bapis—anyone of them—had wanted me to go, my career would have ended that very day. Once again, my fate had been placed in the hands of others, and once again, I was being treated with empathy.

A couple of months later, Dale Frey called again to say the NYSE had agreed to let me stay on. My long nightmare was over.

TWENTY-ONE

Dimple Dell Lane

Suzie and I raised our kids on Dimple Dell Lane. Jesse was nine when we moved in, Cassie seven. Mary had just had her first birthday. I was thirty-one, and Suzie thirty-two. The first few years, the house was really more than we could afford. We were even late on our mortgage payment once. It was my fault, of course. Based on my early success with options, I had thought my money worries over. Plus, in my limited experience, home prices only went up. I was expecting a free ride on the inflation train. Instead, thanks to Ronald Reagan and Paul Volcker, the inflation train was dead in its tracks. If anything, the value of our new home was falling.

Nonetheless, it was a beautiful home in an upscale neighborhood. We were set in a rural enclave with a spectacular view straight up the side of eleven-thousand-foot Lone Peak. There was a cascading creek across the street from the house. Yet shopping and schools were close by. I couldn't think of a better setting for raising our children.

For the first few years, Suzie was a stay-at-home mom. With her education, her ambition, and her gregarious nature, she was well suited to having a career outside the home, but neither of us wanted Mary going to day care. So Suzie focused on preparing wonderful dinners every night and on keeping a clean, well-organized household. As soon as the girls were old enough, she enrolled them in ballet classes, something they all would continue enthusiastically into their teenage years.

Mary was given the added responsibility of piano lessons, though she required considerable prodding. Probably because she spent so much time with her older sisters, Mary was precocious. By the time she was in first grade, it was obvious that Suzie could get a job, if she wanted to, and she did.

In college, Suzie had majored in elementary education. With her love of books and her patience with small children, there is no doubt she would have been an excellent teacher. But I had been a broker long enough by now to realize what a natural Suzie would be at sales, and she agreed to give it a try. She took the necessary training and got herself licensed for selling real estate.

Meanwhile, my own business plan was paying off. I spent the 1980s conducting seminars, teaching people about the "miracle" of compound interest and the importance of setting long-term goals. If their money was in a tax-qualified retirement account, great. We could get busy investing in stocks or mutual funds and have no taxes to worry about—at least not until they retired. If their money wasn't in a qualified account, I would show them how to use what's called a variable annuity to accomplish practically the same thing.

Was I smashing records as a salesman? Far from it. Nick Bapis was down the hall, opening two or three new accounts a day. I was lucky to get ten in a month. I just didn't seem to have what it takes to stand out as a salesman. Nonetheless, I soldiered on. I had my goals, and I believed in what I was doing.

By the way, I am not just talking about sales goals. I also had well-defined investment performance goals. In an ideal world, isn't that what you'd want your broker to focus on? Instead of trying to meet my employer's ever-higher commission targets, why not concentrate on making money for my clients? If I succeeded, I might wind up with plenty of business anyway. I'd also have the satisfaction of making an important difference in other peoples' lives!

By the time I was thirty-five, I had paid off all debts, except for our mortgage, and I had put $6,000 into each of two IRA accounts, one for Suzie, one for myself. I was also having money withheld from my pay to invest in the company retirement plan. My first objective

for the IRAs was to grow them to $100,000 before I turned for-
ty-one, and I was well on my way when I got an unexpected boost.

So far, throughout the Reagan years, the stock market had been
very generous to Wall Street. But toward the end of Reagan's presidency, things got a little dicey. In 1987, government bond prices
started falling. By summer, they were so cheap you could get a 10
percent yield on a ten-year bond. That exceeds the average annual
return on stocks, and it is a lot more dependable than stocks. After
all, if it had to, the government could just print the money to pay
you with.

So I pulled every dollar I could out of the stock market for
myself and my clients. For accounts that could, including my own,
I bought zero-coupon treasuries. Those are government bonds that
pay no interest but are purchased at a deep discount to their face
value. For accounts that were in mutual funds or variable annuities,
there was no treasury bond option, so I merely went to cash.

At first, I looked like an idiot. Throughout July and much of
August, the stock market kept going higher. Clients were starting to
wonder if I knew what I was doing. One client, in fact, asked me to
put his money back into stocks, which I reluctantly did.

In late August, the market began to slip. The weakness continued into September and October. Then came October 19, the
date that would always be remembered as Black Monday. That day,
the Dow Jones Industrial Average fell 22.6 percent, the biggest percentage loss for any single day in the history of the New York Stock
Exchange. And what happened to my zero-coupon bonds? They
exploded higher in price.

Driving home that afternoon with the car windows rolled up,
I turned on the radio and started yelling at the top of my lungs. I
had just dodged the biggest bullet of my career. In fact, I had made
myself, and many of my clients, a bundle. Those who counted on
me to manage their savings were going to be calling tomorrow for a
damage assessment. I had no doubt about that, and it was going to
be awfully sweet surprising them with the news.

Sadly, not everything that happened in 1987 was so happy,
though. First, in June, Suzie's father, Vincent Arthur Albanesi, died.

He had lived his whole life in and around Pittsburgh. During World War II, he had served in the Army Air Corps as a radioman/bombardier on a B-17 flying out of England. The daylight bombing raids made over Germany in those planes were among the most dangerous assignments given anyone in the war. Something like 20 percent of those men never made it home again. Yet they climbed back into those planes time after time to do their duty for their country.

Vince wouldn't talk about his wartime experience. Maybe he was traumatized by it. Then, too, he was a very modest man who rarely spoke about anything. But when he got home from the war, he married Mary McGovern. She was only seventeen, but already she was one of the most beautiful women in Pittsburgh. Together they raised three daughters and a son. Vince supported the family repairing TV sets for thirty-five years.

Vince and Mary came out to visit us in Salt Lake a few times, though they could hardly ever afford to. When they talked about retirement, they dreamed of doing the littlest, most inexpensive things, like taking walks together or maybe riding the public bus into the city to see a movie. With Vince gone now, even those heart-rending dreams would never come true.

He was sixty-five and still working when he was diagnosed with kidney cancer. He and Mary were self-described Born-Again Christians. They had always been Catholic, but after their only son, Vince Jr., died in a 1975 automobile accident, their devotion to Jesus had intensified. For a year, while big Vince kept getting sicker, he and Mary prayed almost constantly, but it was to no avail. He died at home after a long and difficult battle.

Mary was fifty-eight and still as beautiful as ever, but for the rest of her life, she must have cried every single day. I don't think she ever looked at another man.

That same year, on August 8, my last surviving grandparent died. Gladys Ruth Houston Davenport (Gamma, as we called her) was at home in Virginia. My aunt Dorothy Weller and my cousins were holding a party for her under the trees at Nadamar. They were celebrating Gamma's ninety-second birthday. Feeling tired, Gamma went into the house to lie down, and when someone checked on her later, they found her dead.

Gamma had grown up in Detroit, of all places. Her mother, Dora Paul, had immigrated there from Germany in 1885 at the age of fifteen. Sadly, Dora died when Gamma was about ten. Gamma's only sibling, younger sister, Grace, was about six. William Henry Houston, the girls' father, was a sometime jewelry engraver, but he was too much of a boozer to take care of his children. The girls wound up being left with good Samaritans.

Detroit isn't on an ocean, but it is located on the Detroit River, part of the passageway connecting Lake Huron to Lake Erie. Port Detroit is an important stop for ships transiting the Great Lakes, including ships of the US Navy. That was how my grandmother came to meet and marry my grandfather, who was just a sailor at that time.

Eventually, that sailor would become Commander Davenport, skipper of the destroyer USS *Jacob Jones*, but only after performing years of sea duty. When he died in 1948, he was fifty-three, and so was Gamma. By then, my father, their only son, was already pursuing his career that would take him, and us, all over the world. And so, throughout her ninety-two years, Gamma was separated from the most important men in her life. Her father, her husband, even her son, each had abandoned her in his turn. At least that might have been how she saw it. How else to explain her decision to leave all seventeen acres of Nadamar to my aunt Dorothy?

Fortunately, Dad did inherit half of Gamma's $400 thousand stock portfolio. But his sister's inheritance was worth something more like $2 million.

Gamma must have foreseen the rift this would create between Wellers and Davenports. And yet she just couldn't bring herself to let one inch of Nadamar, the ultimate fruit of Robert Earl Davenport's lifetime of hard work, fall into the hands of his only son and namesake, Robert Earl Jr.

Two years before she died, Gamma had warned Dad about this. He jumped on a plane and went back east to see if he could change her mind. Together, they saw her attorney and rewrote the will to provide a more equal split, but that night at dinner, Dorothy and my cousins were begrudging about it. They claimed that by living away from Virginia so many years, Dad had somehow disinherited himself. Cousin Buz even brought up Dad's having missed his father's funeral some four decades earlier as evidence of his supposed indifference.

Dad swallowed his pride and flew back to San Diego. Then, a couple of weeks later, his phone rang, and it was Gamma. She had decided to put the will back in Dorothy's favor.

So when Gamma died, there was already bad blood. I knew Dad was going to be uncomfortable attending the funeral in the presence of the Weller side of the family. I also knew my mother wasn't going to go. She was way too resentful for that. So I volunteered.

Dad and I rendezvoused at National Airport in Washington, DC. He flew in from San Diego, and I from Salt Lake City. We rented a car and drove south into Virginia, looking for a hotel to spend the night. The next morning, we arrived at Nadamar in time for a short visit with the family before heading to the church. Once the service was over, we got in our separate cars and caravanned behind the hearse all the way to Arlington National Cemetery, two hundred miles away. At Arlington, we found Commander Davenport's grave next to the fresh hole that had been dug for my grandmother. Words were spoken, and tears were shed (most notably by me, incidentally), and then Dad and I said goodbye to everyone. The Wellers headed back to Virginia Beach, and we went looking for another hotel.

A few weeks later, Dorothy sent me an unexpected inheritance of $1,000. It wasn't quite enough to cover my expenses for attending the funeral, but I was grateful to have been remembered. I corresponded with Dorothy, mostly by mail, until she died in 2005. I tried communicating with Buz by e-mail for a while, but she showed little interest, so I stopped.

Meanwhile, of course, Wall Street was in turmoil. While the October 19 crash was a boon for my business, you could not say the same thing for my firm. The money lost that day at EF Hutton sent the company reeling. Six weeks later, management reached an agreement to be acquired by Shearson Lehman. The combined firm was to be known as Shearson Lehman Hutton.

I had no problem with the merger, but Nick Bapis didn't want to work for Shearson Lehman, and at our office, he held the cards. As a group, we negotiated a separate deal with another Wall Street firm, Dean Witter. Each broker—and there were about eight of us—was given a large bonus as an inducement.

We made the switch in early 1988. Using part of my bonus, I bought Suzie a two-karat diamond ring, her first, even though we had been married almost nineteen years. Then, with Jesse graduating from high school in June, the five of us celebrated by going on a Caribbean cruise. I was forty years old.

Meantime, Suzie was working hard at her real estate career. No matter what her results from one month to the next, she was delighted to have a reason to dress up and go out to meet the world every day. Jesse had made no decision about college yet, but Cassie was only two years behind, so I figured we were going to be incurring a lot of tuition expenses pretty soon. Even though I was doing well, I welcomed the added income Suzie earned. What I didn't like was her unpredictable schedule. My work was done by the clock in New York, which was two hours ahead of Utah. I would go in at six thirty or seven in the morning and sometimes be finished for the day as early as noon. Suzie's schedule, on the other hand, was concentrated more in the afternoons and on weekends. Nonetheless, we made it work, for a while, at least.

TWENTY-TWO

Salt Lake Magazine

I made a few good friends during my working life. Two who stand out were Frank Briggs and Jim Tybur, neither of whom ever met the other, by the way. I got to know Frank at Merrill Lynch. He was as sweet and innocent a man as I ever knew, not at all the type A personality one associates with stockbrokers. In a way, it was a shame, because real success always seemed just a little out of Frank's reach. Merrill even let him go, eventually, though he did manage to get on at Kidder Peabody and save his career.

I guess I must have seen some of myself in Frank. He was a well-educated man who might have been happier teaching school or doing any number of other things were it not for the money being better on Wall Street. Frank was incapable of hyperbole and utterly without guile, as comfortable as an old shoe, you might say, and I found him immensely admirable.

Jim Tybur, on the other hand, was a brilliant colleague of mine who started after I did at EF Hutton. He built a significant business in municipal bonds, often finding underpriced situations that made his clients a lot of money. He and I both employed his wife, Annette, as our secretary for a number of years. She was a comely blonde who dressed impeccably and had professional ability that was as remarkable as her appearance. The two of them became important friends to Suzie and me. Often, we would go to dinner or take in the Utah Symphony together.

By now, I was pretty secure in my career. Long gone was the fear of failure that had plagued my earlier days. Always a sentimental person, I would think about the good friends I had made in my youth and wonder whatever happened to them. Particularly, I thought of my old girlfriends, Janet Grkovic and Karlana Carpen. And then there was Elias Menkes, the boy who had inspired me so much in Vienna.

I was a vice president at the firm now, and I was getting my share of recognition. I was even called to New York a couple of times to teach my business approach to newer brokers. Was this enough? I wondered how much longer I needed to go on running from my past.

One day, I called the alumni office at Columbia University and asked about Elias. I was told he had gone on to graduate school at the University of Chicago. So I called Chicago. Their records indicated he had finished there and left for medical school at the University of Toronto.

Wow! So Elias was a doctor. The last time I saw him, he said he was thinking about medicine. Now I was getting excited. I called Toronto. I was told he went on from there to the medical school at Harvard University.

Because of the effort required in reaching the right people, these phone calls took me a couple of days to complete. Massachusetts General is the hospital at the Harvard Medical School, and that was where my search finally came to an end. I got to the right person, all right. He was suspicious of my motives at first and did not want to say anything, but I pressed.

Yes, Elias had been at Massachusetts General. He was an anesthesiologist. One day in 1981, he was discovered slumped over in his office. An autopsy revealed he had injected himself with something that stopped his heart.

The year 1981? That was almost ten years ago. He was thirty-two. Are you kidding? Elias was such a well-liked and brilliant young man with so much going for him. I learned he had left an adoring wife behind with two young daughters to raise by herself. Suicide? Him? Why?

I immediately called the only Vienna friend who had stayed in touch with me over the years, Tom Wheeler. I couldn't stop myself from crying as I told him the news. Tom hadn't been close to Elias the way I was, so he didn't take it as hard. But he said, "Dave, you know, I have been thinking, anyway. We are coming up on twenty-five years since we graduated. Why don't we start planning a reunion?"

I liked Tom's idea at once. All afternoon and evening, I thought about how we might go about finding the people necessary to hold such an event. It had taken me two days, after all, just to track down Elias. The rest of these people, no doubt, were scattered all over the planet. The Internet was just now being opened up for public commercial use. I wasn't even familiar with it, and the information I needed wouldn't be there yet, anyway. Even the school wouldn't be much help. I, for one, hadn't stayed in touch. Why would anyone else have?

The next morning, I called Tom, who lived near Washington, DC, and I told him I wanted to get started. My local library had hundreds of phone books from around the nation. Working from our memories of where people had come from all those years before, I might be able to find some of the American males. Their names, at least, would still be the same. Then, each time we found someone, we could pick his brain. Surely, Tom and I weren't the only ones who had stayed in touch with somebody.

I began spending an hour or two every afternoon at the library or on the phone. Within weeks, I had found over eighty people who were at AIS when we were. Not all were in our class, but that didn't matter. Having a reunion was a big deal to us, and we wanted to include as many people as possible.

Soon, Tom printed out a list of the names and contact information, and I sent it out to everyone I had found. I included a cover message in the form of an open letter addressed to my poor, deceased friend.

October 21, 1989
Salt Lake City

Dear Elias,

It's Saturday morning. I'm in the kitchen, having my coffee, listening to Judy Collins on the stereo and thinking about you. I'm the only one up.

It's autumn now. The wind awoke me this morning. Outside it is still blowing. Leaves are everywhere. Halloween is coming. This time of year, my thoughts often turn to our school days, to Salmannsdorferstrasse, to sweaters and books, to glasses of apfelsaft, and to speaking German (which I never did very well). Finally, this autumn, I decided to look for you.

I wonder if, under other circumstances, I ever would have had the courage to explain to you what an impact you had on my life. You, who, at sixteen, already possessed so great a mind and heart. I still think about our first conversations, conversations between an impressionable boy and a young philosopher. On Sunday afternoons, we would walk down cobbled streets, through vineyard and forest, stopping here and there, talking of ideas and feelings and, of course, girls. You always carried a book. In those days, you were reading Dos Passos. Do you remember? Sometimes, at a little shop along the way, you would buy oranges, and we would walk back to the school eating them.

When our time in Vienna was over, we were scattered like the leaves in the wind. You went to New York, where I visited you once, and then, when we were nineteen, we met for what was to be the last time, in Portland. I was on my way to a summer job in Alaska. You were going to take a course at Stanford. That day we spent walking, just the two of us, and talking, as though very little had changed. We saw Reed College, because you wanted to, and when our day was ended, we said our final goodbye.

It was Tom Wheeler who suggested doing the work you'll find enclosed. With his help, and with the help of others, I've put my heart into seeking out our classmates, one by one. Some, we have still yet to locate, though I expect we'll find them all.

Before long, we will schedule a reunion, probably in Vienna. Yes, even we, the class of 1966, and our friends from the American International School, will have a reunion. People will come from around the world to attend, to see what the years have wrought. And when it is over, we shall look into one another's faces and smile and then part again, this time perhaps forever.

I regret to tell you this, Elias, but Mike Valunas will not be invited. Neither will Jim Ward. Those two close friends were casualties of the war in Vietnam. Their names are on the wall at the memorial in Washington, DC. And I'm sorry to say, there are others we will be unable to invite. Sissy Porges, Elizabeth Denchfield, and Butch Rattray are all tragically gone.

And you, my friend? Well, you won't be getting any invitations either. But I want you to know that, like Mike and Jim and Sissy and Beth and Mr. Rattray, you will be there.

With love,
Dave

While I was working on the reunion, Jesse was growing up fast. She had started out bussing tables at La Caille right after high school. La Caille was a high-end restaurant built in the style of a seventeenth-century French farmhouse, with its own vineyard and dozens of exotic animals roaming about the property. It was located less than two miles from our house, and the tips there were well above what Jesse could have earned at any other restaurant. I was glad she was able to get on.

The kitchen manager and head chef at La Caille was a high-energy, supremely self-confident young man named Darren Alder. He was only in his midtwenties, but already he had worked his way up from dishwasher. Darren was going to have everything he wanted in life, and right now what he wanted was Jesse.

The two of them married in 1990, and Jesse gave birth to our first grandchild, a son named Martin Read Alder, in April of that year. I confess, I was very worried about Jesse marrying so young. She just didn't seem ready. Over the decades, though, their marriage would endure, and the two of them would prove to be very successful in businesses they built themselves.

Suzie, of course, was delighted to be a grandmother. With her own children mostly grown now, and with a career of her own, she was experiencing a degree of independence beyond what she had known in the past. She loved her job selling real estate, although I can't say I felt the same.

Because of her hours, I was now the one preparing dinner every night. Weekends? Who knew? Anything was liable to happen. Same thing with vacations. We really couldn't make any plans without fear of having to cancel them at the last minute. And sure, this is the sort of thing hardworking people put up with all the time, but should we? I was, after all, making well into six figures by now, and her job was making it difficult to enjoy life.

Recently, a glitzy new lifestyle magazine had come to town. Called *Salt Lake City*, it was aimed at affluent readers, or at least those who aspired to being affluent. I started encouraging Suzie to find out if they had any openings in their advertising department, and one day she did. The associate publisher there interviewed her and asked if she could start right away. Suzie was off on a new career selling advertising.

There is almost no way of exaggerating what a great fit this new job was going to be for my sweet wife. Suzie would be calling on all the finest dress shops in the city, the luxury car dealers, and the best furniture stores. She would be schmoozing clients over lunch almost every day at some of the finest restaurants in the city. Suzie, a beautiful woman who was outgoing, well-spoken, and ambitious, would be the top ad salesperson at the magazine from the very first issue on.

Meanwhile, just as I had hoped, we held our reunion in Vienna in June of 1991. It was a full week in length, and as expected, nearly one hundred people came from around the world to attend. Among the guests were my Israeli roommate, Mike Nassie, and the cute little ninth grader, Susie Voigt.

By far, however, the most important attendee to me was Janet Grkovic. I must confess, my heart was pounding when I saw her. Yes, I know, I was a married man, and I hope the reader knows how much I adored my wife. But seeing Janet again, especially in Vienna, drew me back to a very special time and place in my life.

Janet was divorced. She was raising two school-age daughters, and she lived in Shelbyville, Kentucky. She had a master's degree in psychology and was working at the University of Louisville. By virtue of a generous divorce settlement, she was in solid financial shape. I learned these things over the course of seven days, during which Suzie and I hung out with her and a girlfriend she had brought along.

Early on the last morning, I helped Janet and her friend get over to the Westbahnhof train station with their luggage. It was a very sad experience for me. I didn't expect I would ever see her again, and I said so. At the last moment, I leaned over and kissed her with all the love I had ever felt before. Then I turned, walked out of the station, and headed back to the hotel.

TWENTY-THREE

On a Roll

I guess you could say we were on a roll in the 1990s. Suzie was flourishing at the magazine. In fact, I had never seen her happier. Jesse and Darren owned their own home and were thriving. On Jesse's way to work in the evenings, she would drop Marty off at our house, which was a joy for Suzie and me.

Cassie had finished up at Alta High School with grades good enough to get her into one of the most selective colleges in the country, the University of California at San Diego. Was I ever proud of that! To make things better, my parents lived in San Diego and could help her out if ever a need arose.

Mary was growing comfortably into her teen years. She was pretty and popular and remarkably poised for a girl her age, which made her very easy to parent.

To top it all off, I was experiencing incredibly good fortune in the stock market. One day, early in the decade, I heard from a friend about a local medical device manufacturer that was supposed to be doing very well. He said he was thinking of applying for work there, and he wondered what I could find out about them. The name of the company was Ballard Medical.

I did some digging, and I was able to find quite a bit of information. Ballard had been started by a man named Dale Ballard, who grew up in Draper, just five miles or so from my house. Clear back in 1955, he and a partner had founded a prior medical device company called Deseret Pharmaceutical. That company eventually went public and was listed on the New York Stock Exchange. After twenty-one years in business, it was acquired by Warner Lambert. Dale Ballard was fifty-four when that happened and already worth millions.

He was in no mood to rest, however. He and his partner had pioneered the very lucrative business of manufacturing cheap disposable plastic devices that would be used by hospitals every day. Now he wanted to repeat this success on his own. The new company was founded in 1978, and by the time I came along, twelve years later, it was the fastest-growing corporation on the New York Stock Exchange.

I bought the stock immediately and started showing it to my clients. Over the next year, I tripled my money in Ballard Medical, which was a windfall to me, because most of what I had was in it.

Meanwhile, Suzie was getting along famously with the owners of her magazine. John and Margaret-Mary Shuff already had years of experience publishing a similar magazine in Boca Raton, Florida, but they were telling Suzie she was the best employee they had ever hired. They got in the habit of inviting her and me out to dinner frequently.

In the course of all this, John and I became good friends. He even transferred his investment account to me. I guess Suzie must have told him I was interested in writing, because one day he asked me if I would like to profile a prominent businessperson for the next issue. The choice of whom to write about was up to me. Knowing just whom to pick, I jumped at the chance. I called Ballard Medical the next day and explained what I was up to. I got an appointment to interview Dale Ballard.

Ballard proved to be an excellent choice. In his heart, he was just an old beet farmer like his daddy. He drove to work every morning in an old pickup truck, stopping at a café along the way to have coffee and a few laughs with some of his seven brothers. And yet his record in business was stellar. A lot of people had become millionaires by investing in his stock.

When the article came out, John Shuff loved it. He wanted me to find more businesspeople to profile, and he wanted me to be a regular contributor to the magazine. Meanwhile, just seeing my byline for the first time was exciting for me.

Salt Lake City magazine was a bimonthly. This meant I would need to have a new article ready every eight weeks. Over the next year or so, I interviewed and wrote about some really accomplished people. One was a man who had built a nationwide business renting hospital equipment. He had just sold the company for $35 million. Another was a lawyer intent upon bringing the mothballed Geneva Steel back to life. Then there was a man who owned casinos in Nevada. For sheer human interest, though, none of these men equaled Dale Ballard.

None, that is, until I met a man named Jay Call.

All I knew about Jay was that he owned the Flying J Travel Plazas that serve the interstate highway system all over America. I learned that from John Shuff. I don't know if Jay was a billionaire or not, but he was certainly up there somewhere. When I talked to his secretary, she told me I could meet him on a Saturday morning at his refinery in Woods Cross, just north of downtown Salt Lake.

The night before we met, I thought, just to be safe, I'd better wash my car. After all, if we were going to meet at his refinery, he was probably going to see me driving in. So I gave the car a good going-over inside and out, and thank goodness! As I pulled in, I saw Jay standing next to his own car, and it was spotless. During the interview, I discovered that cleanliness was a near-obsession with him. Jay, in fact, washed his car nearly every day and considered cleanliness an essential part of his business success.

He started using my name right away. I don't recall any of my other subjects doing that. To them, I guess I was just a generic reporter, but Jay was more personal. As we walked around the refinery, he began telling me his story.

He grew up in the little southeastern Idaho town of Soda Springs, a place so remote you'd wonder how any industrialist could possibly have started there. But Jay's father and uncle were already partners in the successful Caribou Oil Company, which owned a chain of Maverick gas stations. Additionally, Jay's father owned the local Chevrolet dealership, where Jay worked as a boy.

Jay tried going to college, but he had big ideas that just wouldn't wait. At nineteen, he talked his dad into leasing him a gas station in Willard, Utah (population, less than one thousand). Then he moved a house trailer onto the property so he could live on-site and keep an eye out for customers. Soon, he was adding a second station in nearby Brigham City.

When his dad died in 1964, Jay went to work for his uncle at Caribou. After four years of that, though, he was ready to strike out on his own again. He was just twenty-seven when he incorporated the Flying J Oil Company in February of 1968. By the end of the first year, he owned five gas stations and was building six more.

Jay did all his construction in-house. In fact, he did most things that way. He wanted to own the oil wells, the refineries, the delivery trucks, the hotels, the restaurants—you name it. By the time of our interview, his company was twenty-four years old, and it had all those things in large numbers. It was one of the biggest privately owned companies in the world.

For getting his executives to and from the field, Jay owned three corporate jets. He had a couple of pilots on the payroll, but he was a skilled aviator himself, and he often took the controls.

After our tour of the refinery, Jay took me out to the airport to see one of his planes. Oddly, we took my car. He said he wanted me to drive. Years later, I would learn Jay often did that sort of thing. He found getting into your space a good way of sizing you up.

After that, we had one more stop to make. Jay wanted me to see his thirty-acre ranch and meet his wife, Tamra. This was another thing none of my other subjects had done. As I might have expected, Tamra was beautiful. So was the ranch, which, incidentally, was less than five miles away from his very first gas station in Willard.

That night, I told Suzie I had met someone truly extraordinary that day.

In 1994, Suzie and I celebrated our twenty-fifth wedding anniversary by taking our three daughters on a two-week trip to England. Marty was only four years old, so we left him behind to be cared for by Darren. For my money, it was the best anniversary we ever had.

Taking the girls along made it a lot more fun than it would have been otherwise.

The following year, Cassie graduated from UCSD, and the whole family showed up in La Jolla for the ceremony. When they called her name to come up and receive her diploma, I started crying. Getting my kids educated had always been a big deal to me, and I was feeling very proud.

My parents were there, too, of course. Afterward, we all went to an Indian restaurant for lunch. We drank a toast to Cassie and her great accomplishment. Then I proposed another toast, a toast to Cassie's mother. Suzie had always been a great student, too, but years before she had set her dream of graduating aside in order to bear our child. Now, that same child had earned a degree entirely on tuition money provided by Suzie's job. Both women were fulfilling a dream that day, and I wanted to make sure everyone realized it.

After selling my Ballard Medical stock for a triple, I decided to give another local medical products company a try. Utah Medical was essentially a Ballard copycat, but I thought the stock had more room to run. Besides, it had even better earning's growth than Ballard. So I bought it. Shortly thereafter, the CEO was arrested for fraud, and instantly the stock was worth 25 percent less than I paid for it.

Of course, I had plunged on Utah Medical as well, so it was a significant setback. Fortunately, though, my clients were still happy enough about the Ballard gains that they were able to stay with me.

At about this time, new laws were being passed to allow Indian reservations to operate gambling casinos. The leading manufacturer of slot machines was a company called International Game Technologies, and the stock was already hot. So I jumped on board, and again, I plunged, putting almost everything in one stock. Within a year, I had another triple under my belt.

Next, I bought Dell Computer. Everyone was buying personal computers, and Dell was the star of the show. In a matter of months, I made my gains and got out. Then I got an idea it was time for gold to rally. I bought a couple of mining stocks and made something like 50 percent in a matter of months.

Did I have some dogs? Yes, I did. After Utah Medical, two others come to mind. Both were steel companies. One was LTV, and the other was our old friend Geneva Steel. I expected both companies to come back from nearly dead, and neither one of them ever did. In each case, I managed to get out without losing more than about 20 percent. I wasn't going to ride them all the way down. As it was, my clients lost 12 percent overall in 1994, but it was the only losing year we had that decade.

In 1997, Dean Witter purchased Morgan Stanley and took over the name. One of my greatest coups came early that year. A fellow broker tipped me off to something called the millennium problem. All the world's computers were programmed to recognize only the last two numbers in a year. So 1923, for example, was just year 23 to a computer. This meant that when we entered the year 2000 (Y2K), computers would only recognize the two zeros and think it was 1900 again. Everything might go haywire. Supposedly, the fix was going to cost billions of dollars, even hundreds of billions, and supposedly only a handful of companies were positioned to do the work. One of those companies was an outfit called Viasoft.

It was all brand-new to me, but it sounded plausible. When I heard mention of it in the news just a day or two later, I decided to jump. Once again, I put everything I had at risk, and then, only five months later, with the turn of the millennium still more than two years away, I sold it. What? Viasoft's business had barely started to pick up, and clients were really scratching their heads on this one. But there is a lesson here. If you own a stock that may be about to reap a temporary windfall, and if the whole world already knows about it, be sure to sell way before the windfall happens. Remember, nobody is going to pay you top dollar for a stock unless he thinks there is room for him to get rich too. Amazingly, within minutes of my last sale, the stock started falling. I had bought it at 28, and I sold it for 59. It never got that high again. In June of 2000, the company was bought out for a mere $8.40 a share.

At about the same time I was getting out of Viasoft, there was serious trouble brewing in Southeast Asia. Throughout the eighties and nineties, economic growth in that part of the world had been explosive. Comparatively low wages and relaxed business regulations in places like Thailand, Indonesia, and Malaysia were drawing companies away from higher-cost regions like Europe and the United States. Eager to get their share, international banks were making huge loans, and society at all levels, including governments, were overburdened with debt. When concern spread to the currency markets, the Thai baht collapsed, and that was the coup de grâce. Overnight, the whole region was in a severe economic crunch. That started in July.

A month later, Suzie and I were taking Mary to Philadelphia, where she had been accepted at Bryn Mawr College. Before heading home, we stopped in Manhattan to take in *Les Misérables* on Broadway. The next morning, I was up early in our hotel room and I turned on the TV. Princess Diana had died in a horrible car crash in Paris during the night.

When we got home, I started seriously considering owning gold again. Having owned it once before, I felt I understood it pretty well. Some people think gold is the place to be in a panic, but I felt I knew better. When people are losing everything, what they really lust for is cash, not gold, and the cash that sustains the global economic system is the US dollar.

No, what really drives gold in the long run is the level of real interest rates. By that, I mean nominal interest rates minus the rate of inflation. Let me put it this way: if the bank pays you 3 percent on your savings but inflation is running at 5 percent, then your account is losing 2 percent per year in purchasing power. If you are smart, you will look for an alternative, and quite often, that is going to be gold.

Most of the money in the world banking system is actually created through loan demand. Say, you put $50,000 in the bank. They lend it to me. I buy a car. Then the car dealer takes the $50,000 to his bank. Now, both you and the car dealer have $50,000 in the bank, and both of you can go out and spend it!

That is capitalism at its core. The whole system depends upon borrowed money. When the borrowing reaches the limits of what can be repaid, things slow down. That's a recession, and that was what happened in Southeast Asia in 1997.

The whole thing should have served as a warning to Alan Greenspan, the chairman of our Federal Reserve Board. He had been letting our money supply grow at frightening levels for years. Instead, afraid of contagion coming from Southeast Asia, he now allowed the money growth to accelerate. We weren't going to have a recession in the good old USA—not if he could help it!

Meantime, gold had been in a bear market for eighteen years. During that time, it had fallen from $600 an ounce to $250. As far as I was concerned, it was a buy! I had done very well on Wall Street in the nineties, but now I thought the party was getting out of hand, and I didn't want to be left holding the bag.

As it turned out, I was early. The party still had two more years to run. Nonetheless, I stuck to my guns, so much so that more than a decade would go by before I would start buying stocks again. In January 2000, the Dow Jones Industrial Average was at 11,250. Ten years later, in July 2011, it would be at the same level. In the meantime, gold would go from $250 per ounce to $1,250. A year or so after that, it would peak above $1,800, but I would already have sold mine at $1,330. Again, I would be early, but everything I had was in it, and I made five times my money.

The great bull market in gold took longer than I expected. Even so, I never thought it would happen overnight, and I realized I couldn't very well be a stockbroker anymore, not if I was just going to advocate sitting on gold. For that reason, I semiretired at about the time I turned fifty in March of 1998. I would continue to maintain a relationship with Morgan Stanley for five years, but only after turning most of my clients over to other brokers. I never went to the office again.

I also talked Suzie into retiring. It wasn't easy. In seven years, she had risen from selling ads to advertising sales manager, to associate publisher, and she was loving every bit of it. But with Mary away at school now and me semiretired, Suzie's job was the only thing keeping us from doing the sorts of things we had always planned.

Our first big trip was to Southeast Asia. With the economic crisis going on there, I considered it the perfect destination. Things were bound to cost less. Places would be less crowded, and our patronage would be even more appreciated than usual.

In May 1998, we took off for Singapore. I had reservations there at that fabulous old jewel of the British colonial period, the beautifully restored, and now very expensive, Raffles Hotel. We were picked up at the airport in an antique Rolls-Royce, and when we arrived, one of the hotel's famous Sikh doormen was there to greet us.

Singapore 1998 didn't even resemble the place I remembered from the 1950s. Gone were the bicycle-powered rickshaws, the peasants cooking their food in the streets, and the laundry hanging from apartment windows. Gone, too, were the ubiquitous cicaks and the mosquito nets in our hotel room. I would say the city was more modern now, more polished, and more prosperous than any city in America. In an annual survey, the *Wall Street Journal* was regularly listing Singapore among the freest market economies in the world. No socialist economy has ever accomplished this kind of transformation, and I don't see how one ever could.

We ate a lot of wonderful Indian and Chinese food that week, some of it right at the hotel. And of course, we drank Singapore Slings in the famous Long Bar. Sadly for the Raffles, we were practically the only guests on hand due to the economic crisis. Nonetheless, we had a great time. I'd forgotten, though, how quickly and how profusely one perspires in this hot and humid part of the world. Additionally, the smell of smoke was everywhere, thanks to the shameful and deliberate burning of the Sumatran rain forest over two hundred miles away.

Next, we flew to Bali, that mystical island of my youth, and yes, it was still beautiful, though, sadly, not so mystical anymore. Now, instead of wearing batik sarongs and walking about barefooted and bare-breasted, carrying all manner of things upon their heads, the natives were in T-shirts and riding motorbikes. One couldn't blame the people for wanting an easier life, of course, but I wondered if they were really any happier.

We stayed at the beautiful five-star Intercontinental Hotel overlooking Jimbaran Bay. There were four-hundred-plus rooms at the hotel, but I doubt if more than twenty of them were occupied. Again, it was the crisis.

While we were there, riots broke out elsewhere in Indonesia. People had lost their jobs and were going hungry. Much of the violence was aimed at ethnic Chinese, who were resented for their relative prosperity. There was rampant looting and vandalism. Hundreds of women were raped, and fires were set, contributing to the deaths of more than a thousand people. Were we wrong to be in Bali, enjoying the high life the way we were? I don't know.

Our next big trip was to Britain in September 1999. Mary was accepted to the London School of Economics for her junior year of college, so Suzie and I went along for a vacation. After dropping our daughter off, we rented a car and spent a couple of weeks touring England and Scotland. We had such a good time, but when we got home, our house felt pretty empty. Within weeks, we acquired a cute little Wheaten Terrier puppy and named him Chester after one of our favorite stops in England.

TWENTY-FOUR

Retirement

Being retired, or at least semiretired, made life very different for Suzie and me. I set up a workstation in a spare bedroom so I could still manage money for myself and my few remaining clients. When Suzie lost her diamond, I bought her a new one. Then, as a gift to myself, I bought a new Honda Valkyrie motorcycle. It was a big one too, with a 1,500 cc engine that looked like it came out of a car. In April 2001, Suzie and I took off across the nation on it. We went as far as Washington, DC, to visit my old friend Tom Wheeler and another good friend from Vienna, Guido Gale.

The day we set off, it was snowing outside. Suzie thought we were going to postpone. "Oh, no," I said. "This is going to be a long trip with all kinds of weather. We can't just stop every time we don't like how it looks outside. Besides, we ski, and this won't be much different from that."

Well, I was wrong. It was very different. Heading south on I-15, I could barely keep the bike upright. We rode as far south as Spanish Fork and then took Route 89 to Route 6 up over the mountains to Price. Only there did we finally escape the weather. We had gone just a hundred miles, but it had taken almost three hours, and we were wet and shivering.

We stopped at McDonald's to warm up and get something to eat. Then we mounted the bike again and headed for Green River, where we spent the first night. By the time we got there, our clothes had dried out from the wind, and we were feeling a lot warmer.

You get a lot of time to reflect on a motorcycle. What I kept thinking about that first day was how similar our life was now to when we were first married. Back then, we hitchhiked around the country. We had no kids, no money, and not much responsibility to anybody. Becoming parents had put an end to that, but now, in a way, we were back living the original dream, only on a motorcycle and with plenty of money. There were no kids to raise. There was no place we had to be. When I thought about this, I would reach back and place my hand on Suzie's leg. I loved her so.

We completed our trip successfully, even though we had a flat tire near Nashville and fell off the bike near Fort Smith, Arkansas. AAA came out and plugged our tire for us when we had the flat, and we were only going five miles an hour on soft grass when we tipped over. So no harm was done.

Back home in September, I was up early one morning, watching the business channel on television, as always. Suddenly, an image of smoke pouring from the side of 1 World Trade Center came onto the screen. My company, Morgan Stanley, was headquartered at the World Trade Center, and building number 1 was where I had gone to speak on a couple of occasions. So I was immediately interested.

It looked like a plane had hit the building, which was odd, because it was a bright, sunny day. Back in 1945, a B-25 bomber had flown into the Empire State Building, but that was in a thick fog.

Seventeen minutes later, I was still watching when a commercial jetliner seemed to appear from nowhere and crashed into the second tower. Now it was obvious. America was under attack.

Through history, there have been plenty of examples of man's inhumanity to man, but never before had such malevolence been played out on live television in front of millions of people. And to think, it was done in the name of righteousness. Nineteen hijackers had commandeered four jetliners, killing over three thousand people. No doubt, their last words were "Allahu akbar!" God is great! Really?

This was a sad time for Americans, but I will say it unified us more than I'd ever witnessed in my lifetime. Less than a month later, our daughter Jesse ran in the Saint George Marathon, and we were on hand to see hundreds of people flying the American flag from their car windows.

It was Jesse's first and only marathon. She finished in just over four hours and four minutes.

In February, the Winter Olympics came to Salt Lake. During the opening ceremony, a tattered flag was marched into the stadium so the whole world could see it. It was the same Old Glory that flew over the World Trade Center the day of the attacks.

Hosting the Olympics in our hometown was a big deal for all of us. Suzie and I didn't have tickets to any of the events, but we watched as much as we could on television.

At the end of the games, we got in the car and headed back to southern Utah. We had been so impressed by the climate and the scenic beauty down there that we decided to look for a place to retire.

We started in Springdale, near the entrance to Zion National Park, but when we realized how many tourists there would be, we headed for Saint George. There, in a development called Entrada at Snow Canyon, we bought a lot and made arrangements to build a house. The address was 2405 West Entrada Trail, Lot 79.

Entrada was an extraordinary place. It was a gated community with a country club, golf course, and sports facility at its center. It also had numerous manmade ponds and streams that truly made it an oasis in the desert. I knew the cost of such amenities would limit any return on our investment, but I didn't care. I wasn't there to make money; I was there to enjoy our retirement. There would be plenty of opportunities for us to hike in the desert, and motorcycling would be year-round. As if that weren't enough, Las Vegas was less than two hours away.

Back in Salt Lake, we sold the Dimple Dell house and started packing for the big move. It would be months before our new place was ready, but we put our furniture in storage and moved anyway, temporarily renting a house in nearby Kayenta. That summer in the desert, Suzie and I felt like we were on a second honeymoon. We would take Chester for walks in the sand dunes every morning. Then we would go check for progress on the new house.

Cassie came down from Salt Lake one of those days with a young man named Gershon Gaisford. A talented musician from a prominent Mormon family, he said he wanted to marry her. Since our new house was nearing completion and it had a beautiful patio with elaborate waterfalls in back, I offered it as a place to hold the ceremony. It was agreed, and on September 21, 2002, the two of them were married. Suzie and I had been in the house less than a week.

There is no place in America more beautiful than the desert Southwest, and Saint George is in as pretty a spot as any. In the years ahead, Suzie and I would hike to the bottom of the Grand Canyon and back out again twice. We would go on frequent treks in Snow Canyon and Zion National Park. Farther away, but still in Utah, were Bryce Canyon, Capitol Reef, Arches, and Canyonlands. We hiked them all.

We also took long motorcycle trips. In 2009 we traded in the Honda for a new Harley-Davidson, and we rode it up into Canada twice. We even made a second transcontinental trip, stopping in Georgetown, New York, the village where my great-great-grandfather Borden Davenport settled over 150 years earlier.

We went abroad more than ever before. Having grown up traveling the world, I wanted Suzie to see it too. Before we were done, I took her to forty-nine states and thirty-nine different countries. Eventually, I would make it to the last remaining state, Maine, but sadly, I would have to do it without her. My own country list would someday grow to more than sixty.

As it turned out, the best thing about living at Entrada wasn't the scenery, the weather, or the location. The best part was the friends we made. Suddenly we were surrounded by highly accomplished people from all sorts of places and backgrounds. There were business owners, corporate executives, doctors, engineers, airline pilots, educators, even a four-star general. Almost all were retired. Almost all had money, and everyone was looking to have a good time. Wow, what an opportunity!

Two of our closest friends were Don and Barbara Smith. Don was a brilliant engineer who had worked at some of the best corporations. We were also friends with people like John and Sharon Wellsandt, Barry and Carla Cook, and Don and Kay Simon. These are just names, I know, but to us they were real people that we cared about.

Twice a year, these friends, and numerous others, would go on driving expeditions out to some of the remotest areas. We explored many ancient Indian sites and saw a lot of fabulous scenery. The trips were organized by a young ball of energy named Kari Isaksen, and she did such a good job that we always felt lucky to be invited.

One evening, Suzie and I were at a club event, having dinner with a new couple recently moved in from California. Their name was Dredge. He was an airline-pilot-turned-entrepreneur-turned-real-estate-speculator. She had owned her own beauty salon in Temecula. In the course of conversation, we discovered they were best friends with Jay Call, the Flying J founder I had profiled in *Salt Lake City* magazine. In fact, they were married on Jay's yacht in San Diego. They were so pleasant and interesting that, when they asked if we wanted to see the home they were building, we said yes.

It was just a short golf cart ride away, but by the time we got there, it was already growing dark outside. The house was only half-built, but we could see it was going to be bigger, and in many ways, better, than ours. It was clear they were creating something special.

We never really got close to the Dredges. Alan, the husband, was very athletic. He was always challenging himself on long bike rides, and he liked to play golf nearly every day. I didn't even own a bicycle, and I was more in the once- or twice-a-week category when it came to golf. Nonetheless, Alan always seemed happy to see me, and I liked him. Once, he said to me, "You know, Dave, you have a really good-looking wife."

I was so flattered. I said, "Thank you, Alan, so do *you*!"

From that day on, whenever we saw each other, we would compliment one another's wives. Once, I even said, "Alan, your wife has the body of a teenager!" He just laughed, but I winced after I said it. Maybe I crossed the line on that one.

In truth, though, Cheryl, Alan's wife, was beautiful. In fact, she was a knockout. She was maybe fifty at that time, but she had perfect features and a very youthful figure. She wore her striking red hair closely cropped on the sides and in back, but on top it was thick and bouncy. Not even the most devoted husband and father could fail to notice such a woman.

Suzie and I were both golfers now, though neither of us was very good at it. We even used to joke that she was the worst female golfer at our club, and I the worst male. Even so, we always did our best. One year, Suzie was elected to the ELGA board. ELGA stood for Entrada Ladies Golf Association. Suzie's job was to take photographs and arrange prizes for the gals who distinguished themselves on the golf course. Cheryl Dredge was on the board at the same time. She planned all the events. By the end of year, the two of them had been to enough board meetings to know each other pretty well. One day in the future, Suzie would say to me, "Of all the women who took up golf after moving to Entrada, Cheryl Dredge is the only one who ever got any good at it."

I, meanwhile, served four yeats on the board of the homeowner association. I also served for a year on the country club board.

Throughout the first decade of the new millennium, I continued to own gold. By 2010, precious metals had proven to be the single best-performing asset class on Wall Street, making me look like a pretty smart cookie. Stocks, meanwhile, had been on a dreadful roller-coaster ride, thanks partly to the so-called Great Recession that occurred in 2008.

During the decade, we also saw considerable growth in our family. Cassie's first child was a daughter, Stella, born in 2003. Then came Charlotte in 2005. Mary, meanwhile, had met and married a Canadian student named Lee Kane, from Toronto. Together, the two of them would go on to have three children, Sophia in 2004, Luca in 2007, and Mirabelle (Mimi) in 2015. Like me, the Kane kids would grow up living in the Far East and traveling the world. Lee would have a fabulous career as a diplomat in China.

By the year 2000, Jesse's husband, Darren, had already built a successful landscaping business, and Jesse was running her own florist shop. Soon, they were buying up land to develop a much bigger business in Riverton, Utah, called Arbor Day Nursery.

In 2010, we experienced our first death in the family since 1987. It was my mother. A heavy smoker for most of her life, she had been treated for lung cancer a decade earlier. Now it had returned, and her doctor said she only had a few weeks to live.

Upon learning this, Suzie and I packed some bags, jumped in the car, and made it down to San Diego the next day. Likewise, my sister, Dana, who had not spoken to my parents in years, came in from Texas to stay with her daughter, Blythe, in Hemet. For numerous reasons, Dana would not be welcome on Brindisi Street as long as my mother was alive, but she wanted to be nearby, just in case.

My brother, Mark, was working as a heavy equipment operator in Antarctica. As soon as he got word, he came to San Diego too. This meant missing work for the rest of the season, which was a considerable sacrifice.

My father and I did most of the caregiving, but Mark covered for me one week while Suzie and I were in Saint George on some unfinished business. Blythe, meanwhile, was bringing meals to the house almost every day, not letting Mom or Dad know that Dana had really cooked them.

Throughout, my mother was her usual crusty self, barking orders at everyone. Once, while we were gathered around her bed, she heard the first ring of the telephone. "ANSWER THAT PHONE!" she bellowed, as though we were all idiots. This was Ernestine to a tee!

After six weeks, Mom was very near the end and no longer aware of her surroundings. I told Blythe to go ahead and bring Dana over. Against his wishes, Dad agreed to receive her. Now, all of us could be on hand for what was coming. In the wee hours of March 5, 2010, we stood around her bed, our hands upon her, as Mom drew her last breath.

That night, Dana made an Indonesian nasi goreng dinner, for old times' sake. Mark bought some beer, and we had our best family time together ever. I think Mom would have approved.

Dad stayed at the Brindisi Street house in San Diego for two more years, socializing with his neighbors and going for walks. He was an avid reader and a true intellectual, but being alone so much was wearing on him. He and I did keep in constant touch by telephone, but in 2012, when he was eighty-nine, he made the tough decision to sell the home he'd loved for forty years. After weeks spent helping him get it ready, Suzie and I moved him to Saint George, where he could live out his life near his family.

TWENTY-FIVE

A New Life

By 2013, Suzie and I were on top of the world. Two people who had endured poverty together as a young couple, we now had more money than ever. We had three grown daughters making significant headway through life and five grandchildren we loved immeasurably. Dad was living nearby and coming over for dinner every night.

Our home had been built exactly to our specifications. The great room had a massive natural stone fireplace with logs in the ceiling. There were granite tiles on the floors and tumbled travertine in the bathrooms. We had a three-car garage and a spacious covered patio facing a series of waterfalls that emptied into a beautiful backyard lily pond.

In the daytime, we would go our separate ways. Suzie worked out at the gym most mornings, and I would speed-walk for miles. She had her book club meetings and golf days with her friends. I served on the homeowner association board and managed our investments.

As a child, Suzie had been taught by her grandmother to crochet. Throughout her life she had always made scarves, mittens, afghans, and so on for our family. Now, in the evenings, her hands were busy crocheting while we watched movies on television. Chester, our dog, would sprawl out next to us on the floor.

In April of that year, we hiked the ten-mile trail down into the Havasupai Indian Reservation with a group of friends. Suzie was in the best shape of her life. We were both strong hikers. Other people, in fact, often had difficulty keeping up with us. We camped for two nights near the falls at the bottom of the canyon and then started back out on the third day. That was when Suzie got into trouble. She wasn't feeling well that morning, and about five miles up the trail, she started having diarrhea. By the time we reached the car, we were at least an hour behind the rest of the group, and she was utterly done in. I remember thinking, *Well, okay. No more long, arduous hikes for us, I guess.* She was, after all, sixty-six.

Nonetheless, on the fourth of May, Suzie was looking beautiful again at our club's Kentucky Derby party. She was wearing a flamboyant hat we had devised for her and a blue-and-yellow cocktail dress that really showed off her figure. I snapped a picture of her standing out in the sunlight. That day, she won fifty dollars predicting the winning horse.

The next couple of weeks, though, she started complaining about double vision. It was causing her to do things like knock her water glass over at the dinner table. After that happened several times, we called the doctor.

Dr. Taylor said it was vertigo and that it would probably go away after a while. Instead, it got worse. One day, when Suzie thought she was setting a jar of olives on the counter, she let it go and it crashed to the floor, sending wet olives all over the kitchen.

Dr. Taylor ordered an MRI. We were riding in the car when he called with the results. Suzie answered and started listening intently. Then, she asked, "Am I going to die?"

The love of my life had three brain tumors.

Right away, we were referred to a Dr. Lin, oncologist. A CAT scan would reveal that the true source of the cancer was actually in one of Suzie's kidneys. A week later, she was in the Dixie Regional Medical Center, having the offending kidney removed. That night, I held on to her arm as we gingerly walked up and down the hallway outside her hospital room, dragging her IV pole. *My gosh,* I thought, *what are we going to do?*

Right away, the cards and phone calls began pouring in. Ever the optimist, Suzie responded to every one with words of reassurance. "I will beat this thing!" I heard her tell people over and over.

Among the first friends to visit was Diane Mowinski. We had been close to Diane and Jerry from the beginning at Entrada. Another much-appreciated guest was Cheryl Dredge. Poor Cheryl had been through a terrible ordeal when her husband, Alan, died from stomach cancer two years earlier. The strain had been so difficult that a blank expression had taken over her face, and her weight seemed dangerously low. The slightest provocation would break her out in tears.

One morning, Cheryl came around with a gift for Suzie. It was a decorative metal stencil with just one word cut into it: *courage*. I hung it on the fireplace so that Suzie would see it every day.

Then, Cheryl began to cry, as she would on every one of her visits, and I went to get the Kleenex. Before she left, she said to us, "I am really sorry for what you are going to go through."

I thought about Cheryl's ordeal and how it ended with Alan's death. And then I thought, *Don't be so sure, Cheryl. I think Suzie can beat this.*

Years earlier, when Suzie's father had suffered from kidney cancer, although a different type, I had thought the family silly to keep saying he was going to make it. Having talked to his oncologist, I knew better. Now, though, I saw how wrong I'd been. No matter what the odds, some people don't quit. Toward the end, hope will be the only thing they have left. Why would anyone take that away?

With her diseased kidney gone, Suzie now underwent radiation for her brain tumors. We understood the risk associated with damaging healthy tissue, but what choice did she have? We were relieved when it became apparent later that the treatment had done no harm.

Finally, Dr. Lin prescribed an immunotherapy drug called Sutent, which isn't well tolerated by some patients. Nonetheless, it can be effective. Lo and behold, Suzie tolerated it well. So things were looking up.

Well, mostly, anyway. Her body scans were coming in clean, and her brain tumors had been zapped, but she still had the vertigo, and her eyes were growing farther out of alignment, worsening the double vision. I found eye patches online and ordered them.

Covering one eye might be uncomfortable, but at least she would be seeing only one image.

In February 2014, we went on a Caribbean cruise. By now, Suzie would fall down if I didn't hold on to her. People on the ship must have thought she was drunk. One night, I took her out on the dance floor and held her close to me. Suddenly, I realized she was crying, and I asked, "What's wrong?"

She looked up at me, the tears streaming down her beautiful face. "I'm *dancing*!" she said.

Three months later, we went to Italy. Holding on to each other, we walked all over Rome and Venice. It was a happy time, but some not-so-happy news was awaiting us when we got home.

Diane Mowinski had fallen in her bathroom and received a brain hemorrhage. A surgeon had to remove a very large piece of her skull to repair the damage. He patched her up, but the wound became so infected that the skull piece had to be removed and discarded. They didn't dare fit her with a prosthesis until Diane recovered enough to endure more surgery. A long, miserable wait of many months in a rehab facility was just beginning for her.

That summer of 2014, I rented a big house at Entrada. Our three daughters and our grandchildren would have one last vacation with Suzie. Afterward, Suzie and I went back to Pittsburgh to visit her family for the last time. One day, while we were there, we had lunch at her friend Judy Jones's house. Suzie's roommate from many years ago, Raine, was there too. The three of them had been great friends in college.

That was the last trip Suzie and I ever took.

When we got home, Suzie's friends Kay Simon and Barbara Smith were ready for us. They had organized the community to start providing home-cooked dinners. Another friend, Mark Shuler, came over a few times to entertain Suzie on his guitar. Suzie felt the love all around, and she greatly appreciated it.

By December, though, things worsened, and I was forced to cut off almost all the visits. No longer could Suzie leave the house. Hospice was ordered in by Dr. Lin.

Throughout this period, Diane Mowinski's condition also worsened. Jerry brought her over one day in a specially equipped van he had purchased. The two nearly helpless old friends had a chance to say goodbye while Jerry snapped their picture.

On January 14, Mary gave birth to the last of our six grandchildren. Little Mirabelle (Mimi, as she would be called) was born in China. So that Suzie could meet her, Mary made a special trip back to Saint George in February. I took some pictures and a short video clip of Suzie adoring her new grandchild.

On the morning of March 22, my birthday, I went into the bedroom to help Suzie get out of bed. She was tired and confused. "I don't want to go to school today," she said.

"You don't have to go to school, Suzie," I responded. "You can just stay right here and rest."

A few hours later, I was by her side when she awoke again. "You are so good to me, David," she said. "I love you."

"I love you too, Suzie! We all love you! Mirabelle loves you so much she came all the way from China just to see you!"

Suzie smiled and said, "That's funny."

Those were the last words she ever spoke.

EPILOGUE

I sat up with Suzie all night on March 25, holding her hand and caressing her hair. At 7:39 the next morning, the love of my life slipped away forever. My sister, Dana, and her husband, Len, were there, as were my father and our eldest daughters, Jesse and Cassie.

Five days later, on March 31, Diane Mowinski died. From that day forward, Jerry and I would always be close friends.

In the last week of Suzie's life, Cheryl visited several times. There was no doubt her efforts at comforting us benefited her as well. The day before Suzie died, Cheryl said, "I wish there were something I could do to help you, David. I am so sorry. I just don't know what to do."

By this point, I was exhausted from two years of caring for Suzie night and day. I was also fearful of what was coming. I saw myself as a man whose ship was going down. Without hope, I was floating in an open sea. To me, Cheryl was a girl in a lifeboat. Her ship had gone down, too, but she alone could pull me from the water.

"There is something you can do," I said. "When this is over, you can go out with me."

Cheryl recoiled. "Oh, David, I can't do that! That's not why I'm here." I could see in her face how appalled she was that her kindness had been misinterpreted. I dropped the subject.

Shortly after Suzie died, I called her mother in Pittsburgh with the news. By now, she was braced for what was coming and surprisingly calm. "David, I want you to find a good Christian girl and get married again," she said.

She spoke from experience. She had been alone in her widowhood for twenty-eight years.

That same morning, as Jesse and Cassie prepared to head for home, Jesse said, "Dad, we don't want you to be alone. We want you to find a girlfriend."

Suzie's death hit me hard. She was the girl I'd spent most of my life with, and now she was gone. Period. In the days ahead, my family, my friends, the hospice people, the doctors, everyone who helped us through our terrible ordeal would be moving on.

I did take a lady to dinner a couple of times. She was a widow, too, and very nice, but I couldn't see her as a partner.

Meanwhile, Cheryl was dutifully keeping her eye on me. She was concerned my grief might lead me to make decisions I would later regret. Each day, she called to check on me, and each day, my affection for her grew stronger. Then, early one evening, she sent me a text.

"Hey," it said. "You want to go get a burger?"

ABOUT THE AUTHOR

David Dobson Davenport has lived and traveled throughout much of the world. He is a retired first vice president of a major Wall Street firm, where he made millions as a stock trader. Although he has authored numerous magazine articles about prominent businesspeople, this is his first book. A widower living alone in southern Utah, he has three grown daughters and six grandchildren.